THE ŚĀKTA

THE
ŚĀKTA PĪṬHAS

D. C. Sircar
*Carmichael Professor and Head of the
Department of Ancient Indian
History and Culture,
University of Calcutta.*

**MOTILAL BANARSIDASS
INTERNATIONAL
DELHI**

Reprint Edition: Delhi, 2023
Second Revised Edition: Delhi, 1973

© MOTILAL BANARSIDASS INTERNATIONAL
All Rights Reserved

ISBN: 978-81-19196-39-5

Also available at
MOTILAL BANARSIDASS INTERNATIONAL
H. O.: 41 U.A. Bungalow Road, (Back Lane) Jawahar Nagar, Delhi - 110 007
4261/3 (basement), Ansari Road, Darya Ganj, New Delhi - 110 002
203 Royapettah High Road, Mylapore, Chennai - 600 004
12/1A, 2nd Floor, Bankim Chatterjee Street, Kolkata - 700 073
Stockist: Motilal Books, Ashok Rajpath, Near Kali Mandir, Patna - 800 004

No part of this book may be reproduced in any form or by any electronic or mechanical means including information storage and retrieval systems without permission in writing from the publishers, excepts by a reviewer who may quote brief passages in a review.

Printed in India
MOTILAL BANARSIDASS INTERNATIONAL

*Dedicated to the
Sacred Memory of the Late
Professor Louis Renou*

Prācyavidyodadherindorujjvalajñānakarmaṇaḥ /
Sūreḥ Śrīhemacandrasya Rāyacaturdharasya ca //
Bhāṇḍārakaravaṁśābjadevadattasya dhīmataḥ //
pratnalipipragalbhasya svalpajñenāntavāsinā //
kavervaidyāgragaṇyasya Yajñeśvaryasya satpituḥ /
mātuśca Kusumādyāyāḥ kumāryāstanujanmanā //
Dīneśena kṛtiścēyaṁ Kāyasthena samarpyate /
Luvireṇusudhīndrāya vedavidyāvivasvate //

FOREWORD

The Śākta Pīṭhas by Dr. D. C. Sircar, which is limited and precise in scope but has a wide appeal, brings honour to the young historian of Calcutta. Its basis is a critical edition of the *Pīṭhanirṇaya* or *Mahāpīṭhanirūpaṇa* which is a short treatise of the late period describing the fiftyone pilgrim spots associated with the Mother Goddess under some of her various names. Each one of the *pīṭhas* is mentioned along with a particular form of the Goddess and that of Śiva associated with it.

The said text passes as a chapter of the *Tantracūḍāmaṇi* and resembles some others, so that a plausible edition, based on six manuscripts and four source materials which Dr. Sircar's diligence has succeeded in grouping together, was philologically realisable. The editor adds a reconstructed text, based mainly on a Bengali version, and furnishes other useful matters in appendices, one of them containing an index of the *pīṭhas* with necessary identifications of the localities.

But what doubtless deserves much more attention is the erudite study in the introduction, wherein the author recapitulates what is known or may be presumed about the problem of the *pīṭhas*. Leaving aside minor indications, the legend which seeks to explain the origin of the *pīṭhas* is the well-known epicopurāṇic account of Dakṣa's sacrifice, interrupted by Śiva's wrath. The story seems to have developed out of certain allusions in the Brāhmaṇas referring to the peculiar misfortunes of Bhaga and Pūṣan. In the later Purāṇas and the Purāṇa-type Tantras, the image of Viṣṇu cutting off, part by part, Satī's corpse borne on Śiva's shoulder has been grafted on this legend. The severed parts of Satī's body fell on the earth and each formed a *pīṭha*, a cult having come to be crystallised on it. Dr. Sircar recalls in this connection the Buddhist legends about the Buddha's relics and the more distant Greek version of the Osiris myth. We see here, once again, that a cult, quite well localised geographically, develops on absolutely mythical conceptions.

Certain *pīṭhas* appear to be associated more especially with the breasts and the female organ of the Goddess, probably analogous to the conception of the phallic emblem of Śiva. Whatever that may be, the religious crystallisation seems to have taken place originally on the basis of a group of 4 *pīṭhas* at a time which, according to Dr. Sircar, may coincide with the appearance of the early Tantras. These 4 *pīṭhas* are supposed to represent the four cardinal points though, from the beginning, the region of Kāmarūpa (Assam) enjoyed a privileged position in the scheme. Gradually there appeared 7 *pīṭhas*, then 10, then 18 (a sanctified number), ultimately (through the intermediate numbers 42, 50 and 51) as many as 108 (an equally expected number). The *Pīṭhanirṇaya* is based on a list of 42, which was later enlarged, by the inclusion of the 10 *mahāvidyās* of the Mother Goddess, the counterpart of the 10 *avatāras* of the Viṣṇuite cycle.

In an appendix, Dr. Sircar discusses the evidence for determining the date of the celebrated encyclopaedic treatise *Tantrasāra* (first half of the 17th century). Another appendix, the scope of which is more general than novel, deals with the development of the Śakti cult from Vedic times going as far back as the Mohen-jo-daro motifs, the interpretation of which is, however, not quite decisive.

I may specially recommend this study of the *pīṭhas* as a model of accurate and penetrating investigation.

Paris, 1950   LOUIS RENOU

PREFACE TO THE SECOND EDITION

I am thankful to Messrs. Motilal Banarsidass for their kindness in taking up the reprinting of my work entitled *The Śākta Pīṭhas* which was not available in the market for some time. The book is now presented to the students of the religious life and historical geography of ancient and medieval India with some additional matter. It is hoped that the work will continue to prove useful to those for whom it is intended.

The book has been printed in the photolithographic process so that modifications in the text had to be indicated in the *Addenda et Corrigenda*. A large number of these became necessary for the political changes in the country such as the partition of the subcontinent and of certain provinces, districts, etc., as well as the creation of numerous administrative units of different categories resulting from the merger of the Native States, the reorganisation of the railways and the policy of reorganising the provinces on a linguistic basis followed after our independence. In such cases, we have sometimes avoided a change when it appeared to be minor or indicated it in an unorthodox way. Only in a few places of the book, changes were necessitated by new discoveries and further studies.

The index has been compiled by Dr. N. N. Bhattacharya, Senior Research Fellow at the Centre of Advanced Study in Ancient Indian History and Culture, Calcutta University, to whom my thanks are due.

645, New Alipore, Calcutta,   D. C. SIRCAR
15th December, 1971.

PREFACE
First Edition

Tantric studies have not much progressed in India. The author of the present monograph originally approached the Tantra literature as a student of ancient and medieval Indian geography, although the subject under discussion in the following pages soon proved to be equally interesting from the viewpoint of the religious life of India. A Tantra text on the Śākta Pīṭhas, entitled *Pīṭhanirṇya* or *Mahāpīṭhanirūpaṇa*, has been edited here with notes and an attempt has been made in that connection to trace the history of the Pīṭha conception with reference not only to the Puranic legend in theoretical explanation of the origin of the Pīṭhas but also to the real basis of the conception itself. No less than six manuscripts and four published sources have been utilized in editing the *Pīṭhanirṇaya* (*Mahāpīṭhanirūpaṇa*). A reconstructed text of the original work has been given in as Appendix, while a large number of relevant texts has been quoted either in the notes or in the Appendixes. The author has also discussed, however summarily, the location of several hundrdes of *tīrthas* or holy places, mentioned in various works as Pīṭhas. Much, unfortunately, still remains to be done in this direction. Any suggestion form the readers for the improvement of the work will be carefully considered and gratefully acknowledged.

The author is extremely thankful to Prof. H. C. Raychaudhuri and Dr. J. N. Banerjea of the Calcutta University, who have taken interest in the preparation of the monograph and have offered some valuable suggestions. His thanks are also due to Drs. R. C. Majumdar, I. B. Banerji and B. K. Ghosh for some help and suggestions. Mr. S. K. Saraswati has laid the author under a debt of gratitude by lending him a valuable manuscript (MS. G) of the *Pīṭhanirṇaya* from his own collection. As however, the manuscript was received after the monograph had been ready for the press, it has been utilized mainly in the notes on the text and in reconstructing the probable original text of the work for Appendix I—A.

Finally, the author thanks the authorities and managment of the Royal Asiatic Society of Bengal and the Baptist Mission Press, Calcutta.

Department of D. C. Sircar
Ancient Indian History and Culture,
Calcutta University.
September 8, 1948.

CONTENTS

Subject	Page
Foreword (Louis Renou)	vii
The Pīṭhanirṇaya or Mahāpīṭhanirūpaṇa	3
Date of its Composition	4
An Ancient Legend	5
Its Development into the Dakṣa-yajña Story	5
Further Development of the Legend to explain the Origin of the Pīṭhas	6
Conception of the Yonikuṇḍa and Stanakuṇḍa associated with that of the Liṅga	7
Some Early Tīrthas associated with the Limbs of the Mother-goddess	8
The Tradition about Four Pīṭhas	11
The Tantric Schools of North-Western and Eastern India	15
Different Traditions regarding the Number of the Pīṭhas	17
Evidence of the Jñānārṇava and the Tantrasāra regarding the Number of the Pīṭhas	20
The Tradition about 108 Pīṭhas	24
Freedom of the Writers on the Pīṭhas from any common Tradition	32
The List of the Pīṭhas in the Pīṭhanirṇaya (Mahāpīṭhanirūpaṇa)	35
Modification of the Pīṭhanirṇaya (Mahāpīṭhanirūpaṇa) in the Śivacarita	38
List of the Pīṭhas (Mahāpīṭhas) and Upapīṭhas in the Śivacarita	39
Materials utilized in the Present Edition of the Pīṭhanirṇaya (Mahāpīṭhanirūpaṇa)	41
Text of the Pīṭhanirṇaya (Mahāpīṭhanirūpaṇa)	42
Appendix I—A. Probable Original Text of the Pīṭhanirṇaya (Mahāpīṭhanirūpaṇa) Reconstructed on the basis of Manuscript G and the Annadāmaṅgala	59
B. Modified Text of the Pīṭhanirṇaya as found in Manuscript H	61
Appendix II — Puranic Text containing 108 Names of the Mother-goddess (Nāmāṣṭottaraśatam)	66
Appendix III— Evolution of the Dakṣayajña Story (Dakṣayajñakathā-mūlam)	70
Appendix IV—Date of the Tantrasāra	74
Appendix V—An Index of Pīṭhas	80
Appemdix VI—Śiva and Śakti in the Orthodox Indian Pantheon	100

INTRODUCTION.

The Pīṭhanirṇaya or Mahāpīṭhanirūpaṇa.

There are three manuscripts of a very small work entitled *Pīṭhanirṇaya* or *Mahāpīṭhanirūpaṇa* (Nos. 196, 3400 and 5303) in the Government Collection of the library of the Royal Asiatic Society of Bengal. The work describes the fifty-one Pīṭhas (literally, altars or seats)[1] or places of pilgrimage, considered to be the favourite resorts of the mother-goddess who is variously known as Devī, Śakti Durgā, Pārvatī, Umā, Ambikā, Aparṇā, Kālī, Gaurī, etc., and is represented in Indian mythology as the wife of the great god Śiva.[2] The Pīṭhas are mentioned together with the names of particular forms of the Devī and of the accompanying Bhairava (form of Śiva) associated with each of them. It is admitted in the text that it forms a section of a Tantra work entitled *Tantracūḍāmaṇi*. Such works as the *Śabdakalpadruma* (1822-52) and the *Prāṇatoṣaṇī Tantra* (1820), which quote the same text of the descriptive list of fifty-one Pīṭhas, also ascribe it to the *Tantracūḍāmaṇi*. The Bengali poem *Annadāmaṅgala* (1752) by Bhāratacandra refers its section on the 'fifty-one' Pīṭhas, although it actually mentions only forty-two names of holy places and does not

---

[1] In early times altars (*pīṭhas*) appear to have been used as objects of aniconic worship. Sacred spots where particular Yogins or ascetics meditated and succeeded in attaining to *siddhi* or perfection are regarded as *Pīṭha* or *Siddhapīṭha*. The *Sarvā-nandataraṅgiṇī* refers to Mehāra, a Parganā in the Tippera District, as a Pīṭha-sthala, because Sarvānanda attained his Tantric *siddhi* there.

[2] The different names of the mother-goddess appear to have originally indicated different tribal deities who were afterwards identified with the wife of Śiva-Paśupati (Vedic Rudra), a pre-Aryan god, known to have been worshipped by the Mohenjodaro people. *Devī* means the 'goddess *par excellence*'. *Śakti* (force) and *Ādyā Śakti* (the primeval force) indicate the power underlying creation and the controlling energy responsible for the universal order, the first name being often applied to the energizing power of the different gods. The name *Śakti* is also applied to the female organ worshipped by the Śāktas (devotees of the mother-goddess) just as the Śaivas adore the Phallus of Śiva, i.e. Śiva in the form of the Phallus; cf. Apte, Sanskrit-English Dictionary, s.v.; also *yonistotra* quoted in Des. Cat. Sans. MSS., R.A.S.B., VIII, p. 806:

भगरूपा जगन्माया (°म्माता) हृदिस्थितिरुद्यान्विता ।
द्यविद्यास्वरूपाक्षा योगिनीं पातु सर्वदा । See *infra*, Appendix VI.

The names *Durgā* and *Pārvatī* emphasize their relation with inaccessible mountain regions (especially the Himālaya of which the Indian mother-goddess is conceived as a daughter) and suggest that these were originally names of deities worshipped by mountaineers (cf. Śiva's name *Giriśa* meaning a dweller of the mountains). The names *Umā* (cf. Ommo on the coins of Huviṣka) and *Ambikā* are derived from the Dravidian word *amma* (mother) in the sense of the universal mother. *Aparṇā* signifies the deity 'who is without her leaf-cloth', i.e. naked, nakedness being one of the striking characteristics of the Indian mother-goddess. She must have originally been worshipped by a tribe such as the Nagna-Śabara (the naked Śabaras) of the *Bṛihatsaṁhitā*, just as the Buddhist deity Parṇaśabarī was undoubtedly associated with the Parṇa-Śabaras (the leaf-clad Śabaras) of the same work. See J.K.H.R.S., I, pp. 87-88. *Kālī* or the dark-complexioned deity may have been the goddess of some dark-skinned pre-Dravidian tribe; but the name may not be entirely unconnected with the conception of Kāla (time or death) with which Śiva is identified. *Gaurī* means the white-complexioned goddess and possibly points to her original worship among the Mongoloid xanthoderms of the Himalayan region. The name *Mahāmayā* apparently represents the mother-goddess as the spirit guiding the magician priests of primitive peoples. The name was later given a philosophical interpretation. Cf. other names like Yoga-māyā. *Kātyāyanī*, although it may indicate a deified lady or a family or tribal goddess (Aryan ?), means 'a middle-aged widow in red clothes'. Cf. *Dākṣāyaṇī, Kauśikī*. She is also called the 'maiden', the 'angry' or 'fierce' one and 'death' (Kālanidrā).

follow the order in which the Pīṭhas are mentioned in the list of the *Pīṭhanirṇaya*, to the *Mantracūḍāmaṇi Tantra* which would appear to be a mistake for *Tantracūḍāmaṇi*.[1] The library of the Royal Asiatic Society of Bengal possesses a manuscript of the Tantra text entitled *Tantracūḍāmaṇi* (No. I, F3); but, although it gives a list of the Pīṭhas (p. 178) in connection with the later form of a Tantric ritual known as *Pīṭhanyāsa*, that has little to do with the text of the *Pīṭhanirṇaya*. As the *Pīṭhanirṇaya* or *Mahāpīṭhanirūpaṇa*, avowedly a part of the *Tantracūḍāmaṇi*, cannot be traced in the Tantra of this name in the Society's library, one has to suggest alternatively either that there are more than one Tantric text entitled *Tantracūḍāmaṇi* and the *Pīṭhanirṇaya* belonged to a different work of this name, or that the ascription of the *Pīṭhanirṇaya* to the *Tantracūḍāmaṇi*, although it is supported by various sources, is without any real foundation. It is, however, very probable that the author of the *Pīṭhanirṇaya* wanted to credit his small work with a stamp of authority by falsely claiming it to be a part of an earlier Tantra entitled *Tantracūḍāmaṇi* mentioned in the encyclopedia of Tantric knowledge known as the *Tantrasāra* (pp. 515, 948). This is possibly suggested by the uncertainty felt by some writers about the name of the source of the *Pīṭhanirṇaya*, variously given as the *Tantracūḍāmaṇi*, *Mantracūḍāmaṇi*, *Candracūḍāmaṇi*, *Bhāvacūḍāmaṇi* and *Pīṭhamālā* (vide infra, pp. 42, note 2 ; 58, note 10).

Date of its Composition.

The text of the *Pīṭhanirṇaya* or *Mahāpīṭhanirūpaṇa*, which is silent as to the date of its composition, seems to have been prepared in the late medieval period. The number of the recognized Pīṭhas given as fifty-one probably points to the seventeenth or the eighteenth century (vide infra, pp. 23-24). But the problem of its date is involved in a bigger question

---

[1] Cf. Vaṅgavāsī ed., p. 42: यामि कवि मन्त्रचूड़ामणितन्त्र सम । A few manuscripts of the work in question read *Bhāvacūḍāmaṇi* or *Candracūḍāmaṇi* in place of *Tantracūḍāmaṇi*. The *Rājamālā* (a Bengali chronicle of the kings of Tipperah), *Lahara* ascribed usually to the middle of the fifteenth century, quotes verse 18 of the *Pīṭhanirṇaya* (*Mahāpīṭhanirūpaṇa*) but refers it to the *Pīṭhamālā Tantra* which seems to be found in some manuscripts as the name of this small work or that of its source. No such manuscripts are, however, known to us. The *Rājamālā* says,

एककन्या सती यत्र पतन येखाने ।
मद्यापीठनिर्णय मुनि बहिछे पुराचे ।
शिववाक्य पीठमाला तन्त्रेर प्रमाण ।
येद राज्ये येद चक्र येद पीठस्थान ।
येद राज्ये यक देवी मेरव थार जान ।
दुर नामे पीठस्थान करि निरूपण ।
सतीर दशिष पद पड़े निपुराबे ।
निपुरासुन्दरी ख्याति निपुर भूमिवे ।
निपुरेश नामे शिव निपुरा राज्येवे ।

It will be clear from our discussion on the text of the *Pīṭhanirṇaya* (vide infra) that the above passage of the *Rājamālā* could have been written only after the middle of the eighteenth century. It cannot be assigned to the fifteenth century as it follows interpolations in a work written not much earlier than the beginning of the eighteenth century.

Bhāratacandra's section on the Pīṭhas, styled *Pīṭhamālā*, may have given rise to the name of an imaginary *Pīṭhamālā Tantra*.

regarding the origin and evolution of the conception of the Pīṭhas with special reference to their recognized number in different works of various periods.

An Ancient Legend

There is a legend offering a mythological explanation of the origin of the Pīṭhas. The earlier versions have nothing, however, to do with the Pīṭhas. The germ of the legend can be traced in the Ṛgveda (X, 61, 5-7); but it received its final form in the latest Purāṇas and Tantras assignable to the late-medieval period. The Ṛgvedic tradition about the incestuous relation of a father with his daughter was elaborated in the Brāhmaṇas such as the Śatapatha (Mādhyandina version, I, vii, 4, 1-8; cf. II, i, 2, 9; Kāṇva version, II, vii, 2, 1-8; I, i, 2, 5-6) and Aitareya (III, 33-34); cf. also Tāṇḍyamahābrāhmaṇa, VIII, ii, 10-11.[1] According to the story found in these Brāhmaṇas, once Prajāpati, identified with Yajña or sacrifice, committed incest with his own daughter Dyaus or Uṣas. Disgusted at this vile act of their father, the gods approached Rudra and requested him to pierce Prajāpati with his arrow. Rudra discharged an arrow at Prajāpati whereupon the latter's retas (germinal fluid) fell upon the ground. As Prajāpati represents sacrifice itself and as no part of his body could be thrown away without being utilized in the performance of sacrifice, the gods first took Prajāpati's retas to Bhaga who sits on the southern side of the sacrificial ground. Bhaga looked at the thing and at once his eyes were burned. The gods then took it to Pūṣan who, on tasting it, lost his teeth. The concluding part of the story is unnecessary for our purpose. But the first portion of the legend is found a little developed in the Gopatha Brāhmaṇa (II, 1), according to which Prajāpati, while performing a sacrifice, did not offer the requisite share of offerings to Rudra who thereupon 'seizing and piercing it (Yajña or Yajñāṅga) cut off a portion from it'. A look at it is said to have made Bhaga blind and Pūṣan toothless.

Its Development into tne Dakṣa-yajña Story.

The same legend later (sometime before the rise of the Guptas in the fourth century A.D.) developed into the well-known story of the destruction of the sacrifice of Dakṣa-Prajāpati by the god Śiva, also called Rudra. The earliest form of the legend of Dakṣa-yajña-nāśa is probably to be traced in the Mahābhārata (XII, chapters 282-83; cf. Brahma Purāṇa, ch. 39) and a slightly modified form of the same story is found in many of the Purāṇas (Matsya, ch. 12; Padma, Sṛṣṭikhaṇḍa, ch. 5; Kūrma, I, ch. 15; Brahmāṇḍa, ch. 31, etc.) as well as in the Kumārasambhava (I, 21) of Kālidāsa who flourished in the fourth and fifth centuries and adorned the court of the Gupta Vikramādityas. According to this modified version of the legend, the mother-goddess, who was the wife of Śiva, was in the form of Satī one of the daughters of Dakṣa Prajāpati. Dakṣa was celebrating a great sacrifice for which neither Satī nor Śiva was invited. Satī, however, went to her father's sacrifice uninvited, but was greatly insulted by Dakṣa. As a result of this ill-treatment, Satī is said to have died by yoga or of a broken heart, or, as Kālidāsa says, she put herself into fire and perished. In the Mahābhārata version of the story, referred to above, the wife of Śiva is only responsible for pointing out, to her husband, Dakṣa's impertinence in disregarding the great god: but she is neither said to have been Dakṣa's

---

[1] See Appendix II.

daughter nor to have died at Dakṣa's house as a result of the latter's illtreatment. It will be seen that the two strains of the legend as found in the *Brāhmaṇas*, viz. Prajāpati insulting his own daughter and disregarding Rudra-Śiva, have both been cleverly accommodated in the story of the Purāṇas. When the news of Satī's death reached her husband, Śiva is said to have become furious and hastened to the scene with his numerous attendants. The sacrifice of Prajāpati Dakṣa was completely destroyed. Śiva, according to some of the sources, decapitated Dakṣa who was afterwards restored to life and thenceforward acknowledged the superiority of Śiva to all gods. According to some subversions of the story, Dakṣa was punished by the demon Vīrabhadra, created for the purpose by Śiva. The hand of a sectarian devotee of Śiva, eager to glorify his tutelary deity, is quite clear in the above story. It also shows that Śiva was originally a non-Aryan deity who later secured a prominent position in the Brahmanical pantheon. That, however, the story of *Dakṣa-yajña-nāśa* evolved out of the old legend about Prajāpati found in the *Brāhmaṇas* is proved by the fact that the Puranic account (cf. *Bhāgavata*, IV, 5, 20-21; *Kālikā*, XVII, 42-49; etc.)[1] of the destruction of Dakṣa Prajāpati's sacrifice often refers to the blinding of Bhaga's eyes and the breaking of Pūṣan's (or, Sūrya's) teeth, incidents pointedly mentioned in the *Brāhmaṇas*. The sixteenth century Bengali poet Mukundarāma, in the *Dakṣa-yajña-bhaṅga* section of his *Caṇḍīmaṅgala* (Calcutta University ed., I, p. 48) speaks of the blindness of Bhaga and the toothlessness of Pūṣan, both said to have been caused by Vīrabhadra on behalf of Śiva.[2]

Further Development of the Legend to explain the Origin of the Pīṭhas.

In still later times, probably about the earlier part of the medieval period,[3] a new legend was engrafted to the old story simply for the sake of explaining the origin of the Pīṭhas. According to certain later Purāṇas and Tantras (*Devībhāgavata*, VII, ch. 30; *Kālikā Purāṇa*, ch. 18; etc.), Śiva became inconsolable at the death of his beloved wife Satī, and, after the destruction of Dakṣa's sacrifice, he wandered over the earth in mad dance with Satī's dead body on his shoulder (or, head). The gods now became anxious to free Śiva from his infatuation and made a conspiracy to deprive him of his wife's dead body. Thereupon Brahman, Viṣṇu and Śani entered the dead body by *yoga* and disposed of it gradually and

---

[1] Cf. विश्वन्तमेव तं यज्ञे प्रथमं पुरतो भगः |***
तमागतमभिप्रेक्ष्य भर्गोऽपि श्वशुरोपितः ।
षड्भ्यःप्रष्टारेण तस्य नेने अचाल च ॥***
पवनस्तस्य सूर्यस्य मौखं दधभञ्जः।
हन्माल् वरप्रष्टारेण श्वातस्यामास वक्रतः ॥ (कालिकापुराण)
For the evidence of the Bhāgavata, see Appendix II.

[2] भगेर दीषन करिला मोचन
पूषार भाङ्गियाम दन्त । (पश्चीमङ्गल)

[3] The *Brahmavaivarta Purāṇa*, an old work known to Albīrūnī, contains interpolations of a date later than the Muslim occupation of eastern India where the Purāṇa was modified; cf. I, 10, 121 referring to the caste called Jolā (from *Julāhā*, weaver) said to have originated from Mleccha (Mahomedan) father and a girl of the Indian weaver caste. *Op. cit.*, IV, 43, 25, referring to Siddha-pīṭhas associated with Satī's limbs should similarly be assigned to a date not earlier than the 14th or 15th century. For the date of the *Kālikā Purāṇa*, see *infra*, p. 12, note 5.

bit by bit. The places where pieces of Satī's dead body fell are said to have become Pīṭhas, i.e. holy seats or resorts of the mother-goddess, in all of which she is represented to be constantly living in some form together with a Bhairava, i.e. a form of her husband Śiva. According to a modified version of this story, it was Viṣṇu who, while following Śiva, cut Satī's dead body on Śiva's shoulder or head piece by piece by his arrows or his discus. The story of the association of particular limbs of the mother-goddess with the Śākta *tīrthas*, which may have some relation with the Tantric ritual called *Pīṭhanyāsa*,[1] belongs, as already pointed out, to the latest stage in the development of an ancient tale. But the story may have some connection with Buddhist legends regarding the worship of Buddha's corporeal relics and the construction of *Stūpas* in order to enshrine them (cf. *Select Inscriptions*, I, pp. 84, 102ff., 120, etc.) as well as with those concerning the various manifestations of Buddha in the Jambudvīpa (cf. the list of 56 countries in the *Candragarbhasūtra*; *I.C.*, VIII, pp. 34-35; *BEFEO*, V, p. 261f.). One cannot also fail to recall in this connection Plutarch's version of the Egyptian Osiris myth: Osiris's brother Set put Osiris in a wooden coffin which he nailed up and cast into the sea; the waves bore it to Syria where, long after, Osiris's sister and wife Isis found it and took the body to Egypt; there unfortunately Set 'found it and scattered the bones far and wide, whence came the innumerable relics of Osiris shown to the faithful of later days in the temples of Egypt' (*Camb Anc. Hist.*, I, p. 332). The mythological interpretation of the genesis of the Pīṭhas, however, has little bearing on the real origin and development of the Pīṭha conception.

Conception of the Yonikuṇḍa and Stanakuṇḍa associated with that of the Liṅga.

The idea of the Pīṭha, associated with certain limbs of the mother-goddess, seems to be essentially connected with that of the Liṅga or phallus. The worship of the *Liṅga* of the great god Śiva originated from the conception of the god as the father or procreator. But in the matter of the procreation of beings the *Yoni* (*pudendum muliebre*) of the mother-goddess should naturally be regarded as much important as the Liṅga of the father-god. Both the Father-god and the Mother-goddess were worshipped by the pre-Aryan peoples of India.[2] The objects discovered at Mohenjodaro show that Śiva and Śakti were worshipped not only in the human form but also in the symbolic form of the Liṅga and the Yoni the former representing procreation and virility and the latter motherhood and fertility (Marshall, *Mohenjodaro and Indus Civilization*, I, pp. 52ff.). The Ṛgveda (VII, 21, 5; X, 99, 3) speaks in a deprecatory manner of a class of people called *śiśna-deva* in which we have probably the earliest literary reference to the worshippers of the phallus. The actual worship of the *Yoni* of the Divine Mother is referred to in certain later Tantric texts such as the *Yonitantra* (cited *infra*). It is interesting to note that one of the popular names of

---

[1] Vide *Sabdakalpadruma*, s.v. *nyāsa*; cf. *aṅganyāsa* (touching limbs with the hand accompanied by appropriate *mantras*) and *ṣoḍhānyāsa* (six ways of touching the body with mystical *mantras*) from which the *pīṭhavinyāsa* seems to have later evolved. Originally certain limbs were mentioned in connection with a Tantric ritual in which the names of the Pīṭhas were afterwards introduced. In explaining *pīṭhanyāsa*, the *Vācaspatya* says पौड़ेवतानाम् व्याधारप्रक्तिप्रकल्प्यादीनां प्रवशादिहिन्मोजेन हृदये न्यायभेदे तन्यशारः:, etc. The association of the limbs of the *sādhaka* with certain localities may have given rise to the belief regarding the Pīṭhas arising from particular limbs of the mother-goddess.
[2] See *infra*, Appendix VI.

the mother-goddess is *Bhagavatī* (literally, a deity possessing the *bhaga*). As the word *bhaga* is a synonym of *Yoni*, it is possible to suggest (although it is not easy to prove it in the present state of our knowledge) that the expression *Bhagavatī* originally indicated the female deity who was thought to have given birth to all creatures, and that the epithet *Bhagavat*, applied to Śiva and other gods, is merely a masculine form afterwards coined on the basis of *Bhagavatī*. It should also be pointed out that hills or mountain-peaks roughly resembling a human phallus were regarded in ancient times as the *svayambhū* (natural) *Liṅga* of Śiva. There is reason to believe that tanks or pools of a particular shape were often conceived as the *Yoni* of the mother-goddess. A pair of hills or peaks of the shape and position of female breasts appear sometimes to have been likewise regarded as the *Stana* of the goddess; cf. Kālidāsa's description (*Raghuvaṃśa*, IV, 51)[1] of the Malaya and Dardura mountains in the Pāṇḍya country as the two breasts of the lady that is the southern quarter. Water coming out of the springs on such hills could be very naturally taken to be the milk of the mother-goddess. All the three conceptions, viz. those of the *Liṅga* of the father-god and the *Yoni* and *Stana* of the mother-goddess, are based on the bearing the three particular limbs have on the birth and growth of beings as well as on the resemblance that particular natural objects may have with certain human limbs. An idea of the importance the Indians of ancient times must have attached to a bath in the *Yoni-kuṇḍa* and to the drinking of the water of the *Stanakuṇḍa* may be formed from another ritual known as the *Hiraṇyagarbha-mahādāna*, which was conceived in imitation of the *Yonikuṇḍa* of the mother-goddess. A pious prince desiring merit and willing to perform the *mahādāna* is sometimes found to have made a *hiraṇya-garbha* or 'golden womb' which was a big pot made of gold and was three cubits in height. He then entered the pot, of which the priests performed the ceremonies of *garbhādhāna*, *puṃsavana* and *sīmantonnayana*, as they would do in the case of an ordinary pregnant woman. The prince was afterwards taken out of the 'golden womb' and the *jātakarman* and other necessary functions were performed by the priests as if the prince was a newly born child. Thereafter the prince declared, 'O the best of gods, previously I was given birth to by my mother and had only the qualities of an earthly creature; but now owing to my rebirth from your womb I have a celestial body' (cf. *Suc. Sāt.*, pp. 52-54). The celebration of the *Hiraṇyagarbha-mahādāna* was adapted from a ceremonial practice of the devotees of the mother-goddess by the worshippers of the male god Viṣṇu. Just like the concept of the *Liṅga*, that of the *Yoni* and *Stana* of the mother-goddess appears to be very old. The history of the socio-religious life in ancient India suggests that these conceptions, like many others, are due to non-Aryan influence on the culture of the Indo-Aryans.[2]

Some Early Tīrthas associated with the Limbs of the Mother-goddess.

It seems that the association of the *Yoni* and *Stana* of the mother-goddess with certain localities belongs to the earliest stage of the history of the Pīṭhas. The *Tīrtha-yātrā* section in the Vanaparvan of the *Mahābhārata*, which is probably earlier than the rise of the Guptas in the fourth century A.D , refers at least to three Śākta holy places associated with the *Yoni* and *Stana* of Śakti. These are the *Yonikuṇḍas* at the Bhīmāsthāna near the Pañchanada (Punjab) and on the hill or mountain-peak called Udyatparvata, and the *Stanakuṇḍa* on the peak known as Gaurīśikhara

---

[1] स्तनाविव दिशस्तस्याः भ्रोशो मलयदुर्दुरौ ।   [2] See *infra*, Appendix VI.

(cf. *Mahābhārata*, III, 82, 83-85; III, 84, 93-95 and 151-53).[1] The name of the Gaurīśikhara (literally, the peak of Gaurī, a form of the mother-goddess) probably connects the peak with the Himalayas.[2] The *Mahābhārata* seems to locate both the Gaurīśikhara and the Udyatparvata in eastern India, the latter probably in the Gayā region. Their exact location is not beyond doubt, although it is tempting to identify the Gaurīśikhara with the peak of that name placed by the *Pīṭhanirṇaya* in the Kāmarūpa country in the Gauhati region of Assam. The Bhīmāsthāna (literally, the resort of Bhīmā, a form of the mother-goddess) was situated on the Karamar not far from Shahbazgarhi in the Peshawar District of the North-Western Frontier Province. The *Mārkaṇḍeya Purāṇa* (ch. 91, vv. 45-46), an early Śākta work, speaks of the goddess Bhīmādevī of the Himācala (cf. also Appendix II, v. 22 *infra*). In the seventh century, this holy *tīrtha* belonging to the ancient country of Gandhāra (Rawalpindi-Peshawar region) was visited by the Chinese pilgrim Hiuen Tsang. According to the pilgrim, 'About 50 *li* (nearly 8 miles) to the north-east of Palushawas a great mountain which had a likeness of Maheśvara's spouse Bhīmādevī of dark blue stone. According to local accounts this was a natural image (*svayambhū mūrti*) of the goddess; it exhibited prodigies and was a great resort of devotees from all parts of India; to true believers, who after fasting seven days

[1]
(a) अथ पञ्चमदं गत्वा नियतो नियताशनः ।
पञ्चयज्ञमवाप्नोति क्रममो येऽनुकीर्तिताः ।
ततो गच्छेत राजेन्द्र भीमायाः स्थानमुत्तमम् ।
तत्र स्नात्वा तु योन्यां वै नरो भारतसत्तम ।
देव्याः पुत्रो भवेद् राजन् रत्नकुण्डलविग्रहः ।
सर्व मतसत्रस्य फलं प्राप्नोति मानवः ।

(b) उद्यन्तं ततो गच्छेत पर्वतं गीतनादितम् ।
सावित्र्यास्तु पदं तत्र दृष्यते भरतर्षभ ।
तत्र सन्ध्यामुपासीत ब्राह्मणः संशितव्रतः ।
तेन ह्युपास्या भवति सन्ध्या द्वादशवार्षिकी ।
योनिद्वारे तथैव विश्रुतं भरतर्षभ ।
तत्राभिगम्य मुच्यते पुरुषो योनिसङ्कटात् ।
कृष्णशुक्लावुभौ पक्षौ गयायां यो वसेन्नरः ।
पुनात्यासप्तमं राजन् कुलं मास्यच संशयः ।

(c) ततो गच्छेत धर्मज्ञ तीर्थंचैवमतत्परः ।
शिखरं वै महादेव्या गौर्याः लोकविश्रुतम् ।
समारुह्य नरस्तत्र स्नानकृच्छ्रेषु संविशेत् ।
स्नानकृच्छ्रसुपस्पृश्य वाजपेयफलं लभेत् ।
तत्राभिषेकं कुर्वाणः पिष्टदेवार्चने रतः ।
दशमेधमवाप्नोति ब्रह्मलोकंच गच्छति ।

The same section of the *Mahābhārata* (III, ch. 83, verses 51, 58, 94, 99, 102, etc.) speaks of other places of pilgrimage, designated Mātṛ-tīrtha or Devī-tīrtha apparently named after the mother-goddess. It is unknown whether they were associated with any of the limbs of the goddess.

[2] Cf. *Gaurī-guru* (father of Gaurī), an epithet of the Himālaya in *Raghu*, II, 26; *Kirāta*, V, 21; Badal pillar inscription, verse 5 (*Gauḍalekhamālā*, p. 27), etc.

prayed to her, the goddess sometimes showed herself and answered prayers. At the foot of the mountain was a temple to Maheśvaradeva (Śiva) in which the ash-smearing *Tīrthikas* (Pāśupata Yogins)[1] performed much worship' (Watters, *On Yuan Chwang's Travels in India*, I, p. 221).[2] The account of

---

[1] In his description of Benares, Hiuen Tsang again refers to the devotees of Śiva some of whom 'cut off their hair, others made it into a top-knot; some went about naked and smeared themselves with ashes; they were persevering in austerities seeking release from mortal existence' (*loc. cit.*, II, p. 47). For the ash-smearing ascetics, see *Bṛhatsaṃhitā*, ch. 60, verse 19:

विश्वोभीगवतान् मगांश्च सवितुः मन्त्रीः सभञ्जद्विज्ञान्
मानूत्वामपि माळमण्डलविदो विप्रान् विदुर्मेक्षणः ।
माख्यान् सर्वचितस्य माःसमनसो लग्रान् जिनानां विदु-
र्ये यं देवसुपाश्रिताः स्वविधिना तेऽसष्य काश्चीः क्रियाः ॥

While annotating this verse, Albīrūnī (*op. cit.*, p. 121) refers to the devotees of Mahādeva (Śambhu-Śiva) as 'a class of saints, anchorites with long hair, who cover their skin with ashes, hang on their persons the bones of dead people, and swing in the pools'. They are the Śiva-bhāgavatas described by Patañjali in his commentary on Pāṇini, V, 2, 76, and were related to the Kāpālikas known from works like the *Pañcatantra* as characterized by carrying skulls of men in the form of garlands and eating and drinking from them. For this sect, cf. the *Mattavilāsaprahasana* attributed to Pallava Mahendravarman I (c. 600-35 A.D.), Bhavabhūti's *Mālatīmādhava* (eighth century), an Early Calukyā inscription, dated 639 A.D. (referring to the worship of the god Śiva Kāpāleśvara, i.e. lord of the wearers of skull-garlands, and to the maintenance of the Mahāvratins, i.e. observers of the great vow characteristic of the Kāpālikas or Kālāmukhas, who resided in the temple of the god), etc. See R. G. Bhandarkar, *Vaiṣṇavism, Śaivism*, etc. (Poona ed.), pp. 165ff.

Bhavabhūti's *Mālatīmādhava* speaks of a woman styled *yoginī*, who performed the *Kāpālikavrata* at the Śrīparvata and illustrates the *vrata* by the horrible activities of Aghoraghaṇṭa and his female disciple Kapālakuṇḍalā who are represented as coming from the Śrīparvata and staying near the *mahāśmaśāna* (at Padmāvatī in the Gwalior State) containing a temple of Cāmuṇḍā to whom they were going to offer the girl Mālatī in sacrifice. This eighth century authority not only testifies to the prevalence of human sacrifice before the mother-goddess, but also to the interesting fact that the Kāpālikas were devoted to both Śiva and Śakti. The practices of the Kāpālikas are often called *Vīrācāra* and *Vāmācāra*.

'From the *Mattavilāsa-prahasana*, it becomes clear that, to a Kāpālika, the *Kapāla* is as essential as is a sacred thread to a Brāhmaṇa. If he loses it, he should provide himself with another in a stated time. He should cover his body with ashes and make himself hideous, and drink liquor from the skull of a human being..... One of the articles of faith is that the effect always resembles, to a certain extent, the cause; therefore from the practice of austerities in this life one cannot obtain bliss in another life, since austerities and bliss are of opposite nature. The Kāpālikas carried in addition to the *Kapāla* a cow's horn both for blowing during their worship and drinking from. The people of this faith associated freely with women Kāpālikas.' Cf. R. Gopalan, *History of the Pallavas*, pp. 94-95. The *Kūrma Purāṇa* (cf. I. 16, 117, etc.) distinguishes the Kāpālikas from the Pāśupatas as well as from the other Śaiva sects and says that 'the Pāśupatas hate those sects which are guided by the Tantras' (R. C. Hazra, *Purāṇic Rites*, p. 64; also *Ṣaṭtriṃśanmata* quoted at p. 201). Cf. the words *pākhaṇḍa* and *pākhaṇḍin* in the sense possibly of the Kāpālikas in the *Mālatīmādhava*, V, 24 and the *Mitākṣarā* on Yāj., III, 6. The *Rāj. tar.* (III, 267) refers to Śrīparvata as a centre of the Pāśupatas and also to their existence in Kashmir (I, 17; V, 404). The doctrines and practices of the Pāśupatas (distinguished from the Kāpālikas) as described in the *Kūrma Purāṇa* show that they were not extremists like the latter with whom they were sometimes identified. For the *Atharvaśiras Upaniṣad* on the early doctrine of the Pāśupatas, see Bhandarkar, *Vaiṣṇavism*, etc., pp. 158ff.

[2] While describing the Gandhāra country, Hiuen Tsang elsewhere (Watters, *op. cit.*, p. 215) says that at the distance of 50 *li* (about 8 miles) to the north-west of certain monasteries (including the Aśoka *stūpa* at Puṣkalāvatī, modern Mirziyarat-Charsadda area near Peshawar) there was a *stūpa* at the place where the Buddha converted the 'Mother of Demons' (the Buddhist goddess Hārītī) and that the people of the country worshipped this Demon-mother and prayed to her for offspring. The deity was apparently an aspect of the mother-goddess. The *stūpa* is now called Sāre Mākhe Ḍherī.

the foreign traveller points clearly to the importance and popularity of the ancient Bhīmā *tīrtha*. The existence of the temple of Śiva at the foot of Bhīmā's peak probably suggests that the association of a Bhairava with the Śākta Pīṭha is earlier than the seventh century. But it is not definitely known whether the Bhīmāsthāna, Udyatparvata and Gaurīśikhara were styled Pīṭhas in the technical Tantric sense of the term and whether they were counted among the recognized Pīṭhas in the days of Hiuen-Tsang.[1]

The Tradition about Four Pīṭhas.

Some of the early *Tantras* refer to four Pīṭhas. This *Catuṣpīṭha* conception may have been associated with a conception of the Sahajayāna school of the Buddhists, according to which one can rise to eternal bliss from sexual pleasure. A Sahajayāna text entitled *Catuṣpīṭhatantra* and its commentaries (one of which was copied in 1145 A.D.; cf. H. P. Sastri, *Cat. Palm-leaf and Selected Paper Manuscripts belonging to the Durbar Library, Nepal*, II, p. viii) speak of the four Pīṭhas as Ātmapīṭha, Parapīṭha, Yogapīṭha and Guhyapīṭha and deal with the various kinds of Vajrasattva's intercourse with the Yoginīs, such as Prajñāpāramitā and others. This philosophical concept of the *Catuṣpīṭha* was either the cause or the effect of the early recognition of four holy places as Pīṭhas.[2]

---

[1] See *infra*, Appendix VI. For the association of Śiva with the Pīṭhas, cf. *Devī-bhāgavata*, Bk. VII, ch. 30, verses 44–50:

अपश्यतां पतौ वह्नौ दह्यमानाम् चितृकटाम् ।
अन्वेष्यारोपयामास वा सतीति वदन् मुह्यः ॥
बभ्राम ध्यानचित्तः सम्भ्रान्तादेषु प्रद्धरः ।
तदा ब्रह्मादयो देवाश्चिन्नामापुरनुत्तमाम् ॥
विष्णुस्तु तरसा तत्र धनुष्ठद्भ्यां मार्गयेः ।
चिच्छेदावयवान् सत्याष्ठतत्वाानेषु तेऽपतन् ॥
तत्तत्स्थानेषु सदाश्रीष्ण्णान्यमूर्तिधरो हरः ।
अवाप च ततो देवान् स्थानेष्वेतेषु मे शिवास् ॥
भजन्ति यरया भक्त्या तेषां किञ्चिन्न दुर्लभम् ।
नित्यं सन्निहिता यत्र निजांशेषु पराम्बिका ॥
स्थानेष्वेतेषु मे मर्त्त्याः पुरश्चरणकर्मिणः ।
तेषां मन्त्राः प्रसिध्यन्ति मायाबीजं विशेषतः ॥
रत्युक्ता मद्गरक्षेषु स्थानेषु विरन्नातुरः ।
कालं निव्यै तपस्येह अपध्यानसमाधिभिः ॥

[2] It is difficult to determine what relation the Catuṣpīṭha could have with the Catuṣpīṭha-parvata near Jajpur in Orissa and with other Sahajayāna conceptions of 'four', e.g. the Caturānanda. The *Caṇḍamahāroṣaṇatantra* (Sastri, *Cat.*, pp. ix-x) is said to have been uttered by Vajrasattva (Buddha) when he was staying in the female organ of Vajradhātvīśvarī. The first verse uttered is:

भावाभावविनिर्मुक्तचतुरानन्दतत्परः ।
निष्प्रपञ्चस्वरूपोऽहं सर्वसङ्कल्पवर्जितः ॥

Caturānanda, i.e. the pleasures of four kinds, has been explained as embracing, kissing, pressing the breast, and pricking with the nails (i.e. imprinting nail-marks). These are said to last as long as the *thunderbolt* is in union with the *lotus*.

In the opinion of some writers, the *Hevajra Tantra* of the Buddhists was composed shortly before 693 A.D.[1] But according to Buddhist tradition, Padmavajra, author of the *Hevajra Tantra*, was the preceptor of Anaṅgavajra, a son of king Gopāla[2] who founded the Pāla dynasty in Bengal about the middle of the eighth century A.D. If this tradition is to be accepted, the composition of the *Hevajra Tantra* may be assigned to the same century. This early work enumerates the following four holy regions as Pīṭhas: (1) Jālandhara, (2) Oḍiyāna (Uḍḍiyāna in the Swat valley),[3] (3) Pūrṇagiri and (4) Kāmarūpa[4] Exactly the same tradition is followed in the *Kālikā Purāṇa* (ch. 64, 43–45)[5] according to which the four Pīṭhas were: (1) Oḍra, seat of the goddess Kātyāyanī and god Jagannātha,[6] in the west, (2) Jālaśaila, seat of the goddess Caṇḍī and god Mahādeva in the north, (3) Pūrṇa or Pūrṇaśaila (Pūrṇagiri), seat of the goddess Pūrneśvarī and god Mahānātha, in the south, and (4) Kāmarūpa,

---

[1] Cf. B. Bnattacharya, *Sādhanamālā* (G.O.S.), II, p. xliii.
[2] *Op. cit.*, pp. l-li.
[3] The suggestion that Oḍḍiyāna was situated in eastern India and is no other than Oḍra (Orissa) is unworthy of any serious consideration. Cf. Lévi, *Journ. As.*, 1915, pp. 105–10; P. C. Bagchi, *Studies in the Tantras*, I, pp. 37ff., 42. For some other unwarranted theories about the location of Uḍḍiyāna, see *I.H.Q.*, XI, pp. 142ff.; *J.As.R.S.*, V, pp. 14ff. For a discussion on the expressions *uḍḍiyānabandha*, *jālandharabandha*, etc., see *J.Or.Ac.*, II, pp. 55–68.

[4] Cf. पीठं जालन्धरं ख्यातं ओड्डियानं तथैव च ।
पीठं पूर्वगिरिं चैव कामरूपन्तथैव च ।

quoted by Bagchi (*op. cit.*, p. 38) from the seventh Paṭala of the *Hevajra Tantra*.
[5] Cf. Vaṅgavāsī ed., p. 410:

ओड्रस्य प्रथमं पीठं द्वितीयं जालशैलकम् ।
तृतीयं पूर्वपीठन्तु कामरूपं चतुर्थकम् ॥
ओड्रपीठं पश्चिमे तु तथैवोग्रेश्वरीं शिवाम् ।
कात्यायनीं जगन्नाथमोग्रेशञ्च प्रपूजयेत् ॥
उत्तरे पूजयेत् पीठं प्रशस्तं जालशैलकम् ।
जालेश्वरं महादेवं चण्डीं जालेश्वरीं तथा ॥
दौर्घिकादौषधच्छाय तथैव परिपूजयेत् ॥
दक्षिणे पूर्वशैलन्तु तथा पूर्वेश्वरीं शिवाम् ।
पूर्णनाथं महानाथं सरोजामथ षष्ठिकाम् ॥
पूजयेदुमरीं देवीं ब्राह्मीमपि तथा शिवाम् ।
कामरूपं महापीठं तथा कामेश्वरीं शिवाम् ॥
नीलस्य पर्वतश्रेष्ठं नाथं कामेश्वरं तथा ।
पूजयेद्द्वारि पूर्वे तु क्रमादेभ्यांश्च भैरव ॥

The *Kālikā Purāṇa*, quoted by Nānyadeva (c. 1097–1133 A.D.) in his *Bharatabhāṣya* and by Aparārka (c. 1115–40 A.D.) and Ballālasena (c. 1159–85 A.D.), seems to have been originally incorporated in the *Rudrayāmala Tantra*; cf. *Des. Cat. Sans. MSS.*, *R.A.S.B.*, VIII, p. 70. This *Purāṇa* (really an Upa-Purāṇa) is earlier than 1000 A.D. according to Gode, *J.O.R.*, X, pp. 289ff.; *J.Or.Ac.*, II, p. 60. Cf. Hazra, *op. cit.*, p. 53; *infra*, p. 17, note 4. Some sections may, however, have been later added to the original *Purāṇa*.
[6] Cf. the god Jagannātha in the Puri temple in Orissa (Oḍra). For the confusion of Oḍra and Oḍḍiyāna, see *infra*.

seat of the deities Kāmeśvarī and Kāmeśvara [1] in the east. That Oḍra in the list is a mistake for Uḍḍiyāna and that Jālaśaila is the same as Jālandhara are clear from another section of the same Purāṇa (ch. 18, 42-44 and 49-51) [2] representing the goddesses- Kātyāyanī and Caṇḍī as the presiding deities respectively of Uḍḍiyāna and Jālandharagiri.[3] Other Buddhist works such as the Sādhanamālā (G.O.S., pp. 453, 455) give the four names as (1) Oḍiyāna or Uḍḍīyana, (2) Pūrṇagiri, (3) Kāmarūpa or Kāmākhyā, and (4) Śrīhaṭṭa or Sirihaṭṭa. Śrīhaṭṭa has been substituted in this list

---

[1] Cf. reference to Mahāgaurī (Kāmākhyā) and Kāmeśvara (on the Kāmakūṭa hill) in some early records of Assam; see infra. The identification of Mahāgaurī with Bhuvaneśī (I.H.Q., XXIII, p. 324, Kālikā P., 62, 127) on the top of the Kāmakhyā hill is rendered doubtful by her association with Kāmeśvara. The boundaries of Kāmarūpa are indicated by the Yoginītantra (Paṭala XI) quoted in Ep. Ind., XII, p. 68:

नेपालस्य कञ्चनाद्रिं ब्रह्मपुत्रस्य सङ्गमम् ।
करतोयां समारभ्य यावद्दिक्करवासिनीम् ॥
उत्तरस्यां कञ्जगिरिः करतोया तु पश्चिमे ।
तीर्थश्रेष्ठा दिक्षु नदी पूर्वस्यां गिरिकन्यके ॥
दक्षिणे ब्रह्मपुत्रस्य लाक्षायाः सङ्गमावधिः ।
कामरूप इति ख्यातः सर्वशास्त्रेषु निश्चितः ॥

This Kāñcana or Kañja Mount is probably the Kunchenjinga. The Dikṣu, which may be associated with Dikkaravāsinī although the latter is located at Dikrang near Sadiya in north-eastern Assam, is the modern Dikhu falling in the Brahmaputra near Sibsagar. The confluence of the Lākṣā (Lakhyā) and the Brahmaputra is in the Mymensing District. The Karatoyā which now runs through North Bengal and falls in the Yamunā in the Pabna District, was the western boundary of Kāmarūpa also according to Chinese sources. A manuscript of the Yoginī Tantra (R.A.S.B., No. I. B. 29, p. 33) reads: नेपालस्य च कान्तद्रिं । Some writers prefer the reading: उत्तरस्यां कुञ्जगिरिः । For Kāmarūpa's four divisions (Pīṭhas), viz. Kāma, Ratna, Bhadra or Suvarṇa and Saumāra, see Gait, Hist. As., p. 11. Kāmarūpa is also called Kubjikā Pīṭha (Kālikā P., 62, 58, etc.).

[2] Cf. Vaṅgavāsī ed., pp. 79-80:

देवीकूटे पादयुग्मं प्रथमं न्यपतत् किल ।
उड्डियाने चोध्वयुग्मं चिताय आगतं ततः ॥
कामरूपे कामगिरौ न्यपतद् योनिमण्डलम् ।
तच्चैव न्यपतद् भूमौ पूर्वस्यां नाभिमण्डलम् ॥
जालन्धरे स्तनयुगं सर्वश्रृङ्गारविभूषितम् ।
षड्ङ्गश्रीवं पूर्वगिरौ कामरूपान्ततः शिरः ॥ * * *
देवीकूटे मद्दादेवी मद्दाभागेति गीयते ।
सतीपादयुगे श्रोणी योगनिद्रा जगत्प्रभुः ॥
कात्यायनी चोड्डियाने कामाख्या कामरूपिणी (°रूपके) ।
पूर्णेश्वरी पूर्णगिरौ चण्डी जालन्धरे गिरौ ॥
पूर्णान्ते कामरूपस्य देवी दिक्करवासिनी ।
तथा क्षतिकान्तेति योगनिद्रा प्रगीयते ॥

For details of other Pīṭhas mentioned here, see infra, p. 17. For the same confusion between Oḍra (placed in north-western India) and Uḍḍiyāna in early literature, see Mahābhārata, II, 47, 19.

[3] The location of the Oḍra (Orissa) country in the western part of India has also to be noted. This points actually to Uḍḍiyāna in north-western India.

for Jālandhara which, however, seems to have been recognized as one of the four Pīṭhas even down to the late medieval period.[1] Abul Fazl's *Ain-i-Akbarī*, composed about the end of the sixteenth century at the court of the Mughal emperor Akbar (1556-1605), contains an interesting description of the Pīṭha near Nagarkot together with the legend about the origin of the four Pīṭhas as known to the author. In this connection Abul Fazl says, 'Nagarkot is a city situated on a hill; its fort is called Kangrah. Near the town is the shrine of Mahāmāyā (a name of the Indian mother-goddess indicating "the goddess having great magical powers") which is considered as a manifestation of the divinity. Pilgrims from distant parts visit it and obtain their desires. Strange it is that in order that their prayers may be favourably heard, they cut out their tongues; with some it grows again on the spot, with others after one or two days. Although the medical faculty allow the possibility of growth in the tongue, yet in so short space of time it is sufficiently amazing. In the Hindu mythology Mahāmāyā is said to be the wife of Mahādeva, and the learned of this creed represent by this name the energizing power of the deity. It is said that on beholding the disrespect (shown to herself and her husband Śiva) she cut herself in pieces and her body fell in four places; her head and some of her limbs in the northern mountains of Kashmir near Kāmrāj and these relics are called Śāradā: other parts fell near Bījāpūr in the Deccan and are known as Tuljā (Turjā) Bhavānī. Such portions as reached the eastern quarter near Kāmarūpa are called Kāmākhyā, and the remnant that kept its place is celebrated as Jālandharī which is this particular spot. In the vicinity torch-like flames issue from the ground in some places, and others resemble the blaze of lamps. There is a concourse of pilgrims and various things are cast into the flames with the expectation of obtaining temporal blessings. Over them a domed temple has been erected and an astonishing crowd assembles therein. The vulgar impute to miraculous agency what is simply a mine of brimstone' (Jarrett's trans., II, pp. 312-14). The four Pīṭha-devīs recognized in the sixteenth century account are, therefore, (1) Śāradā at modern Sardi in northern Kashmir, (2) Tuljā Bhavānī in a locality in the medieval kingdom, the capital of which was at Bijapur in the southern part of the Bombay Presidency, (3) Kāmākhyā in Kāmarūpa, and (4) Jālandharī near Nagarkot in the Punjab. Abul Fazl has substituted Kashmir for Uḍḍiyāna. He refers to Jvālāmukhī and not to the neighbouring Jālandhara Pīṭha.[2] The Pīṭha that he

---

[1] For the tradition of the four Pīṭhas, cf. षड्दर्शनीं प्रवक्ष्यामि जघान्यं पीठचतुष्टयम् । पूर्णगिरिश्च प्रथममुड्डीयानं द्वितीयकम् । जालन्धरं ततीयपं कामरूपं चतुर्थकम् ।..... मग्ने: सर्वशरीरं यत् पीठं पूर्णगिरिः शृतम्। तस्या: शिरस्य सुभगे उड्डीयानं प्रकीर्तितम् ॥ स्तनो जाल-
ध्वरं ज्ञेयं कामरूपं भगस्थचा ॥ (*Samayācāra Tantra* quoted in the *Prāṇatoṣaṇī Tantra*, Vasumatī ed., p. 548); also पुण्यतीर्थं कुरुचन्द्रे देवीपीठचतुष्टये । प्रयागे श्रीगिरौ काम्यां
काञ्चीकाञ्चं न घोषयेत् ॥ (*Yāmala* quoted in the *Tantrasāra*, Vaṅgavāsī ed., p. 40). Vide the two *Pīṭhatattvanyāsas* mentioning the four Pīṭhas by name in the *Tantra-sāra*, pp. 419-20, 451-52. The Pūrṇagiri Pīṭha is in these cases called *Uḍḍīśanāthāt-maka*. For a tradition about five Pīṭhas accommodating the claim of both Jālandhara and Śrīhaṭṭa, cf. पट चक्रं मेदःपद्मं उड्डीयानं तथैव च । जालन्धरः कामरूपः पूर्णपीठ: (°गिरिः) श्रीपद्मकः ॥ quoted from the sixth Paṭala of the Tattvasāra in the *Prāṇatoṣaṇī Tantra*, pp. 39 and 40.

[2] For some foreign notices of Jvālāmukhī, see *Hobson-Jobson*, s.v. *Jowalla Mookhee*. In the third quarter of the fourteenth century, Shams-i-Shirāj 'Afīf (Elliot, *Hist. Ind.*, III, p. 318) mentions the idol Jvālāmukhī much worshipped by the

places in the Bijapur region may be the same as Pūrṇagiri mentioned in the other texts. The shrine of Bhavānī stands at Tuljapur to the south of Osmanabad in the Hyderabad State. Such was the celebrity of this goddess that, when Śivājī built the fort of Pratāpgarh near Javli, he set up there an image of his patron-deity Bhavānī as the Bhavānī of Tuljapur was beyond easy reach to him (J. N. Sarkar, *History of Aurangzib*, IV, p. 32). It is well known that the Thuggees (both Hindus and Muslims), many of whose organizations belonged to Western India and the Deccan, were followers of the goddess Bhavānī irrespective of their personal religious beliefs. This fact points also to the importance of the mother-goddess in the religious life of that part of India. The Śāradā-maṭha on the borders of Kashmir is mentioned in such other works as the *Śaktisaṅgama Tantra* (*I.C.*, VIII, pp. 38, 49). About 1030 A.D., Albīrūnī says (Sachau, *Alberuni's India*, I, p. 117), 'In inner Kashmir, about two or three days' journey from the capital in the direction towards the mountains of Bolor, there is a wooden idol called Śāradā, which is much venerated and frequented by pilgrims.' The temple of Śāradā is also mentioned in Kalhaṇa's *Rāj. tar.*, VIII, 2556, 2706. The ruins of Sardi, where the shrine of Śāradā stood, lie at the confluence of the Kishengaṅga and Kankatori rivers. The old shrine is substituted by the late Śāradā temple at Gusha (old Ghoṣa) which is now visited by pilgrims. See Stein, *Rāj. tar.* (trans.), II, pp. 279–89.

The Tantric Schools of North-Western and Eastern India.

Two things are apparent from the accounts of the four Pīṭhas. In the first place, Kāmarūpa has a prominent place in all the lists of four. This fact may suggest that the Kāmarūpa Pīṭha became unrivalled as a centre of Tantric culture by absorbing the popularity of the other Yoni *tīrthas* of ancient India at a fairly early date. The name of Kāmarūpa, with which that of the goddess Kāmākhyā (the original name probably being *Kāmā*, a shortened form of *Kāmarūpā*)[1] seems to be intimately associated, is mentioned in the Allahabad pillar inscription (middle of the fourth century A.D.) of Samudragupta. But the holy seat of the goddess near Gauhati in Assam does not appear to be mentioned in the *Tīrthayātrā* section of the Vanaparvan, even if the Stanakuṇḍa at Gaurīśikhara is located in the neighbourhood. The Chinese pilgrim Hiuen Tsang who lived for some time at the court of the Kāmarūpa king Bhāskaravarman (*c*. 600–50 A.D.) in the seventh century, is also silent about the goddess Kāmākhyā. It is, therefore, not improbable that the presiding deity of Kāmarūpa did not quite attain to her pre-eminence in the days of Hiuen Tsang.[2] Worship of the mother-goddess was, however, widely prevalent among some of the primitive tribes of ancient Assam. The following note on the religious life of the Chutiyas of Assam throws interesting light on the subject: 'The religion of the Chutiyas was a curious one. They worshipped various forms of Kālī with the aid, not of Brāhmaṇas, but of their tribal priests or Deoris. The favourite form in which they worshipped this deity was that of Kesāi

---

infidels and situated on the road to Nagarkot and says, 'Some of the infidels have reported that Sulṭān Fīrūz went specially to see this idol and held a golden umbrella over its head.... Other infidels said that Sulṭān Muḥammad Shāh bin Tughlak Shāh held an umbrella over this same idol; but this also is a lie.'

[1] The name of the goddess is traced to the Austric words *Kāmoi* (demon), *Kāmoit* (devil), *Komin* (grave), *Kamet* (corpse in Khasi), *Kamru* (a god of the Santals), etc. Cf. C. B. Kakati in *Assam Tribune*, October 22, 1947.

[2] Kāmākhyā seems to be called Mahāgaurī in the records of Vanamāla (end of the 9th century) and Indrapāla (12th century), kings of Kāmarūpa. See *infra*, Appendix VI.

Khāti, "the eater of raw flesh", to whom human sacrifices were offered. After their subjugation by the Ahoms, the Deoris were permitted to continue their ghastly rites; but they were usually given, for the purpose, criminals who had been sentenced to capital punishment. Failing them, victims were taken from a particular clan, which in return was accorded certain privileges. The person selected was fed sumptuously, until he was in sufficiently plump condition to suit the supposed test of the goddess, and he was then decapitated at the Copper Temple at Sadiya, or at some other shrine of the tribe. Human sacrifices were also formerly offered by the Tipperas, Kachāris, Koches, Jaintias and other Assam tribes' (E. Gait, *History of Assam*, 1926, p. 42; *J.A.S.B.*, 1898, p. 56).[1] It may be pointed out in this connection that the Chinese pilgrim noticed the influence of the Pāśupatas or Tīrthikas, with whom the Tantric devotees of Śakti and Śiva were associated, all over India—in Jālandhara, Ahicchatra (?), Malakūṭa (in the Far South), Mālava, Benares, Maheśvarapura (on the Narmadā), the land about eastern Makran, Bannu (?) and even Khotan (in Central Asia); cf. *loc. cit.*, I, 296, 331; II, 47, 229, 242, 251, 257, 262, 296, etc. Bhavabhūti's *Mālatīmādhava* not only speaks of a great centre of the Kāpālikas (cf. *supra*, p. 10, note 1), apparently devoted to the god Śiva Mallikārjuna, at Śrīparvata (Śrīśaila in the Karnool District, Madras Presidency), but also of their devotion to an image of the mother-goddess Cāmuṇḍā (another name of Tārā or Kālī according to the *Kālikā Purāṇa*, ch. 61, 85–91), entitled Karālā, in a temple at Padmāvatī (Padampawaya near Narwar in the Gwalior State).

Another point of interest in the account of the four Pīṭhas is the importance of the Gandhāra, Uḍḍiyāna, Jālandhara and Kashmir countries of north-western India as centres of Tantricism. Hiuen Tsang not only noticed the prevalence of Śakti worship in Gandhāra, but has also left an account of the popularity of Tantric practices among the people of Uḍḍiyāna. According to the pilgrim, 'The people (of Uḍḍiyāna) were pusillanimous and deceitful; they were fond of learning but not as a study, and they made the acquisition of magical formulae their occupation' (Watters, *op. cit.*, p. 225). Uḍḍiyāna's eminence in the Tantric world is also indicated by the recognized association of its name with the worship of the Buddhist deities Mārīcī, Kurukullā (identified with Kālī in some passages cited in the *Tantrasāra*), Lokeśvara and Ūrdhvapāda-Vajravārāhī (cf. *Sādhanamālā*, G.O.S., pp. 80, 83, 283ff., 361, 439). Indrabhūti, the Buddhist king of Uḍḍiyāna, was a celebrated Tantric teacher who composed the *Jñānasiddhi* and other works. He was the father of Padmasambhava, the famous teacher of the Yogācāra doctrine, who was responsible for the popularity of Buddhism in Tibet and established in that country the great Bsam-yas monastery in *c.* 787 A.D. with the help of a Bengali (?) Buddhist teacher named Śāntarakṣita or Śānti . The lady Lakṣīṃkarā, a sister of king

---

[1] Cf. 'When the new temple of Kāmākhyā was opened, the occasion was celebrated by the immolation of no less than a hundred and forty men, whose heads were offered to the goddess on salvers made of copper. Similar sacrifices were offered to various aboriginal deities. According to the *Haft Iqlim*, there was in Kāmarūpa a class of persons called Bhogīs, who were voluntary victims of a goddess named Ai who dwelt in a cave; from the time when they announced that the goddess had called them, they were treated as privileged persons; they were allowed to do whatever they liked, and every woman was at their command; but when the annual festival came round, they were killed. Magic also held an important place in the estimation of the people, and in the '*Ain-i-Akbarī* they were accused, among other practices, of divination by the examination of a child cut out of the body of "a pregnant woman who has gone her full term of months"' (*History of Assam*, p. 58).

Indrabhūti, composed the Buddhist Tantra work entitled *Advayasiddhi*.[1] The rule of the Turkish Musalmans, that spread over north-western India from the tenth century, led to the gradual decline of the once flourishing Tantric culture in that part of India.

Different Traditions regarding the Number of Pīṭhas.

Although four Pīṭhas were associated roughly with the northern, southern, eastern and western regions of India,[2] writers on the subject are not, unanimous as regards the exact number of the seats of the mother-goddess. The *Kālikā Purāṇa* account of the four Pīṭhas has been already noticed; but a different section of the same Purāṇa (ch. 18, verses 42–51) gives an account of seven Pīṭhas (including the four seats of the goddess described above), no less than three of which are located in Kāmarūpa. According to this section, the Pīṭhas are: (1) Devīkūṭa (i.e. Devīkoṭṭa, modern Bangarh in the Dinajpur District of Bengal) where Sati's two feet fell on the ground and where the Devī is Mahābhāgā; (2) Uḍḍiyāna where the two thighs fell and where the Devī is Kātyāyanī; (3) Kāmagiri in Kāmarūpa where the *pudendum muliebre* fell and the Devī is Kāmākhyā; (4) a locality on the eastern border of Kāmarūpa where the navel fell and where the Devī is Dikkaravāsinī; (5) Jālandhara where the two breasts fell and where the Devī is Caṇḍī; (6) Pūrṇagiri where thè neck and shoulders fell and where the Devī is Pūrṇeśvarī; and (7) a locality on the borders of Kāmarūpa where the head fell and where the Devī is Lalitākāntā.[3] A Tantra work entitled *Rudrayāmala*, which seems to have been composed considerably earlier than 1052 A.D.,[4] mentions ten holy places as the 'principal' Pīṭhas. These ten Pīṭhas, which include the celebrated four discussed above are: (1) Kāmarūpa, (2) Jālandhara, (3) Pūrṇagiri, (4) Oḍḍiyāna (Uḍḍiyāna), (5) Vārāṇasī (Benares), (6) Jvalantī (probably Jvālā-mukhī of later texts), (7) Māyāvatī (near Hardwar), (8) Madhupurī (Muttra), (9) Ayodhyā (near Fyzabad, U.P.), and (10) Kāñcī (Conjeeveram in the

---

[1] Cf. Bhattacharya, *op. cit.*, pp. li–liv. Bhattacharya gives the date of the foundation of the Bsam-yas monastery as 749 A.D. But the period of Padmasambhava's stay in Tibet is usually assigned to *circa* 780–95 A.D. by recent writers on the subject (F. W. Thomas, *Indianism and its Expansion*, p. 79).

[2] As the number 3 had a mystic significance with many ancient peoples of the world (cf. the Trimūrti, Triratna, Tribhuvana, etc., of the Indians, the Anu-Bel-Ea trinity of the Babylonians, and the Osiris-Isis-Horus triad of the Egyptians), there was also a tradition about three Pīṭhas; cf. *Ānandārṇava Tantra* quoted in *Des. Cat. Sans. MSS.*, R.A.S.B., VIII, p. 213:

विद्या***पीतांलिपीठांछिदभाम्मरे ।
कामरूपक-जालन्ध-पूर्णभूपुर(भूभर)सञ्ज्ञकान् ॥

[3] *Supra*, p. 13, note 2. A passage (probably adapted from the *Kālikā Purāṇa*) in the sixth Paṭala of the *Bṛhan-Nīlatantra* refers to the same five Pīṭhas:

देवीकोटे मदमागा उड्डीयाने च भैरवी ।
योनिमुद्रा कामरूपे मदिषासुरमर्दिनी ॥
कात्यायनी कामभूमौ कामाख्या कामरूपिणी ।
जालन्धरे (पूर्णशैले) च पूर्वशैलौ पूर्व शैले (जालन्धरे) च षष्टिका ॥
कामरूपे ततो देवी पूज्या दिक्करवासिनी ॥

The temple of Dikkaravāsinī is usually located at Dikrang near Sadiya. Lalita-kāntā is now popularly associated with the hill-streams Sandhyā, Lalitā and Kāntā not far from Gauhati.

[4] The *Rudrayāmala* is mentioned in the *Brahmayāmala*, a manuscript of which was copied in 1052 A.D. (Bagchi, *op. cit.*, pp. 6–7). Cf. *supra*, p. 12, note 5.

Chingleput District, Madras Presidency).[1] The language of the *Rudra-yāmala* suggests that its author had knowledge of some other Pīṭhas of lesser importance. A passage from this work quoted in the *Kulārṇava Tantra* (*Des. Cat. Sans. MSS.*, R.A.S.B., VIII, pp. 110-11) actually speaks of the following 18 Pīṭhas: (1) Uḍḍiyāna, (2) Devīdaikoṭha (Devīkoṭṭa), (3) Hiṅgulā, (4) Koṭimudrā, (5) Jālandhara, (6) Vārāṇasī, (7) Antarvedī, (8) Prayāga, (9) Mithilā, (10) Māgadha, (11) Mekhalā (Mekalā), (12) Aṅga, (13) Vaṅga, (14) Kaliṅga, (15) Siṃhala, (16) Strīrājya, (17) Rādhā and (18) Gauḍa. That, however, the list of even the *pradhāna* Pīṭhas were drawn arbitrarily without any basis of accepted tradition is clearly demonstrated by the discrepancy among similar lists of Pīṭhas found in different works. A passage of the *Jñānārṇava Tantra* (Ānandāśrama ed., Paṭala V, verses 66-67), which was composed considerably earlier than the middle of the sixteenth century,[2] enumerates eight important Pīṭhas in the following order: (1) Kāmarūpa, (2) Malaya, (3) Kaulagiri, (4) Kulāntaka, (5) Cauhāra (not mentioned in the *Jñānārṇava* list of 42 Pīṭhas and may be a result of misreading), (6) Jālandhara, (7) Uḍḍiyāna, and (8) Devakūṭa (Devīkoṭṭa).[3] As a matter of fact, there are only a few common names in the lists of the *Rudrayāmala* and the *Jñānārṇava*. Such is also the case with other lists of the Pīṭhas which usually contain only a number of common names.

There is a very small work entitled *Aṣṭādaśapīṭha* incorporated in Manuscript No. 5913 in the library of the Royal Asiatic Society of Bengal. This work, which is full of textual errors, is ascribed to Śaṅkarācārya (probably the same as Śaṅkara Āgamācārya, the Bengali author of the *Tārā-rahasya-vṛttikā*, an R.A.S.B. copy of which was made in Śaka 1583 = 1661 A.D.) and mentions eighteen Pīṭhas together with the Pīṭha-devīs. Although some of these names are apparently doubtful, it is interesting that the list of eighteen Pīṭhas includes: (1) Laṅkā—Śaṅkarī, (2) Ālāpura—Yugalā, (3) Śrīśaila—Bhramarāmbikā, (4) Kolhāpura—Mahālakṣmī, (5) Vārāṇasī—Viśālākṣī, and (6) Kāśmīra—Sarasvatī (Śāradā). The location of Bhramarāmbikā on the Śrīśaila and of Mahālakṣmī at Kolhapur in the southern part of the Bombay Presidency is specially interesting because Bhramarāmbā, still worshipped on the Śrīśaila, is not mentioned in the other texts, while Kolhapur reminds one of Kolvagiri, etc., and of Mahālakṣmī or Mahā-lakṣmīpura (cf. *I.C.*, VIII, p. 49). The interesting work on the eighteen

---

[1] Vide *tārā-śodhā* in the *Rudrayāmala*, quoted in the *Tantrasāra*, Vaṅgavāsī ed., pp. 521-22:

मूलाधारे कामरूपं हृदि जालन्धरं तथा ।
भ्रूद्वाटे पूर्णगिर्याख्यमुड्डीयानं तदूर्ध्वके ॥
वाराणसीं भ्रूर्मध्ये व्यक्तनीं कोषनचये ।
मायावतीं सुषुम्णे कण्ठे मधुपुरीं ततः ॥
अयोध्यां नाभिदेशे च कर्ण्यां काञ्चीं विनिर्दिशेत् ॥
दशैतानि प्रधानानि पीठानि क्रमतो विदुः ।
स्कन्धौघ्रेष्वङ्गमेषोस्त्रैः क्रमतो न्यसेत् ॥

[2] The *Jñānārṇava* is largely quoted by the Tantrācāryas Brahmānanda and Pūrṇā-nanda in the sixteenth century.

[3] कामरूपं च मलयं ततः कौलगिरिं तथा ।
कुलान्तकं च चौहारं जालन्धरमतःपरम् ॥
उड्डीयानं देवकूटं पीठाष्टकमिदं क्रमात् ॥

Pīṭhas is said to have been written down by one Sambhunath Kar of Calcutta in Samvat 1863 = 1806 A.D. from the dictation of an Utkala Brāhmaṇa who was an inhabitant of Jahājapura (Jājpur) on the Vaitaraṇī.[1]

Another Tantra text entitled *Kubjikā Tantra*, usually supposed to be a fairly early work, enumerates the following Siddha-Pīṭhas: (1) Māyāvatī, (2) Madhupurī, (3) Kāśī, (4) Gorakṣakāriṇī or Gorakṣacāriṇī, (5) Hiṅgulā, (6) Jālandhara, (7) Jvālāmukhī, (8) Nāgarasambhava, (9) Rāmagiri, (10) Godāvarī, (11) Nepāla, (12) Karṇasūtra, (13) Mahākarṇa, (14) Ayodhyā, (15) Kurukṣetra, (16) Siṃhanāda or Siṃhala, (17) Maṇipura, (18) Hṛṣīkeśa, (19) Prayāga, (20) Badarī, (21) Ambikā, (22) Vardhamāna or Ardhanālaka, (23) Triveṇī (probably Muktaveṇī near Calcutta and not Yuktaveṇī at Prayāga which is separately mentioned), (24) Gaṅgā-sāgara-saṅgama, (25) Nārikela, (26) Virajā, (27) Uḍḍiyāna, (28) Kamalā, (29) Vimalā, (30) Māhiṣmatī, (31) Vārāhī, (32) Tripurā, (33) Vāgmatī, (34) Nīlavāhinī, (35) Govardhana, (36) Vindhyagiri, (37) Kāmarūpa, (38) Ghaṇṭākarṇa, (39) Hayagrīva or Akṣayagrīva, (40) Mādhava, (41) Kṣīragrāma, and (42) Vaidyanātha.[2]

मद्दाकाल्यै नमः । अष्टादशपीठानि लिख्यन्ते ।
लङ्कायां शङ्करी देवी कामाख्या काषिकापुरी ।
प्रद्युम्ने सिंग(ंघ)लद्वीपे चामुण्डा कुच्चपट्टने (क्रौञ्च°?) ॥
चाञ्चापुरे (हट्टा°?) युगला देवी श्रीशैले अमराम्बिका ।
उज्जयिन्यां महाकाळी माकरे (सह्याद्रौ ?) एकवीरका ॥
उत्कले विरजा देवी माणिक्यां(?) चक्रकोटिन्यौ(?) ।
चयद्येने कामरूपौ(?) प्रयागे माश्ववेश्वरी ॥
ज्वालायां वैष्णवी देवी गया माङ्गल्यकोटिका(?) ।
वाराणस्यां विशालाक्षी काश्मीरे तु सरस्वती ॥
अष्टादशानि पीठानि योगिनां ध्यानिर्मितम्(?) ।
तेषां पठनमात्रेण अरद्दारिद्यनाशनम् ॥

इति शङ्कराचार्यविरचितम् अष्टादशपीठं सम्पूर्णम् । इति श्रीसम्भुनाथकर (°करेण) उत्कलदेशस्य ब्राह्मण-बेलंपुरोकर-अदजपुरीय-वैतरणीय-ब्राह्मणाच्छ्रुत्वा लिखितम् । संवत् १८६३ पौषस्यैकादश्याः प्रज्ञे लिखितं कलिकातास्थपट्टने । प्रभवस्तु सर्वजगताम् ॥

[2] Cf. *Kubjikā Tantra* (Paṭala VII), Manuscript No. 3174 (R.A.S.B.); the same quoted in the *Prāṇatoṣaṇī Tantra* (Vasumatī ed., p. 234) and in the *Vācaspatya*, s.v. *pīṭha*.

मायावती मधुपुरी काश्मी गोरचकारिषी (v.l. °चारिषी) ।
चिङ्गुला च महापीठं तथा जालन्धरं पुनः ॥
ज्वालामुखी महापीठं पीठं नागरसम्भवम् (v.l. नगर°) ।
रामगिरिसंद्वापीठं तथा गोदावरी प्रिये ॥
नेपालं कर्णसूत्रञ्च महाकर्णं तथा प्रिये ।
अयोध्या च कुरुच्चेवं सिंहलाख्यं (v.l. सिंहनादं) मनोरमम् ॥
मणिपुरं हृषीकेशं प्रयागञ्च तपोवनम् ।
बदरी च महापीठमम्बिका अर्धनालकम् (v.l. अम्बिकाम्बर्धनालकम्) ॥
त्रिवेणी च महापीठं गङ्गासागरसङ्गमम् ।
नारिकेलस्य विरजा उड्डीयान महेश्वरि ॥

This list, probably composed in eastern India, speaks rather independently of about forty-two Pīṭhas some of which seem to represent actually the names of deities. Reference to the Vindhyan region as a Pīṭha in this list no doubt points to the resort of the celebrated non-Aryan goddess Vindhyavāsinī (identified with the Indian mother-goddess) whose temple stands near modern Mirzapur in the United Provinces. The antiquity of the worship of this goddess is proved by the fact that, according to Vākpatirāja's *Gauḍavaha*, king Yaśovarman (c. 730-53 A.D.) offered his homage to Devī Vindhyavāsinī in connection with his expedition for the conquest of the quarters. In the twelfth century, Kalhaṇa (*Rāj. tar.*, III, pp. 394-431) seems to refer to the same deity as Bhramaravāsinī [1] in connection with a sixth century Kashmirian king named Raṇāditya. The celebrated Śākta work entitled *Caṇḍī*, incorporated in the *Mārkaṇḍeya Purāṇa*, gives evidence to the cult of the goddess Vindhyavāsinī (cf. ch. 91, v. 37). That the resort of this early and important deity is not mentioned in all the different lists of Pīṭhas containing even names of lesser importance, indicates the absence of recognized traditions and the freedom an author may have exercised in this matter

Evidence of the Jñānārṇava and the Tantrasāra regarding the Number of Pīṭhas.

Eight Pīṭhas mentioned in the *Jñānārṇava Tantra* have been mentioned above. It is interesting to note that a different section of the same work definitely gives the recognized number of Pīṭhas as fifty only.[2] These fifty Pīṭhas are: (1) Kāmarūpa, (2) Vārāṇasī, (3) Nepāla, (4) Pauṇḍravardhana (Mahasthan in the Bogra District, North Bengal), (5) Kashmir, (6) Kānyakubja, (7) Purasthita (v.l. Purasthira), (8) Carasthita (v.l. Candrāsthira, Carasthira), (9) Pūrṇaśaila, (10) Arbuda, (11) Āmrātakeśvara, (12) Ekāmra (Bhuvaneśvar in Orissa), (13) Trisrotaḥ (the Tista river in north-eastern

कमला विमला चैव तथा माङ्गिभती (v.l. माङ्गिबरी) पुरी ।
वाराणी त्रिपुरा चैव वाम्पती नौक्षवाणिनी ॥
गोवर्धनं विन्ध्यगिरिः कामरूपं कम्बोजे युगे ।
षष्ठाकर्षे चयप्रौवी (v.l. °चयप्रौवी) माधवस्य सुरेश्वरि ॥
चौरप्रामं वेद्यानाश्च ज्ञानीयादामलीयने ॥

This list can hardly be very early. But the idea (*Rājamālā*, I, ed. K. P. Sen, p. 124) that the *Kubjikā* speaks of 127 Pīṭhas is due to the wrong impression created by the *Prāṇatoṣaṇī* which quotes several lists from the *Bṛhan-Nīlatantra*, without reference to the source, in continuation of the *Kubjikā* list.

[1] The name has, as the *Rāj. tar.* seems to imply, bearing on the condition of the Vindhyan forests infested with bees. The Indian mother-goddess is given the name Bhrāmarī in some texts (*Mārkaṇḍeya Purāṇa*, 91, 49; *Devībhāgavata*, X, 10, 13); cf. the name of Bhramarāmbā on the Śrīśaila. The *Pīṭhanirṇaya* locates this deity in northern Bengal and in the Nasik region of the Bombay Presidency. It is interesting to note that certain forms of the mother-goddess in western Asia, such as Nanaia and Artemes, had the bee for their symbol. The Indian mother-goddess riding a lion reminds one of the Cappadocian Ma who stands on a lioness or panther. Like Śiva, Ma's consort Teshub also rides on a bull and has the three-pronged thunder-bolt (cf. *triśūla*) as his distinctive weapon. See Raychaudhuri, *D. R. Bhand. Volume*, pp. 301-03. The goddess Vindhyavāsinī is possibly called Śūlinī in the *Tantrasāra*, p. 193. The *Gauḍavaha* (verses 285-347) identifies Vindhyavāsinī with Kālī or Pārvatī, associates her with the Kols and Śabaras, and refers to human sacrifices offered to her. For the goddess, fond of wine and flesh and worshipped by the Śabaras, Pulindas and Barbaras, see *Hariv.*, II, iii, 7-8.

[2] Cf. the expressions *pañcāśat-pīṭha-sañcaya* (v.l. *pañcāśat-sthāna°*) and *pañcāśat-pīṭha-vinyāsa* in the *Jñānārṇava* (Ānandāśrama ed., Paṭala XIV, verse 112); quotation from the same work in the *Tantrasāra*, p. 427n.; *Tantracūḍāmaṇi* (MS. No. I, F 3 in the library of the R.A.S.B.), p. 515.

THE ŚĀKTA PĪṬHAS

India), (14) Kāmakoṭṭa (v.l. °koṭa), (15) Kailāsa, (16) Bhṛgu, (17) Kedāra, (18) Candrapura, (19) Śrīpīṭha (probably, Śrīhaṭṭa), (20) Oṅkāra, (21) Jālandhara, (22) Mālava (v.l. Mānava), (23) Kulānta (v.l. Kūpānta), (24) Devakoṭṭa, (25) Gokarṇa, (26) Māruteśvara, (27) Aṭṭahāsa, (28) Virajā, (29) Rājagṛha, (30) Kolvagiri (Kaulagiri), (31) Elāpura (Ellora), (32) Kāleśvara (v.l. Kāmeśvara), (33) Jayantikā (Jayantī), (34) Ujjayinī, (35) Kṣīrikā (Kṣīragrāma), (36) Hastināpura, (37) Uḍḍīśa (from Prakrit *Oḍḍaviśa, Oḍḍaīsa* > Sanskrit *Oḍraviṣaya*, i.e. Orissa), (38) Prayāga, (39) Vindhya, (40) Māyāpura, (41) Jaleśvara (in Orissa), (42) Malaya, (43) Śrīśaila, (44) Merugiri, (45) Mahendra, (46) Vāmana, (47) Hiraṇyapura, (48) Mahālakṣmī, (49) Uḍḍiyāna, (50) Chāyāchatrapura.[1] It is doubtful whether all the

---

[1] The same passage is also found in the manuscript of the *Tantracūḍāmaṇi* (pp. 515-16) in the R.A.S.B. library and in Brahmānanda's *Śāktānandataraṅgiṇī*, ch. 15 (referring to the *Gāndharva Tantra*).

कामरूपं महापीठं पीठं वाराणसीं तथा ।
नेपालञ्च तथा पीठं तथा वै पौण्ड्रवर्धनम् ॥
काश्मीरञ्च महापीठं कान्यकुब्जमतः परम् ।
पुरस्थितं (v.l. °स्थिर°) तथा पीठं चरस्थितमथापरम्
(v.l. चरस्थिर°, चन्द्रास्थिर°) ॥
पूर्णशैलं महापीठसर्वुद्धं ततः परम् ।
व्याघ्रातकेश्वरं पीठमेकाम्रञ्च ततःपरम् ॥
(v.l. दार्व्यकेश्रं महापीठम् एकाम्रञ्च तथा शिवे ।)
विख्यातः पीठमनघं कामकोष्ठं (v.l. °टि°) मतःपरम् ।
कैलाशं भृगुपीठञ्च (v.l. °नगरं) केदारं चन्द्रपुरकम् ॥
(v.l. कैलाशभृगुकेदारं पीठं वन्द्रपुरं ततः ॥)
श्रीपीठञ्च (श्रीहट्टञ्च ?) तथोद्गारं जालन्धरमतः परम् ।
मालवञ्च (v.l. मानवञ्च) तथा पीठं कुलान्तं (v.l. कूपान्तं)
देवकोट्टकम् (v.l. देवी°, °कोटकम्, °कोटरम्) ।
(v.l. कैलाशं भूतनगरं केदारं पीठमुत्तमम् ।
श्रीपीठञ्च कुलान्तञ्च देवमाल्कमेव च ॥)
गोकर्णञ्च महापीठं मारुतेश्वरमेव च ।
अट्टहासञ्च विरजं राजगृहमथापरम् (v.l. महापथम्) ॥
पीठं कोल्वगिरिं प्रोक्तमेलापुरमथापरम् ।
कालेश्वरं (v.l. कामेश्वरं) महापीठं महापीठं (v.l. प्रणवाख्यं) जयन्तिकाम् ।
पीठमुज्जयिनीञ्चैव विचित्रं क्षीरिकाभिधम् ।
दक्षिणपुरपीठञ्च (v.l. पुरकं पीठम्) उड्डीशञ्च प्रयागकम् ॥
विन्ध्यञ्चैव (v.l. षष्ठीश्रञ्च, कान्यकुब्जं) महापीठं मायापुरजलेश्वरौ ।
मलयञ्च महापीठं श्रीशैलं मेरुकं गिरिम् ॥
महेन्द्रं वामनञ्चैव (v.l. माहेन्द्रं वाहनं°) हिरण्यपुरमेव च (v.l. हिरण्यं) ।
महालक्ष्मीञ्च (v.l. °पुरं) पीठउड्डीयानमतः परम् ॥
छायाछत्रपुरं पीठं तथैव परमेश्वरि ।
पञ्चाशत्पीठविन्द्यासं मातृकावद्व्रजेत् सदा ॥

places mentioned were Śākta *tīrthas*. In some cases there seems to be an attempt to trace Śākta influence in not only Śaiva but also Vaiṣṇava holy

---

The same passage is found in the fifth Paṭala of the *Bṛhan-Nīlatantra* in a modified and corrupt form (cf. *infra*, p. 37, note 1 for the emendations):

कामरूपं प्रियं वाराणसी मैथाह्नमेव च ।
पौण्ड्रं वर्धमपीठच्च पावकं (पारखं) कान्यकुब्जकम् ।
पुष्याद्रिमर्वुदञ्चैव (पुष्या°) शकाचमान्वकेश्वरम् (°वैकाचमाघातके°) ।
चेपुरं कामकोटच्च तथा गुप्तपुरं (श्चगु°) वरम् ॥
कैलासं पीठकेदार(°र) च्चम्भचन्द्रपुरं तथा ।
श्रीपुरं च तथा काल्याः (कन्या°) पुरं ज्वालम्बरं तथा ॥
मानवं (माहवं) विल्वपीठच्च देवीकोट तथैव च ।
गोकर्णं माषतेजच्च तथाङ्गच्छमेव च ।
ह्यमुकानासगोनच्च (विरजापुरच्चेनच्च) शङ्खापुरमस्ति प्रियम् ।
मन्दापद्मपुरच्चैव चौड्रारपुरमेव च ॥
जयद्रच्च जयपुरम् ञ्जजयिनीपुरं तथा ।
हरिद्रापीठकच्चैव प्रिय(यं)जीरपुरं प्रियम् ॥
मज्ञाक्षयपुरच्चैव उड्डीनपुरमेव (उड्डीम°) च ।
प्रयागच्च तथा वच्छौपुरमेव शिवप्रदम् ॥
मायापुरमतिश्रेष्ठं पुरच्च परमेश्वरम् (श्रमने° ?) ।
श्रीमेकलमेवपीठच्च विमाच्नयमन्तगिरिम् ।
मन्द्रेन्द्रपुरपीठच्च तथा बलिपुरं प्रियम् ।
विरिच्चपुरपीठच्च मच्चालक्षौपुरं तथा ॥
चण्डीपुरमतिश्रेष्ठं (चण्ड°?) तथा च्छायापुरं (च्चायाक्तपुरं) प्रिये ॥

To give the above passage an appearance of an original composition, it is preceded in the *Bṛhan-Nīlatantra* by the following verses which mention certain Pīṭhas in the alphabetical order:

श्रमरेशपुरच्चैवासुराज्ञकपुरं तथा ।
श्रम्बिकापीठमत्यनमनमपुरमेव च ॥
श्रनिरुद्धपुरं वेतृषि तथादितिपुरं परम् ।
श्रविमादिपुरच्चैव श्रश्वमेघपुरं परम् ॥
श्रन्नपूर्णामच्चपीठमम्बुजाच्चपुरन्तथा ।
श्रादिपौञ्चानन्दपीठौ श्रामोद्रावादिच्चकरौ ॥
श्राम्रसिद्धिपुरच्चैव यथाद्यकपुरं सुखम् ।
श्रकम्पादित्यपीठौ च श्राद्यादिनाथपीठकौ ॥
इष्टनाम(°नाम°)पुरच्चैव रन्दिरापुरमेव च ।
इक्षोदयगिरिर्च्चैव रक्षाक्लेष्पुरे प्रिये ॥
रन्द्राच्चीन्द्रौश्वरच्चैव रन्द्रानन्दपुरन्तथा ।
परमिन्द्रवतौ नाम तवेन्द्रविजयं पुरम् ॥
ईश्वरेश्वरयोगी च ईशानेश्वौरपुरम् ।
ईश्वान्येशपुरं देवि कथितं पीठमुत्तमम् ॥

Some of the names mentioned appear to have been fabricated by the author and to have had no real existence.

places. This attempt may possibly be attributed to eastern India. The above list has been quoted and utilized in a *Piṭhanyāsa* section of the *Tantrasāra* by the Bengali Tantric teacher Kṛṣṇānanda Āgamavāgīśa in the seventeenth century.[1] Curiously enough the *Tantrasāra*, in spite of its clear recognition of the number of Pīṭhas to be fifty only in accordance with the *Jñānārṇava Tantra*, actually makes fifty-one Pīṭhas out of the fifty enumerated above. This has been done strangely by splitting the name of one of the fifty Pīṭhas, viz. Merugiri (No. 44) into two names, viz. Meru Pīṭha and Giri Pīṭha,[2] in the formal *nyāsa* associating certain limbs with the Pīṭhas.[3] The anomaly was probably the result of a modification of the text of the *Tantrasāra* by later hands. What is, however, more interesting is that the *Pīṭhanirṇaya* or *Mahāpīṭhanirūpaṇa*, which has been quoted in the *Prāṇatoṣaṇī Tantra* by Rāmatoṣaṇa Vidyālaṅkāra, who was seventh in descent from the compiler of the *Tantrasāra*, in 1820 adheres exactly to this modified number of the Pīṭhas, viz. fifty-one, although the list itself is independent of the earlier lists of Pīṭhas. As this work is not quoted in the *Tantrasāra* or any other earlier Tantra dealing with the Pīṭhas, it seems that the *Pīṭhanirṇaya* was composed or became popular in eastern India shortly after the compilation of the *Tantrasāra* by Kṛṣṇānanda Āgamavāgīśa (seventeenth century) but before that of the *Prāṇatoṣaṇī Tantra* by Rāmatoṣaṇa in 1820. As the work was utilized by Bhāratacandra in his *Annadāmaṅgala* (1752), it must have been composed earlier than the middle of the

---

[1] For a detailed discussion on the date of the *Tantrasāra*, see Appendix IV.

[2] Cf. *Tantrasāra*, p. 426: लं लं लं मेरुपीठाय नमः ककुदि; वं वं वं गिरिपीठाय नमो वामकक्षे ।

[3] Cf. *loc. cit.*; also the Rudrayāmala passage quoted above. The *Tantrasāra* associates the following limbs with the following Pīṭhas: (1) कामरूप—limb not mentioned; according to the *Rudrayāmala* मूत्राधार (region of the organ of generation); (2) वाराणसी—मुखाग्रम ; (3) नेपाल—दक्षचक्षुः (दक्ष = right); (4) पौण्ड्रवर्धन—वामचक्षुः ; (5) काश्मीर—दक्षकर्ण ; (6) कान्यकुब्ज—वामकर्ण ; (7) पूर्णशैल—दक्षिणनस् (नस् = nostril) ; (8) चरस्थित—वामनस् ; (9) पूर्णशैल—दक्षगण्ड ; (10) शर्वत—वामगण्ड ; (11) आम्रातकेश्वर—ओष्ठ ; (12) एकाम्र—अधर ; (13) विश्वोत्तः—अर्ध्वदन्त ; (14) कामकोट—अधोदन्त ; (15) कैलाश—भ्रुवन्तरम् ; (16) भृगु—मुख ; (17) केदार—दक्षबाहुमूल ; (18) चन्द्रपुर—दक्षकूर्पर ; (19) श्री—दक्षमणिबन्ध ; (20) ओड्रर—दक्षिणाङ्गुलिमूल ; (21) जालन्धर—दक्षाङ्गुल्यग्र ; (22) मालव (मानव)—वामबाहुमूल ; (23) कुलान्तक (कूपान्तक)—वामकूर्पर ; (24) देवीकोट—वाममणिबन्ध ; (25) गोकर्ण—वामाङ्गुलिमूल ; (26) मारतेश्वर—वामाङ्गुल्यग्र ; (27) अट्टहास—दक्षपादमूल ; (28) विरज—दक्षजानु ; (29) राजगृह—दक्षगुल्फ ; (30) कोलागिरि—दक्षपादाङ्गुलिमूल ; (31) एलापुर—दक्षाङ्गुल्यग्र ; (32) कालमेश्वर (कालेश्वर)—वामपादमूल ; (33) जयन्ती—वामजानु ; (34) उज्जयिनी—वामगुल्फ ; (35) चौरिका—वामपादाङ्गुलिमूल ; (36) क्षितिमापुर—वामपादाङ्गुल्यग्र ; (37) उड्डीश—दक्षिणपार्श्व ; (38) प्रयाग—वामपार्श्व ; (39) विन्ध्य—पृष्ठ ; (40) मायापुर—नाभि ; (41) जलेश्वर—उदर ; (42) मलय—हृत् ; (43) श्रीशैल—दक्षस्कन्ध ; (44) मेरु—ककुत् ; (45) गिरि—वामस्कन्ध ; (46) महेन्द्र—हृदादिदक्षकर ; (47) वामन—हृदादिवामकर ; (48) विरंजपुर—हृदादिदक्षपाद ; (49) मधाङ्कीपुर—हृदादिवामपाद ; (50) उड्डीयान—हृदादिदर ; (51) कायाक्षचपुर—हृदादिमुख । It should be noted that the association of a Pīṭha with a limb in the *nyāsa* was suggested differently by different writers.

eighteenth century. The composition of the *Pīṭhanirṇaya* or *Mahāpīṭhanirūpaṇa* may therefore be assigned to the closing years of the seventeenth century or more probably to the early years of the eighteenth (c. 1690-1720). The reference to Kālīghāṭa, whose popularity seems to be associated with the foundation of Calcutta (1690) and whose mention in earlier works is rare,[1] possibly supports this date. The important feature of this work, as it is usually accepted in Bengal, is that its list of Pīṭhas together with the names of the Devī and the Bhairava, includes a number of places in the rural areas of Bengal. The language is in some cases greatly influenced by Bengali. The history of the literature on the Pīṭhas no doubt points unmistakably to the great contribution Bengal must have made to the Tantric literature and culture in the medieval period. The greatest centre of Tantricism seems to have originally been in north-western India. Before the medieval period, the Tantric school of north-eastern India rose to eminence and became a great rival of the north-western school. With the gradual decline of Tantric culture in the north-west as a result of foreign occupation, Bengal seems to have come to the forefront as the abode of great leaders of Tantric thought.

The Tradition about 108 Pīṭhas.

The uncertainty about the recognized number of the Pīṭhas in the medieval period is also demonstrated by another fact. The number 108 had some importance in India to the sectarian worshippers who often attempted to endow their respective deities with 108 names.[2] In the list of such 108 names of a particular deity, names or epithets of various other deities were appropriated, the underlying idea being that the latter are only different manifestations of the former. The love of system and concord, which is a feature of the Indian mind, inspired theologians to harmonize Brahman, Viṣṇu and Śiva in the compound form of the Trimūrti, Viṣṇu and Śiva in that of Hari-Hara, and Śiva and Śakti in that of Ardha-nār-īśvara. The theory of the ten Avatāras of Viṣṇu was likewise the result of an attempt at harmonization of different religious sects worshipping different cult-deities.[3] Even in recent times, the Bāuls of Bengal, both Muslim and

---

[1] There is no mention of Kalighat as a Pīṭha in the *Caṇḍīmaṅgala* (16th century) by Mukundarāma of the Burdwan District. But Vipradāsa's *Manasāmaṅgala* (1495 A.D.) mentions Kālikā of Kalighat, Sarvamaṅgalā of Citpur (now included in Calcutta) and Betāi-Caṇḍī of Betor (near Sibpur in the Howrah District). Even if this reference is not an interpolation, it does not prove that Kalighat was regarded as an important *tīrtha* in the fifteenth century. The sixteenth century author Vaṁśīdāsa of Mymensing does not regard Kalighat as a Pīṭha. See *infra*, p. 33 and note 3.

[2] Cf. the list of various names of Śiva in the Sanatkumāra-saṁhitā section (ch. 31) of the *Śiva Purāṇa* and in the Kedārakhaṇḍa subsection of the Māheśvarakhaṇḍa section of the *Skanda Purāṇa*. For a list of the different names of Brahman, see *Padma Purāṇa*, Sṛṣṭikhaṇḍa, ch. 34; *Skanda Purāṇa*, Prabhāsakhaṇḍa, ch. 107. The idea seems to have originated from the Śatarudrīya section of the *Yajurveda* (Taittirīya Saṁhitā, IV, 5, 1; Vājasaneyī Saṁhitā, ch. 16). A Bengali text entitled *Śrīkṛṣṇa-śatanāma* (literally, the 100 names of Lord Kṛṣṇa) is very popular in Bengal and is daily recited by many pious people. There are also later lists of the 1,000 names of some gods, notably Viṣṇu. See *Des. Cat.*, R.A.S B., VIII, pp. 173, 500, 812, 815, 820ff., 842, etc. For two lists of the *sahasranāma* of Viṣṇu and Śiva, see *Mahābhārata*, XIII, chs. 149 and 17. For the importance of the numbers 108 and 1008, see *Tantrasāra*, pp. 48, 116, 131, 157, 538, 652, 733, 761, 781, 825-26, 903, 905, 918, 920, 973, etc., and 83, 157, 906-07, 928, etc. The importance of the number 108 is clearly demonstrated by the fact that even today the revered names of many religious teachers are mentioned as prefixed by the word *Śrī* for no less than 108 times, although in actual practice *Śrī* for 108 times is indicated by the expression '*śrī* 108'.

[3] See Sircar, 'Sectarian Difference among the Early Vaiṣṇavas' in *Bhār. Vid.*, VIII, pp. 109-11.

Hindu, have been declaring in their songs the absolute identity of Rāma and Rahim, of Christ (Beng. *Khṛṣṭa*) and Kṛṣṇa (vulgo *Kṛṣṭa*), of Śiva and 'Alī, and of Durgā and Fatīma. A section of the devotees of the mother-goddess is known to have endowed their cult-deity with 108 names attempting thereby to identify her with various goddesses and with the female forms (Śaktis or energizing powers) of many gods worshipped in different parts of India. An early list of this nature can be traced in the *Mahābhārata* (VI, ch. 23); but a complete list of the 108 names of the mother-goddess with the specification of her association with particular holy places is probably to be found for the first time in the *Matsya Purāṇa*, ch. 13, the particular section, however, being assignable to the early medieval period.[1] The same text has been quoted in the description of the various manifestations of Bhadrakarṇikā (a form of the mother-goddess) in the Revākhaṇḍa subsection of the Āvantyakhaṇḍa in the *Skanda Purāṇa* (which in its present form is not earlier than the twelfth century)[2] as well as in the enumeration of the different names of the goddess Sāvitrī, the wife of Brahman, in the Sṛṣṭikhaṇḍa section (ch. 17) of the *Padma Purāṇa*. The same text is also quoted in the *Devībhāgavata* (VII, ch. 30) which, unlike the *Matsya*, *Skanda* and *Padma Purāṇas*, refers to the holy places, associated in this work with the different manifestations of the mother-goddess and of her consort, as Pīṭhas without, however, mentioning the particular limbs of the goddess and the particular Bhairavas, although it says that the list contains the names of some Pīṭhas in addition to those that 'sprang from' the limbs of Satī.[3]

---

[1] Ch. 13 of the *Matsya Purāṇa* refers to Vṛndāvana as the resort of Rādhā and to Puruṣottama. There is no genuine evidence to show that Rādhā was recognized as a divinity earlier than the post-Gupta period and that Puruṣottama (Purī) attained to any eminence before the days of Anantavarman Coḍagaṅga (1078–1147 A.D.) who laid the foundation of the great temple of Jagannātha at Purī. Cf. also reference to Māṇḍavyapura (Mandor in the Jodhpur State), Vaidyanātha, etc., which do not appear to be early, although the *Matsya Purāṇa* in some form must have existed in earlier times.

[2] Cf. references to Rāmānuja (Viṣṇukhaṇḍa, ch. 21) who flourished in the age of the Choḷa King Adhirājendra (c. 1070 A.D.) and the Hoysaḷa Viṣṇuvardhana (c. 1106–41 A.D.), to the Gurjara-Pratīhāra King Bhoja I (c. 836–85 A.D.) and to King Āma of Kanauj who was either the same as Āma (c. 753–65 A.D.), son of Yaśovarman (c. 730–53 A.D.) or as Āma-Nāgabhaṭa II (c. 805–33 A.D.), grandfather of Bhoja I. Vide Prabhāsakhaṇḍa-Vastrāpathamāhātmya, ch. 1ff.; Brahmakhaṇḍa-Dharmāraṇya-khaṇḍa, ch. 36ff. These, however, do not prove that the *Skanda Purāṇa* did not exist in any form in earlier times. In the first-half of the 11th century, Albīrūnī had no information about the 18 *Purāṇas* including the *Skanda* (Sachau, *loc. cit.*, pp. 130-31). For a Bengal manuscript of this *Purāṇa* 'written in Gupta hand, to which as early a date as the middle of the seventh century can be assigned on palaeographical grounds', see *JRAS*, 1903, p. 193; Smith *EHI*, 1924, p. 23.

[3] A later list of 108 Pīṭhas is found in the *Prāṇatoṣaṇī Tantra*, p. 236 (cf. *Vācaspatya*, s.v. *pīṭha*). The verses appear to have been quoted from the *Bṛhan-Nīlatantra* (Paṭala V) which was known to the Prāṇatoṣaṇī (cf. p. 2). As there are several lists in it, the *Bṛhan-Nīla*, itself a late-medieval work, probably also drew from some slightly earlier sources. If it is the same as the *Mahā-Nīlatantra*, it must be regarded as earlier than c. 1550 A.D. when Brahmānanda mentioned it in his *Tārārahasya* (Paṭala I). But this date is doubtful, as the *Bṛhan-Nīla* quotes one list of 52 Pīṭhas.

[पीठानां परमं पीठं कामरूपं मद्दाफलम् ।]
* * * * * * *
पीठप्रमद्दादेवीशि पीठानि शृणु भैरवि ।
* * * * * * *
पुष्करं गयाचैनं अच्चयाख्यवटस्य या (v.l. अच्चयाद्य॰) ।
वराहपर्वतच्चैव तीर्थंनामरकण्टकम् (v.l. शिवष्टा॰) ॥

This interesting list of the 108 names of the mother-goddess and those of as many holy places in different parts of India includes the following names:

नर्मदा यमुना पिङ्गा गङ्गाद्वारं तथा प्रिये ।
गङ्गासागरसङ्गञ्च कुमारवनमेव विश्वकम् ॥
श्रीनीलपर्वतञ्चैव कलम्बकुञ्जके (v.l. °कुञ्जिके) तथा ।
भृगुतुङ्गञ्च (v.l. °भ्रष्टञ्च) केदारं सर्वप्रियमहालयम् (v.l. ° चलम्) ॥
कलिता च सुगन्धा च माकभरीपुरं प्रियम् ।
कर्णतीर्थं महागङ्गा कुग्रिकाश्रम (नग्रिका° ?) एव (v.l. °मेव) च ॥
कुमाराख्यप्रभासौ च तथा धन्या सरस्वती ।
चावक्यात्रममिदं (v.l. चमस्या°) मे कन्याश्रममतः (v.l. कम्या°, काण्ठा°) परम् ॥
कौशिकीसरयूशोषज्योतिःसरपुरःसरम् ।
कामोदकं (v.l. कालोदकं) प्रियं श्रीमत् प्रियमुत्तरमानसम् ॥
मानतुङ्गवापी सप्तार्चिर्मेचाविष्णुपदं (v.l. °सन्ध्यविष्णु°) महत् ।
वैद्यनाथं महातीर्थं प्रियः कालञ्चरो गिरिः ॥
रामोच्छेदं गर्गच्छेदं शरोच्छेदं महावनम् ।
(v.l. बामो° ; रामोद्भेदं गर्गोद्भेदं शरोद्भेदं महावनम् ।)
भद्रेश्वरं महातीर्थं लक्ष्मणोच्छेदमेव (v.l. लक्ष्मणोद्भेद°) च ॥
ज्ञानोदि प्रियश्रेष्ठा (v.l. °सठा) च कावेरी कपिलोदका ।
सोमेश्वरं शुक्लतीर्थं कण्व्यवेण्या (v.l. °वेण्या°) प्रभेदकः ॥
पाठला च सद्बोधिनमतीर्थं महन्निका (v.l. °निके) ।
पुण्यं रामेश्वरं देवि तथा मेघवनं वरैः ॥
रेलं रमणकञ्चैव (v.l. रेलेयकवन्चैव) गोवर्दनमजप्रियम् ।
चरिचन्द्रं पुरञ्चन्द्रं प्रद्युदकमये प्रियम् (v.l. °मथ प्रिये ; त्रियम्) ॥
दन्द्रनौलं महानादं तथैव प्रियमेलकम् ।
पक्षाचरं (v.l. पक्षाचर°) पक्षवटी वटौ(ट)पर्वतिका तथा ॥
गङ्गाविल्वं प्रसह्रञ्च (v.l. °विल्वञ्च प्रा°) प्रियमाद्वटं तथा (v.l. °ढस्था) ।
गङ्गावामाचलञ्चैव (v.l. गङ्गाराम°) तथैव ऋषभोचमम् ॥
गौतमेश्वरतीर्थञ्च वशिष्ठतीर्थमेव च ।
द्वारीतथ (v.l. °तर्क) तथा देवि ब्रह्मावर्तं शिवप्रियम् (v.l. °प्रदम्) ॥
कुशावर्तमतिश्रेष्ठं चन्तीर्थं तथैव च ।
पिण्डारकवनं (v.l. °षकरणं) ख्यातं हरिद्वारं तथैव च ॥
तथैव बदरीतीर्थं रामतीर्थं (v.l. °बाम°) तथैव च ।
जयन्तं विजयन्तं च सर्वकख्याणदं प्रिये ॥
विजया सारदातीर्थं भद्रकालेश्वरं तथा ।
चयतीर्थं सुविख्यातं तथा वेदशिरः प्रियम् (v.l. वेदशिराप्रियः ; देवि
                                                          शिवप्रियम्) ॥
चोधवती नदी चैव तीर्थमश्वप्रदं (v.l. °स्य पदं) तथा ।
जामलिङ्गं माठगणं करवीरपुरं तथा ।

(1) Viśālākṣī—Vārāṇasī, (2) Liṅgadhāriṇī—Naimiṣa, (3) Lalitā—Prayāga, (4) Kāmākṣī, Kāmukā or Kāmukī—Gandhamādana, (5) Kumudā—Mānasa, (6) Viśvakāyā or Viśvakāmā—Ambara, (7) Gomatī—Gomanta, (8) Kāmacāriṇī—Mandara, (9) Madotkaṭā—Caitraratha, (10) Jayantī—Hastināpura, (11) Gaurī—Kānyakubja, (12) Rambhā—the Malaya or Amala mountain, (13) Kīrtimatī—Ekāmra, (14) Viśvā or Vilvā—Viśveśvara, (15) Pūruhūtā—Puṣkara, (16) Mārgadāyinī—Kedāra, (17) Nandā or Mandā—the Himalayas, (18) Bhadrakarṇikā or Bhadrakālikā—Gokarṇa, (19) Bhavānī—Sthāṇvīśvara or Sthāneśvara, (20) Vilvapatrikā—Vilvaka or Vilvala, (21) Mādhavī—Śrīśaila, (22) Bhadrā or Bhadreśvarī—Bhadra, Bhadreśvara or Madreśvara, (23) Jayā—Varāhaśaila, (24) Kamalā—Kamalālaya, (25) Rudrāṇī or Kalyāṇī—Rudrakoṭi, (26) Kālī—Kālañjara, (27) Kapilā—Mahāliṅga, (28) Mukuṭeśvarī or Maṅgaleśvarī—Koṭa, Markoṭa, Mākoṭa or Karkoṭa, (29) Mahādevī—Śālagrāma or Śāligrāma, (30) Jalapriyā—Śivaliṅga, (31) Kumārī—Māyāpurī, (32) Lalitā—Santāna, (33) Utpalā or Utpalākṣī—Sahasrākṣa, (34) Mahotpalā—Sahasrākṣa or Hiraṇyākṣa, (35) Maṅgalā—the Gaṅgā or Gayā, (36)Vimalā—Puruṣottama, (37) Amoghākṣī—Vipāśā, (38) Pāṭalā—Puṇḍravardhana or Puṇyavardhana, (39) Nārāyaṇī—Supārśva, (40) Bhadrasundarī or Rudrasundarī—Trikūṭa, (41) Vipulā—Vipula, (42) Kalyāṇī—Mānasācala or Malayācala, (43) Koṭavī—Koṭitīrtha, (44) Sugandhā—Mādhavavana or Madhavīvana, (45) Trisandhyā—Godāśrama, Godāvarī or Kubjāmraka, (46) Ratipriyā or Haripriyā—Gaṅgādvāra, (47) Śivānandā, Śubhānandā, Sunandā or Sabhānandā—Śivakuṇḍa, Śivakuñja or Śivacaṇḍa, (48) Nandinī—the bank of the Devikā, (49) Rukmiṇī—Dvāravatī, (50) Rādhā—Vṛndāvana, (51) Devakī—Mathurā, (52) Parameśvarī—Pātāla, (53) Sītā—Citrakūṭa, (54) Vindhyavāsinī—the Vindhyas, (55) Ekavīrā—the Sahyādri (Western Ghats), (56) Candrikā—Hariścandra or Harmacandra, (57) Ramaṇā—Rāmatīrtha, (58) Mṛgāvatī—the Yamunā, (59) Mahālakṣmī—Karavīra, (60) Umā or Rūpā—Vināyaka, (61) Arogā or Ārogyā—Vaidyanātha, (62) Maheśvarī—Mahākāla, (63) Abhayā—the Uṣṇatīrthas, or Puṣpatīrtha, (64) Amṛtā, Nitambā or Mṛgī—the Vindhyan cave, (65) Māṇḍavī or Māṇḍukī—Māṇḍavya or Māṇḍava, (66) Svāhā—Māheśvarapura or Māheśvarīpura, (67) Pracaṇḍā—Chāgalāṇḍa, Chagalaṇḍa, Chāgaliṅga or Vegala, (68) Caṇḍikā—Amarakaṇṭaka, Makarandaka or Marakaṅkaṭa, (69) Varārohā—Someśvara, (70) Puṣkarāvatī—Prabhāsa, (71) Devamātā—Sarasvatī, (72) Mātā, Pārā or Pāvā—the shore of the sea or the bank of the Pārā, (73) Mahābhāgā or Mahāpadmā—Mahālaya, (74) Piṅgaleśvarī—the Payoṣṇī, (75) Siṃhikā—Kṛtaśauca, (76) Yaśaskarī, Śaṅkarī or Atiśaṅkarī—Kārttikeya, (77) Lolā—Utpalāvartaka,

---

सप्तगोदावरं तीर्थं लिङ्गाख्यं सर्वमोचनम् (v.l. सर्वधर्मफलप्रदम्) ।
[अयोध्या मथुरा माया दुर्गा द्वारवती (v.l. द्वारा°) परैः ॥
विद्यापुरमवन्ती च काञ्ची मङ्गलकोष्ठकम् (v.l. °कोटरम्; °कुट्टकम्; मकुट-
कोटरम्; मकुटकोटरम्) ॥
काञ्चीघट्टं गुप्ततीर्थं पिडाख्यं (v.l. लिङ्गाख्यं) सर्वमोचनम् ॥]
किरीटमुमरे (v.l. °रा°) तीर्थं दक्षिणे (v.l. °या°) तीर्थमुत्तमम् ।
विशालनौीर्थं काख्यात्र वन इन्द्रावनं तथा ॥
व्याघ्रासुखी पिङ्गला च मङ्गतीर्थं गणेश्वरम् ।
ज्ञानीहि सर्वसिद्धीनां (v.l. °तीर्थानां; °सिद्धानां) हेतुस्थानानि सुन्दरि ॥

The text is not free from defects. Names like Aila, Kuśāvarta, etc., have been duplicated.

(78) Subhadrā—Śoṇasaṅgama or Sindhusaṅgama, (79) Mātā Lakṣmī or Umā Lakṣmī—Siddhapura, Siddhavana or Siddhavaṭa, (80) Aṅganā, Anaṅgā or Taraṅgā—Bharatāśrama, (81) Viśvamukhī—Jālandhara, (82) Tārā—the Kiṣkindhya hill, (83) Puṣṭi—Devadāruvana, (84) Medhā—Kāśmīra, (85) Bhīmā—the Himalayas, (86) Puṣṭi or Tuṣṭi—Vastreśvara or Viśveśvara, (87) Śuddhi or Śuddhā—Kapālamocana, (88) Mātā—Kāyāvarohaṇa, (89) Dhvani or Dharā—Śaṅkhoddhāra, (90) Dhṛti—Piṇḍāraka, (91) Kālā or Kalā—the Candrabhāgā, (92) Śivakāriṇī, Śivadhāriṇī, Siddhidāyinī or Śaktidhāriṇī—Acchoda, (93) Amṛtā—the Beṇā, (94) Urvaśī—Badarī, (95) Oṣadhi or Auṣadhi—Uttarakuru, (96) Kuśodakā—Kuśadvīpa, (97) Manmathā—Hemakūṭa, (98) Satyavādinī—Mukuṭa or Kumuda, (99) Vandanīyā or Vandinīkā—Aśvattha, (100) Nidhi—in the home of Vaiśravaṇa, (101) Gāyatrī in grammar, (102) Pārvatī in the company of Śiva, (103) Indrāṇī in the world of gods, (104) Sarasvatī in the mouths of Brahman, (105) Prabhā (light) in the solar orb, (106) Vaiṣṇavī among the Divine Mothers,[1] (107) Arundhatī among chaste women, (108) Tillottamā among beautiful girls, (109) Brahmakalā in the hearts of men, and (110) Śakti (strength) in the living beings.[2] It will be seen that the names are actually more

---

[1] They are usually regarded as seven or eight in number.

Cf. ब्राह्मी माहेश्वरी चैव कौमारी वैष्णवी तथा ।
माहेन्द्री चैव वाराही चामुण्डा सप्त मातरः ॥ or
ब्राह्मी माहेश्वरी चण्डी वाराही वैष्णवी तथा ।
कौमारी चैव चामुण्डा चर्चिकेत्यष्ट मातरः ॥

(Apte, *Sanskrit-English Dictionary*, s.v. *mātṛ*). In place of Cāmuṇḍā of the first list, the *Mārkaṇḍeya Purāṇa* (ch. 88) gives Nārasiṃhī. These seven names are found in the list of the eight *nāyikās* or *yoginīs* to be worshipped along with the form of the mother-goddess called Kauṣikī-Caṇḍikā in the *Kālikā Purāṇa*, ch. 61, 84:

ब्राह्मी प्रथमा प्रोक्ता ततो माहेश्वरी मता ।
कौमारी चैव वाराही वैष्णवी पञ्चमी तथा ।
नारसिंही तथैवेन्द्री शिवदूती तथाष्टमी ॥

For Śivadūtī, cf. *Mārkaṇḍeya Purāṇa*, loc. cit.

In place of Carcikā of the second list, the *Tantrasāra* (pp. 314, 320) reads Caṇḍikā or Mahālakṣmī. It is not known if they are associated with the eight Bhairavas:

चण्डिताङ्गी खड्गपड: क्रोधोन्मत्तभैरवः ।
कपाली भीषणैव संहारस्याष्टभैरवाः ॥ (*ibid.*, pp. 332f.)

For a list of sixteen Mothers, see *Prāṇatoṣaṇī Tantra*, p. 146.

[2] See the text of the list edited in Appendix I. The *Bṛhan-Nīla* (Paṭala V) and *Prāṇatoṣaṇī* (pp. 237-38) *Tantras* supply a later list of similar nature.

Cf. पुष्करे कमलाक्षी च गयायां गयेश्वरी ।
अच्छया अच्युतवटेऽमरेशोऽमरकण्टके (v.l. अच्युताच्यवटकोमरेश्वरमर°) ॥
वराहपर्वते च लं वाराही भरणीप्रिया ।
नर्मदा (v.l. सुनर्मदा) नर्मदायां कान्तिर्दे यमुनाञ्जले ।
त्रिवास्तुता च गङ्गायामम्बा ऐरङ्गिकाश्रमे (v.l. ते°) ।
कुमारश्रमे कौमारी प्रभासे सुरपूजिता ॥
काम्यांश्चैवाद्रपूर्णां च द्राविडे च सरस्वती ।
महाविद्या सप्तमेधा अगस्त्याश्रमके तथा ॥

than 108 in number, but that a number of the holy places are **only imaginary**. The fact that even in an attempt to find out 108 actual *tīrthas* that

---

कौशिकिप्रियं नाम कौशिकास्त्रं(v.l. वृत°)कौशिके ।
शारदा शरयूतीरे शोणे च कनकेश्वरी ।
श्रप्रकाशा यदा (v.l. सदा) देवी ज्योतिर्मध्यज्योतिसंगमे ।
(v.l. स्वप्रकाशयशादेवि ज्योतिर्मती ज्योतिसंगमे ।)
श्रीनाभा (v.l. श्रीरदे) श्रीगिरी चैव काञ्ची कालोदके तथा ।
महोदरी महालोर्ये नौलो (v.l. महादेवी महावृद्धिर्मौ°) चोत्तरमानसे ।
मातङ्गी स्वार्मातङ्गे (v.l. मातङ्गिनी मतङ्गे; स्वाम्भतङ्गे) च गुप्तार्चिर्विष्णुपादुके
(v.l. °पादुके) ॥
खगंदा खगंमार्गे च गोदावर्यां गवेश्वरी ।
विमुक्तिश्चैव गोमत्यां विपाश्रायां (v.l. विप्रगा वा) महाबला ॥
शतद्रवा (शतद्रौ; v.l. शतद्रूं; शतप्रभा) शतरूपा च चन्द्रभागा च तत्र वै ।
रेवायत्याख (दरा°) ईर्गा सिद्धिदा सिद्धितीरके ॥
दक्षपदनरे चैव दक्षिणा लं प्रकीर्तिता ।
चौरसे (v.l. चौजवे; चौजिवे) वीर्यदा च लं सङ्गमा लौर्यसङ्गमे ।
वाङ्कदायासनम्ला (v.l. °सम्ना) लं कुरुचेचे रचेचया (v.l. °उचेचया; व[रु?]
चेचया) ।
तपखिनी पुष्पतमा भारती भरतात्रमे ।
सुकथा नैमिषारण्ये पाण्डौ च पाण्डरागना (v.l. °बामना) ।
विश्वाच्यायां (v.l. दिव्याच्याख) विश्वाङ्गाची सुपुष्पहत्ते शिवाम्बिका ॥
श्रद्धा कनखले तीर्यं श्रद्धवृद्धिर्मुनीश्वरे ।
सुवेशा सुमना गौरी मानसे च सरोवरे ॥
नन्दापुरे महानन्दा ललिता ललितापुरे ।
ब्रह्माणी ब्रह्मशिरसि महापातकनाशिनी ॥
पूर्णिमा चेन्दुमत्यां (v.l. चेन्दुमत्यादी:) विश्वयक्षी (v.l. विश्वीरति°)
प्रिया सदा ।
जाह्नवीसङ्गमे दग्निः (v.l. दग्निः) स्वभा लं पिष्टपिष्टदा ।
पुष्पा लं वेणुवत्यां च (v.l. वङ्कवितायां) प्रपार्यां पापनाशिनी ।
शंखसंचारिणी (v.l. °संवरचे) चैव घोररूपा महोदरी ॥
खर्मोच्छेदे (v.l. खर्मोद्धेदे) महारात्रिः प्रवक्ता च महावने ।
भद्रा च भद्रकाखी च भद्रेश्वरीश्वरप्रिया ।
भद्रेश्वरे रमा विष्णुप्रिया विष्णुपदे तथा ।
दाश्चा नर्मदोच्चेदे (v.l. °ह्रदे) कावेर्यां कपिलेश्वरौ ।
भेदिनी कृष्णवेणायां शंभेदे शुभवाहिनी ।
श्रदा च श्रुङ्कतीर्ये च प्रभासे पेश्वरे तथा ॥
(श्रदा च श्रुङ्कतीर्ये च प्रभा रामेश्वरे तथा ॥)
महाशोधी महावज्रिः पाटले पाटलेश्वरी ।
सुरसा (v.l. सुबला) नागतीर्ये च नागेश्वरी नागवन्दिता ॥

could be associated with Śakti rather arbitrarily the author does not refer to Kāmarūpa and Uḍḍiyāna may point to the author's aversion for these

---

मद्मे च मद्नो च प्रमद्रा च मंदन्तिका ।
मेघखमा मेघवने (v.l. °वासे ; मेघखना मेघवने ; मेघवह्ना) विद्यत्
सौदामिनी च्छठा ॥
रामेश्वरे मद्दासिद्धिर्वीरा (v.l. मद्दाबुद्धि° ; °र्वारा) चैत्नापुरे सतौ ।
प्रिया रमण्डके (v.l. प्रिये ; विद्याह्नमार्गके) दुर्गा सुवेशा सुरसुन्दरी ॥
कात्यायनी मद्दादेवी गोवर्डने तथाम्बिका (v.l. °खिन्नाम्बिका ; °गेऽम्बिका तथा) ।
भ्रभेखरे चरिचन्द्रे पुरचन्द्रे पुरेखरी ॥
प्रथूदके मद्दावेगा सेंनाकेऽखिल्लवर्दिनी ।
रन्द्रनीले मद्दाकाल्ली (v.l. °कान्ता) रलवेशा सुशोभना ॥
मारेखरौ मद्दानादे मद्दावेजा मद्दावले (°वने ; v.l. °बह्ना) ।
पम्पासरसि सारङ्गा (v.l. पद्मासरसि ; सारङ्गा) पद्मवर्या (v.l. °कर्या) तपस्विनी ॥
वटौपर्वतिकायाद्द (वटपर्वतिका° ; v.l. वटौश्रौ°) पद्मवर्गा (v.l. सर्ववर्षे)
सुरङ्गिनी ।
षह्मे विन्ध्यगङ्गायां (v.l. गङ्गाख्या) विन्ध्ये (v.l. विन्ध्य°) श्रीविन्ध्यवासिनी ॥
मद्दानन्दा नन्दतटे (v.l. °वटे) गङ्गावामाच्वले (v.l. वाटाच्वले) प्रिवा ।
चार्यावर्ते मद्दार्या लं विमुक्तिक्षेपमोच्ने ॥
चद्दवासे च चामुखा तन्वे श्रौगौतमेखरौ (v.l. तन्वेश्रौ) ।
वेदमयौ ब्रह्मविद्या वशिष्ठे (v.l. वाशिष्ठे) लसरस्वती ॥
चारीते चरिचाच्रौ च ब्रह्मावर्ते ब्रजेखरी (v.l. व्रते°) ।
गायत्रौ चैव सुविचौ कुशावर्ते कुशप्रिया ॥
षंसेखरौ मद्दातीर्थे परखंसेखरेखरौ (v.l. परखंसेखरौति च) ।
पिण्डारकवने (v.l. पिण्डावकरणे) धन्या सुरसा सुखदायिनी ॥
नारायणौ बैंख्यौवी च गङ्गाद्वारे विमुक्तिदा ।
श्रीविद्या वद्रीतीर्थे रामतीर्थे (v.l. वाम°) मद्दाधृतिः ॥
जयन्तौ च जयन्ते लं विजयन्तेऽपराजिता ।
विजया च मद्दामुदिः शारदायाद्द शारदा ॥
सुभद्रे भद्रदा भव्या भद्रकालेखरे तथा ।
मद्दाभद्रा (v.l. मद्दाभद्रौ) भद्रकाल्लौ (v.l. मद्दाकाल्लौ) चरतीर्थे (v.l. चय°)
गवौखरौ ॥

वेदद्रा वेदमाता च वेदेशा (v.l. विदेशे) वेदमस्तके ।
श्रोघवत्यां (v.l. युवत्याद्द) मद्दाविद्या मद्दानद्या मद्दोद्या ॥
चण्डा च विपदे (v.l. चाचपदे) चैव कामलिङ्गे वलिप्रिया ।
माद्दद्मे (v.l. °द्रिये) जगन्माता करवौरपुरे स्तौ ॥
मालिनौ (v.l. मान्त्तवे) रल्लिनौ वामा परमा परमेखरी ।
पक्षगोद्वारे तीर्थे देवर्षिरखिलेखरौ (देवी श्रौर° ; v.l. देवर्षिवे° ; देवर्षौश्रा°) ॥
चयोध्यायां भवानौ च जयदा जयमङ्गन्ना ।
माधवौ मधुरायाद्द देवकी यादवेखरौ ॥

out-and-out Tantric *tīrthas*. It cannot possibly be held that the text was composed before Uḍḍiyāna and Kāmarūpa attained to eminence.

वृन्दागोपेश्वरौ (v.1. गोपीश्वरौ) राधा रासवन्दावने रये (v.1. रमा) ।
कात्यायनी मन्नामाया भद्रकाली कलावती ॥
चन्द्रमाला मन्नाप्ताग्निर्मद्यायोगिन्यधीश्वरी (v.1. मन्नायोगा म°) ।
त्र्यनेश्वरौ यशोदेति ब्रझश्रीगोकुलेश्वरी ॥
काच्यां कनककाच्यौ स्यारवन्त्यामनिपावनी (v.1. स्याद्°) ।
विद्या विद्यापुरे चैव विमला नीलपर्वते ॥
रामेश्वरौ सेतुबन्धे (v.1. राजेश्री क्षेत्रगर्देश्री) विमला पुरुषोत्तमे ।
विरजा यागपुर्यां च (v.1. नागपुर्यां च) भद्रेऽपि (v.1. भद्राचे; भद्रेश्री)
                                                                भद्रकर्षिका ॥
तमोलिङ्गे तमोब्री च खान्दा सामरलङ्गमे ।
कुलश्रीर्यंशठ्दिश (v.1.° वंश°) माधवी माधवप्रिया ॥
मङ्गला मङ्गले कोटे राढे मङ्गलचण्डिका ।
ज्वालामुखी शिवापीठे मन्दरे (v.1. मन्दारे) भुवनेश्वरी ॥
कालीघट्टे (v.1. °घाटे) गुह्यकाली किरीटे च मन्नेश्वरौ ।
किरीटेश्वरौ मन्नादेवो लिङ्गाख्यो लिङ्गवासिनी ॥

    *   *   *   *   *

त्र्यमरेश्वरमन्नापीठे कुशमृङ्कारसंज्ञकः (v.1. ईशदुङ्कार°) ।
तत्र दुर्गादर्य नाम चण्डिका च मन्नेश्वरौ ॥
प्रभासे सोमनाथोऽसौ (v.1. °नाथादौ) देवी च पुष्करेक्षणा ।
देवदेवाधिपः ब्रह्मानैमिषे च मन्नेश्वरः ॥
तत्र प्रज्ञा च देवी च शिवानी लिङ्गधारिणी ।
पुष्करे च राजमन्निः पुरङ्कता मन्नेश्वरी ॥
श्रीपर्वते प्रियं नाम (v.1. त्रिया नाम्ना) शङ्करत्रिपुरान्तकः ।
मायावी शङ्करौ (v.1. माया विष्कुरौ) तत्र भक्तानामभिलाषदा ॥
अच्छेश्वरे मन्नास्थाने शङ्करौ च विशृङ्खिनी ।
विष्णुलौ (v.1. विष्णूल:) शङ्करस्त्वत्र सर्वपापविमोचकः ॥
त्र्यम्बाकपुरे (v.1.° तर्केश्वरे) रुद्राः रुद्राख्या परमेश्वरौ ।
(मन्नाकाले मन्नाकालो मन्नाकाली मन्नेश्वरौ ॥
मध्ये शिवस्य [v.1. शिवस्य] सर्वज्ञ सर्वाणी परमेश्वरौ ।
केदारेश्वर ईशानो देवी मन्नार्गदायिनी ॥
मेरवे भैरवः ब्रह्माभैरवी परमेश्वरौ ।)
गर्गचंचे (v.1. गण्°) भद्रकाख्या शिवोऽयं प्रपितामहः ॥
कुरुच्छे शिवः स्थाणुः शिवा स्थाणुप्रिया परा ।
रुद्रनाभे स्वयंभूश्च देवी स्वायम्भुवा मता ॥
पद्मः कमलजे प्रोक्षः शिवोग्रे (शिवोग्रा; v.1. शिवोपः) शिवबल्लभा ।
विमलेश्वरे विश्वप्रभुर्विश्या (v.1. °विश्वस्तु; °रिष्टा) विश्वप्रिया सदा ॥

Freedom of the Writers on the Pīṭhas from any Common Tradition.

We have seen that the lists of the Pīṭhas and those of the Devīs and Bhairavas connected with each of them are variously prepared by different authors and have a great deal of discrepancy among them. There was apparently little influence on these writers of something like a recognized tradition about the number of the Pīṭhas, the names of the deities worshipped at them, and their association with particular limbs of the mother-goddess. Names of the *tīrtha*, Devī and Bhairava were often fabricated by the writers and the association of a *tīrtha* with one of Satī's limbs was also determined usually by their individual imagination. The fact that in many cases entire countries are mentioned as Pīṭhas suggests that the writers had only vague ideas about some of the *tīrthas* and often took resort to imagination. That medieval writers on the subject of the Pīṭhas took the greatest liberty in these respects is clearly demonstrated by the sixteenth century Bengali

अहद्दाये महानन्दो महामन्दा महेश्वरी ।
महान्नको महेन्द्रे च पार्वती च महान्नका ।
भीमेश्वरी भीमपीठे शिवा भीमेश्वरी तथा ।
वज्रपादे (वज्रापथे ?) भवनाम भवानी भुवनेश्वरी ॥
चन्द्रिकूटे महायोगी वज्राषी परमेश्वरी ।
चविसुज्ञे महादेवो विशाखाची शिवा परा ॥
महाक्षये (v.l. महासामे) षरो वज्रो महाभागा शिवा तथा ।
महाचक्षस्य गोकर्वे शिवभद्रा (v.l. शिवा ज्येष्ठा) च षष्ठिका ॥
भद्रकर्णे महादेवी भद्रा च कर्षिका तथा (च भद्रकर्षिका) ।
सुपर्णाख्ये (v.l. सुवर्णाख्ये) षट्स्याच षत्यक्षा परमेश्वरी ॥
स्थाणुसंज्ञे शिवस्या श्रीस्वरस्या (स्थाणुसंज्ञः शिवः स्थाणीश्वरः; v.l. स्थाणुसंज्ञे
शिवस्या श्रीस्वरः स्थानीस्वरा; शिवः स्थाणुतीर्थस्या) श्रीभरा शिवा ।
कमलालये (v.l. कमलाख्ये) महास्थाने (v.l. °स्थाने) कमलाची महेश्वरः ॥
कमलाची महेश्वानि सकलार्थप्रदायिनी ।
जगलाख्ये (v.l. जगला तु) कपर्दी च प्रसरा (v.l. प्रसभा) च महेश्वरी ॥
जर्हुरेता वरिष्ठे (v.l. तरष्ठे; षरष्ठे) च सन्ध्याख्या परमेश्वरी ।
माकोटाख्ये (माकोटाख्ये; v.l. षाकोटे च) महाकोटः शिवा च सुपक्षेश्वरी ॥
(मण्डलेश्वरपीठे च शङ्करः खाण्डवी शिवा ॥)
(काकड्वरे नीलकण्ठो वर [षरः] काची शिवा मता ।
स्थलेश्वरे (v.l. °श्वरी) स्थलोनाम्ना स्थलाख्या परमेश्वरी ॥)
मण्डलेश्वरपीठे (v.l. मालुले°) च करवीराचलेश्वरः (v.l. °रार्च्यश्वरा) ।
श्रीमद्द्व्याम्रपुरे षाच्चादरनामा सभापतिः ॥

* * * *

यस्मिन् महोत्तमे स्थाने शिवमङ्गाख्यमद्भुतम् ।
तडागमस्ति तत्तीरे दक्षिणे त्यतौश्वरः ॥

* * * *

[षष्टोमरुएछचन्न् अपेक्षडामुदान्वितः ।]

poet Mukundarāma in the *Dakṣa-yajña-bhaṅga* section of his *Caṇḍīmaṅgala*. According to an interpolated passage found in some manuscripts of this work, the following nine places are the Pīṭhas where Satī's limbs fell: (1) Ghāṭaśilā (between the Kharagpur and Tatanagar Railway Stations on the B.N.R.) where Satī's left foot fell and where the Devī is Rukmiṇī (apparently the Sanskritized form of the name of the aboriginal deity Raṅkiṇī whose worship is widely prevalent in the Burdwan Division of Bengal and the adjoining region of the west),[1] (2) Yājapura (in Orissa) where the right foot fell and where the Devī is Virajā, (3) Rājabolahāṭa (near Serampur in the Hooghly District) where the left hand fell and where the Devī is Viśālocanī, (4) Bālidāṅgā (near Dhaniakhali in the Hooghly District) where the right hand fell and where the Devī is Rājeśvarī, (5) Kṣīragrāma (near Katwa in the Burdwan District) where the back fell and where the Devī is Yogādyā, (6) Nagarakoṭa where the head fell and where the Devī is Jvālāmukhī, (7) Hiṅglāja (in Baluchistan) where the navel fell,[2] (8) Kāmākhyā where the central part of Satī's body fell and where the Devī is Kāmarūpa-Kāmākhyā, and (9) Vārāṇasī where the chest fell and where the Devī is Viśālākṣī.[3] Needless to say that the unimportant

---

[1] For human sacrifices in the Raṅkiṇī temple at Burdwan, see an instance cited in the newspapers in January, 1837, and quoted by B. N. Banerji in *Saṃvādpatre Sekāler Kathā*, Vol. II, pp. 532-34.

[2] Owing to defect in the text, the name of the Devī at Hiṅglāja cannot be determined.

[3] Cf. Calcutta University ed., pp. 49-50:

যত্র কৌটব্য ভরি   মরীরে প্রবেশ করি
    পন্থে পন্থে কাটিতে লাগিল ।
বামবরষ নিভা   পতিত যে ঘাটশিলা
    তার নাম রুক্মিণী পরল ॥
দক্ষিণ চরণবরে   পতিত যে যাজপুরে
    তার নাম পরল বিরজা ।
দেবতা সকল মেলি   সিদ্ধপীঠ তারে বলি
    সুরপতি তারে করে পূজা ॥
বক্ষ সব বাম কাঁধে   পড়ে রাজবোলহাটে
    বিশালোচনী মহেশ্বরী ।
ধনৌর দক্ষিণ পায়   বালিডাঙ্গায় এই পাত
    রাজেশ্বরী বলি নাম ধরি ॥
নবে সদাশিব পায়   মহাপরিশ্রম পায়
    ক্ষীরগ্রামে করিলা বিশ্রাম ।
তারে পৃষ্ঠদেশ পড়ে   দেবের বাম্য বাড়ে
    যোগাদ্যা পরল তার নাম ॥
নবে প্রভু ভূর্জণ্ডে   মেলেন নগরকোটে
    দিবসেক রহিলা পিশাচী ।
মস্তক কাটে বজ্রকোট   বের মধ্যে সিদ্ধপীঠ
    তার নাম হৈল আজ্ঞাসুৱী ॥

rural *deva-sthānas* in Rādha, such as Rājabolahāṭa and Bāliḍāṅgā, received the status of Pīṭha in the hands of Mukundarāma merely because the poet was originally an inhabitant of the village of Dāmuṇyā in the Burdwan District. The *Pīṭhanirṇaya* (in its accepted form), likewise, includes in the list of Pīṭhas Chittagong, Tipperah, Nalahati, Vakresvara, Kiritakona, Jessore, Kalighat, etc., which are late and unimportant *deva-sthānas* in Bengal,

তবে ত দেবের রাজ 	তনরিজ্ঞা দিক্ষাজ
নাভিক্ষল পড়িল তথায় ।
দেবরে তন্নমান (?) 	ষেব মবানওজক্ষান
অপিলে পামব নাম পায় ॥
ইমানে ইমান যায় 	তনরিজ্ঞা কামিক্ষায়
তথা ষৈল দেবীপ্রিযক্ষান ।
মধ্য বব কাডে কৌত 	ষের মবাসিবপীত
কাবরূপ কামাক্ষা তার নাম ॥
তবে ন ক্রীডাবসাবী 	তনরিজ্ঞা বারাবসী
বচঃক্ষল পড়িল মাগাবে ।
বিশ্বাক্ষাবী রূপ বৈন্ত 	সবং দেব পূজা কৈল
পঠে মিব মূল করি বানে ॥
মন্তু মূল মূন্য দেখি 	কেরেতে সজল বাঁচি
বক্ষিবক্ষ পারল মূলষামে ।
কাবব পদান্যবলি 	ষের বক্ষি কঞ্চে ধরি
ধান করি বসিলেন যোমে ॥

It is very interesting to note that the name of Kālīghāṭa near Calcutta is not found in this list prepared in South-west Bengal possibly a little later than the composition of the *Caṇḍīmaṅgala*. The popularity of Kālīghāṭa is probably later than the foundation of Calcutta by Job Charnock in 1690. Cf. *supra*, p. 24, note 1. Certain editions of Vaṃśīdāsa's *Manasāmaṅgala*, said to be composed in 1570 A.D., has:

হতেক গুনিযা বরি বক্রকৌত বরযা ।
খণ্ড খণ্ড করি কাটে বল্লে প্রবেশিযা ॥
সতীর সাথার কেম পড়িলেক যথা ।
কাশী নামে তীর্থ ষৈল পূজযে দেবতা ॥
বক্তগুহা বসিযা যে পড়িল যেখানে ।
তপ্রতারা নাম তীর্থ বিক্ষাত ভুবনে ॥
সুবব'তে জিক্ষা পড়িল যেথা থাকি ।
দেবের দুক্ষম তীর্থ নাম ব্যাক্ষামুষী ॥
নাভি কাডিযা বিষ্ণু পড়িল যেখানে ।
নাভিমথা নাম তাষা বিক্ষাত ভুবনে ॥
দুর বব বাযে মাব কেব নাবি বাড়ে ।
নীচাচল গিরি গিযা যোনিমুদ্রা পড়ে ॥
কামাক্ষা নাম তার চারিবেদে গাব ।

Note the non-mention of Kalighat and the differences of this account from the other. Mahal Kalkattā in Sarkār Sātgāon is, however, mentioned in the '*Ain-i-Akbarī* as paying in 1582, together with two other Mauzas, a land revenue of Rs. 23,905 (*J.A.S.B.*, 1873, p. 217).

but omits such important old names as Uḍḍiyāna and Pūrṇagiri. The absence of such celebrated deities as Vindhyavāsinī is also striking. Some obscure names, e.g. Maṇiveda, Ratnāvalī, etc., do not appear in the earlier lists. Another feature of the list is that it (in its usually accepted form) not only regards the Devī's *hāra* (necklace), *kuṇḍala* (ear-ring) *kirīṭa* (crown) and *nūpura* (anklet) as so many of her limbs but, strangely enough, even includes in the same category her *manas* (mind). The author's knowledge of Sanskrit was probably poor, while the copyists and modifiers of the work could hardly claim any knowledge of the language. As a result of this, different versions of the text before us are full of discrepancies and mistakes often of an extremely baffling nature. In some manuscripts of the work the text is found in an exceptionally modified form. It will be interesting to compare the probable original text of the *Pīṭhanirṇaya* (reconstructed on the basis of Manuscript G and the *Annadāmaṅgala*) with the late modification in Manuscript H both quoted in Appendix I (A and B).

The List of Pīṭhas in the Pīṭhanirṇaya (Mahāpīṭhanirūpaṇa).

Reserving for the foot-notes on the text discussion on the discrepancies as regards the names of the Pīṭhas, the Pīṭha-devatās (forms of the Devī), the Kṣetrādhīśas (Bhairavas) and the Devī's *aṅga-pratyaṅga* (limbs including ornaments, etc.), the descriptive list supplied by the *Pīṭhanirṇaya* (*Mahāpīṭhanirūpaṇa*) may be offered in a tabular form.

Number	Pīṭha	Aṅga-pratyaṅga	Devī	Bhairava
1.	Hiṅgulā Hiṅgulāṭa	Brahmarandhra	Koṭṭarī Koṭṭavī Koṭṭarīśā	Bhīmalocana
2.	Karavīra Śarkarāra	Trinetra	Mahiṣamardinī	Krodhīśa Krodheśa
3.	Sugandhā	Nāsikā	Sunandā Sugandhā	Tryambaka
4.	Kāśmīra	Kaṇṭha	Mahāmāyā	Trisandhyeśvara Trinetreśvara
5.	Jvālāmukhī	Jihvā	Siddhidā Ambikā	Unmatta
6.	Jālandhara	Stana	Tripuramālinī Tripurāśinī	Bhīṣaṇa Īśāna
7.	Vaidyanātha	Hṛdaya	Jayadurgā	Vaidyanātha
8.	Nepāla	Jānu	Mahāmāyā	Kapālī
9.	Mānasa Mālava	Dakṣiṇa-hasta	Dākṣāyaṇī	Hara Hari Amara
10.	Virajākṣetra in Utkala	Nābhi	Vimalā Vijayā	Jagannātha Jaya
11.	Gaṇḍakī Gaṇḍaka	Gaṇḍa	Gaṇḍakī Caṇḍī	Cakrapāṇi Jagannātha
12.	Bahulā Bāhulā	Vāma-bāhu	Bahulā Bāhulā	Bhīruka Tīvraka
13.	Ujjayinī Ujānī Ujjanī Urjanī Urjayinī	Kūrpara	Maṅgalā Maṅgalacaṇḍī	Kapilāmbara Kapileśvara

Number	Pīṭha	Aṅga-pratyaṅga	Devī	Bhairava
14.	Caṭṭala (Candraśekhara)	Dakṣiṇa-bāhu	Bhavānī	Candraśekhara
15.	Tripurā	Dakṣiṇa-pāda	Tripurā Tripurasundarī	Nala Tripureśa Tripurākṣa
16.	Trisrotā (Sans. *Trisrotas*) Tirotā	Vāma-pāda	Bhrāmarī Amarī	Īśvara Ambara Amara
17.	Kāmagiri in Kāmarūpa (Ten Pīṭhas were originally located here)	Mahāmudrā (Yoni)	Kāmākhyā	Umānanda Śivānanda Rāmānanda Rāvānanda
18.	Yugādyā (Kṣīragrāma)	Dakṣiṇa-pādāṅguṣṭha	Yugādyā (Yogādyā)	Kṣīrakhaṇḍa Kṣīrakaṇṭha
19.	Kālīpīṭha Kālapīṭha (Kalighat)	Dakṣiṇa-pādāṅguli	Kālī	Nakuleśa Nakulīśa Nalīśa
20.	Prayāga	Hast-āṅguli	Lalitā	Bhava
21.	Jayantī Jayantā	Vāma-jaṅghā	Jayantī	Kramadīśvara
22.	Kirīṭa Kirīṭakoṇā	Kirīṭa	Bhuvaneśī Vimalā	Siddhirūpa Saṃvarta
23.	Maṇikarṇikā at Vārāṇasī	Kuṇḍala	Viśālākṣī	Kāla
24.	Kanyāśrama (see p. 37, note 1)	Pṛṣṭha Dṛṣṭi	Sarvāṇī	Nimiṣa
25.	Kurukṣetra	[Dakṣiṇa]-gulpha	Sāvitrī	Sthāṇu Snāyu
26.	Maṇiveda Maṇivedika Mānavedaka	Maṇibandha	Gāyatrī	Sarvānanda
27.	Śrīśaila Śrīhaṭṭa	Grīvā	Mahālakṣmī Mahāmāyā	Saṃvarānanda Samarānanda Sarvānanda
28.	Kāñcī	Kaṅkāla	Devagarbhā	Ruru
29.	Kālamādhava	Nitamba	Kālī	Asitāṅga
30.	Narmadā Śoṇa Śaila	Nitamba	Śoṇā Narmadā	Bhadrasena
31.	Rāmagiri Rājagiri Rāmākiṇī	Stana Nāsā Nalā	Śivānī	Caṇḍa
32.	Vṛndāvana (Umāvana) Keśajāla	Keśa	Umā Kātyāyanī	Bhūteśa Kṛṣṇanātha
33.	Śuci Anala	Ūrdhva-danta	Nārāyaṇī	Saṃhāra Saṃkrūra
34.	Pañcasāgara	Adhodanta	Vārāhī	Mahārudra
35.	Karatoyātaṭa	Vāma-karṇa Talpa Gulpha	Aparṇā	Vāmana Vāmeśa

THE ŚĀKTA PĪṬHAS

Number	Pīṭha	Aṅga-pratyaṅga	Devī	Bhairava
36.	Śrīparvata	Dakṣiṇa-karṇa Talpa [Dakṣiṇa]-gulpha	Sundarī	Sundarānanda Sunandānanda
37.	Vibhāsa	Vāma-gulpha	Bhīmarūpā Kapālinī	Kapālī Sarvānanda
38.	Prabhāsa	Udara Adhara	Candrabhāgā	Vakratuṇḍa
39.	Bhairavaparvata Bhīruparvata	Ūrdhvoṣṭha Oṣṭha Tuṇḍa	Avantī	Lambakarṇa Namrakarṇa
40.	Janasthāna Jala-sthala	Civuka	Bhrāmarī	Vikṛta Vikṛtākṣa
41.	Godāvarītīra	[Vāma]-gaṇḍa	Viśveśī Rākiṇī	Viśveśa Daṇḍapāṇi Vatsanābha
42.	Ratnāvalī Ratnavatī	Dakṣiṇa-skandha	Kumārī Śivā	Śiva Kumāra
43.	Mithilā	Vāma-skandha	Umā Mahādevī	Mahodara

(The following Pīṭhas were omitted in the original text which located ten Pīṭhas in Kāmarūpa.)

Number	Pīṭha	Aṅga-pratyaṅga	Devī	Bhairava
44.	Nalāhāṭī	Nalā	Kālī	Yogīśa Yogeśa
45.	Kālīghāṭa (Kālīpīṭha)	Muṇḍa	Jayadurgā	Krodhīśa Krodheśa
46.	Vakreśvara	Manas	Mahiṣamardinī	Vakranātha
47.	Yaśora	Pāṇi	Yaśoreśvarī	Caṇḍa Caṇḍeśa
48.	Aṭṭahāsa	Oṣṭha	Phullarā	Viśveśa
49.	Nandipura	Hāra	Nandinī	Nandikeśvara
50.	Laṅkā	Nūpura	Indrākṣī	Rākṣaseśvara Nandikeśvara
51.	Virāṭa	Padāṅguli	Ambikā	Amṛta Amṛtākṣa[1]

---

[1] For Manibandha, a name created out of a confused text, and for Magadha and Karṇāṭa, interpolated by later modifiers of the text who could not make out 51 names from the text before them, see foot-notes on the text. Bhāratacandra omitted the last eight names together with Vārāṇasī and Kanyāśrama but recognized the ficticious Manibandha, while our G text omits only the last eight names and thus makes the number of Pīṭhas 52 (with Vārāṇasī and Kanyāśrama and with the extra nine Pīṭhas located at Kāmarūpa). It seems that the original text made a reference either to Kanyāśrama or to Vārāṇasī. The fifth Paṭala of the late Bṛhan-Nīlatantra contains no less than five lists of Pīṭhas. Four out of them together with another from the sixth Paṭala of the same Tantra have already been quoted (see above, pp. 21, note 1; 25, note 3; 28, note 2). A list like the following one quoted from the Bṛhan-Nīla may be regarded as the source of the belief, prevalent in some parts of Bengal, that the number of Pīṭhas is fifty-two (cf. our G text enumerating fifty-two Pīṭhas owing to confusion).

कामेशा कामरूपे लं पूर्वां काम्यां विषु लिङ्ग:
नेपाले पुखड़ा पुण्या दुर्गश पौडुवर्धने ॥

Modification of the Pīṭhanirṇaya (Mahāpīṭhanirūpaṇa) in the Śivacarita.

An attempt was made to utilize and improve upon the text of the *Pīṭhanirṇaya (Mahāpīṭhanirūpaṇa)* by the author of the *Śivacarita* which

धर्मबुद्धिः सुखा चैव सुखदा पापमोचनी ।
पारस्ये परमानन्दा ब्रह्माणी कान्यकुब्जके ॥
पुण्याद्रौ च महापुण्या पूर्णा यज्ञफलेश्वरी ।
कात्यायन्यर्बुदे देवि धनदा शिववल्लभा ॥
एका चैकाम्रके देशे सुरूपेयाम्रकेश्वरे ।
त्रिपुरे सुन्दरी दिव्यरूपाखिलमनोहरा ॥
कामकोटे महापीठे प्रमदा मदनालसा ।
कामेश्वरी रतिश्चैव श्रृङ्गुर्यां त्रलोकेश्वरी ॥
ब्रह्मेशा च तपोलक्ष्मीः कैलासे भुवनेश्वरी ।
केदारे वरदा चैवास्तता चन्द्रपुरे चित्रा ॥
कलावती प्रभेशा च श्रीपुरे श्रीरमा प्रिया ।
कुमारी ब्रह्मचर्या च कन्या च कन्यकापुरे ॥
जालन्धरे महापीठे नामर्याग्निमुखी प्रभा ।
व्यालामुखी छोछ्छिष्का सुवेशा च सुरद्विषी ॥
मालवे च महाविद्या बिल्वपीठे च रूपिणी ।
रूपवती महादेवी देवीकोठेऽखिलेश्वरी ॥
मोक्षर्ये प्रियपीठे लं श्रद्धाधी सर्वमङ्गला ।
पवने वरपीठे च मनस्त्रीष सुगन्धिका ॥
षड्दशे महापीठे भौमकाली च कालिका ।
विरजे सुश्रिहेतुश्च नमःश्लिखामयी ॥
जयश्रीराजलक्ष्मीश्च सुवेशा राजपर्वते ।
रक्तपुरे महासम्यत् भावेश्वरी महापथे ॥
गायत्री ब्रह्मरूपा च तत्त्वद्वारपीठके ।
जया जयपुरे देवी जयदा जयमङ्गला ॥
विजया मङ्गला गौरी उज्जयन्यां सदाशिवा ।
गौरीश्वरी महादेवी हरिद्रापीठके शिवा ॥
क्षौरपीठे युगाद्या च क्षौराष्ट्रा नियमप्रभा ।
राजेश्वरी महालक्ष्मीरंक्षिमापुरवासिनी ॥
कमला विमला भक्ती रौद्री च नीलपर्वते ।
थाजेश्वरी चित्रवेशी च चित्रोत्था ब्रह्मरूपिणी ॥
चिभ्रम्भला कामधेनु षष्ठी षष्ठीपुरे प्रिये ।
माया मायापुरे देवी सुरभौ सौरभेश्वरी ॥
विलासिनौ महानन्दा प्रियचन्दनपर्वते ।
महाब्रजेश्वरी श्रेष्ठा श्रमनेश्वरपीठके ॥
भवानी भवभक्ता च श्रौमैसे शिववल्लभा ।
देवता या धर्मलक्ष्मीः कनकामरपर्वते ॥

has been analyzed by N. N. Vasu in the *Viśvakoṣa*, s.v. *pīṭha*. This work supplies a list of 51 Mahā-Pīṭhas (great Pīṭhas) and another of 26 Upa-Pīṭhas (Pīṭhas of lesser importance). Although the word *upapīṭha* is traced in such works as the *Sādhanamālā* (p. 479), no early lists of the less important Pīṭhas are known to us. The *Śivacarita* closely follows the text of the *Pīṭhanirṇaya* in regard to 41 (actually 42, but the name Maṇibandha is due to textual confusion) out of the 51 great Pīṭhas, the remaining 10 names as given in the latter not being found in that work. It is interesting to note in this connection that Bhāratacandra, who mentions 42 Pīṭhas (including Manibandha) by name and locates 10 Pīṭhas at one of them to make the number 51, closely follows in his *Annadāmaṅgala* the readings of the *Śivacarita* in spite of his avowed indebtedness to the *Mantracūḍāmaṇi* (for *Tantracūḍāmaṇi*) *Tantra*. These facts suggests that the original text of the *Pīṭhanirṇaya* actually but partially followed the *Kubjikā Tantra* in offering only the names of 42 Pīṭhas, while the number of the Pīṭhas was made 51 by locating the ten Mahāvidyās (manifestations of Śakti conceived in imitation of the Daśāvatāra of Viṣṇu) at Kāmarūpa. If such was the case, it is tempting to suggest that some verses containing the names of certain obscure Pīṭhas especially in the concluding part of the *Pīṭhanirṇaya* text (cf. verses 48-55) were added to the original text at a later date. They may have been inspired and influenced by the *Śivacarita*. The above suggestion seems to be strongly supported by the fact that verses 48-55 of our *Pīṭhanirṇaya* text containing the names of Nalāhāṭī, Kālīghāṭa, Vakreśvara, Yaśora, Aṭṭahāsa, Nandipura, Laṅkā and Virāṭadeśa (including the variants Karṇāṭa and Magadha) are conspicuous by their absence from some manuscripts of the *Pīṭhanirṇaya*; cf. our G text.

The evidence of the *Annadāmaṅgala* has been quoted in the foot-notes on the text of the *Pīṭhanirṇaya*, while the descriptive list of the *Śivacarita* is offered below in a tabular form.

List of the Pīṭhas (Mahāpīṭhas) and Upapīṭhas in the Śivacharita.

A—*Mahāpīṭhas*

Number	Pīṭha	Aṅga-pratyaṅga	Devī	Bhairava
1.	Hiṅgulā	Brahmarandhra	Koṭṭarī	Bhīmalocana
2.	Śarkara	Trinetra	Mahiṣamardinī	Krodhīśa
3.	Tārā	Netrāṃśa-tārā	Tāriṇī	Unmatta

जमा गौरी सती सत्या पार्वती हिमपर्वते ।
रम्भेश्वरी दुरारात्या भावेन्द्रे जगदीश्वरी ॥
वज्जा भोगेश्वरी नित्या श्रीमद्विंडुरे शिवा ।
सुवर्णा कमका रामा विरष्ठुरपीठके ॥
मष्ठलक्ष्मीमंत्रेमानी मष्ठलक्ष्मीपुरेऽम्बिका ।
चच्चुरे प्रचण्डा च चण्डा चण्डवती शिवा ॥
वज्रे मेघखना चैव मायाजनेश्वरी (काया° ?) तथा ।
कालीघट्टे मष्ठापीठे काली कालास्मिका तथा ॥
विक्राण्डे मेरवी विद्या विजया ज्ञाङ्कवीहटे ।
इति ते कथितं दिव्यं पीठत्रममुदाहृतम् ॥

It is to be noted that the six lists of Pīṭhas found in the *Bṛhan-Nīlatantra* do not agree fully with one another and are not free from mistakes.

Number	Pīṭha	Aṅga-pratyaṅga	Devī	Bhairava
4.	Karatoyātaṭa	Vāma-karṇa	Aparṇā	Vāmeśa
5.	Śrīparvata	Dakṣiṇa-karṇa	Sundarī	Sundarānanda
6.	Sugandhā	Nāsikā	Sunandā	Tryambaka
7.	Vakranātha	Manas	Pāpaharā	Vakranātha
8.	Godāvarī	Vāma-gaṇḍa	Viśvamātṛkā	Viśveśa
9.	Gaṇḍakī	Dakṣiṇa-gaṇḍa	Gaṇḍakī	Cakrapāṇi
10.	Anala	Ūrdhva-danta	Nārāyaṇī	Samkrūra
11.	Pañcasāgara	Adho-danta	Vārāhī	Mahārudra
12.	Jvālāmukhī	Jihvā	Ambikā	Vaṭakeśvara Unmatta
13.	Kāśmīra	Kaṇṭha	Mahāmāyā	Trisandhya
14.	Śrīhaṭṭa	Grīvā	Mahālakṣmī	Sarvānanda
15.	Bhairavaparvata	Oṣṭha	Avantī	Namrakarṇa
16.	Prabhāsa	Adhara	Candrabhāgā	Vakratuṇḍa
17.	Prabhāsakhaṇḍa	Marma	Siddheśvarī	Siddheśvara
18.	Janasthāna	Civuka	Bhrāmarī	Vikṛtākṣa
19.	Prayāga	Dvi-hast-āṅguli	Kamalā	Veṇīmādhava
20.	Mānasa-sarovara	Dakṣiṇa-hastārdha (Vāmahasta)	Dākṣāyaṇī	Hara
21.	Caṭṭagrāma	Dakṣiṇa-hastārdha	Bhavānī	Candraśekhara
22.	Mithilā	Vāma-skandha	Mahādevī	Mahodara
23.	Ratnāvalī	Dakṣiṇa-skandha	Śivā	Śiva Kumāra
24.	Maṇibandha	Vāma-maṇibandha	Gāyatrī	Śaṅkara Sarvāṇa
25.	Maṇiveda	Dakṣiṇa-maṇibandha	Sāvitrī	Sthāṇu
26.	Ujānī	Vāma-kaphoni	Maṅgalacaṇḍī	Kapilāmbara
27.	Raṇakhaṇḍa	Dakṣiṇa-kaphoni	Bahulākṣī	Mahākāla
28.	Bahulā	Vāma-bāhu	Bahulā	Bhīruka
29.	Vakreśvara	Dakṣiṇa-bāhu	Vakreśvarī	Vakreśvara
30.	Jālandhara	Vāma-stana	Tripuramālinī	Bhīṣaṇa
31.	Rāmagiri	Dakṣiṇa-stana	Śivānī	Caṇḍa
32.	Vaivasvata	Pṛṣṭha	Tripuṭā	Śamanakarman Nimiṣa
33.	Vaidyanātha	Hṛdaya	Navadurgā Jayadurgā	Vaidyanātha
34.	Utkala	Nābhi	Vijayā	Jaya
35.	Haridvāra	Jaṭhara	Bhairavī	Vakra
36.	Kōkāmukha	Kōk (Sans. Kukṣi)	Kōkeśvarī	Kōkeśvara
37.	Kāñcī	Kaṅkāla	Vedagarbhā	Ruru
38.	Kālamādhava	Vāma-nitamba	Kālī	Asitāṅga
39.	Narmadā	Dakṣiṇa-nitamba	Śoṇākṣī	Bhadrasena
40.	Kāmarūpa	Mahāmudrā (Yoni)	Kāmākhyā Nīlapārvatī	Rāvānanda Umānanda
41.	Mālava	Vāma-jānu	Śubhacaṇḍī	Tāmra
42.	Trisrotā (Sans. *Trisrotas*)	Dakṣiṇa-jānu	Caṇḍikā	Sadānanda
43.	Jayantī	Vāma-jaṅghā	Jayantī	Kramadīśvara
44.	Nepāla	Dakṣiṇa-jaṅghā	Mahāmāyā Navadurgā	Kapālī

THE ŚĀKTA PĪṬHAS

Number	Pīṭha	Aṅga-pratyaṅga	Devī	Bhairava
45.	Trihuta (Sans. Tīrabhukti)	Vāma-pāda	Amarī	Amara
46.	Tripurā	Dakṣiṇa-pāda	Tripurā	Nala
47.	Kṣīragrāma	Dakṣiṇa-pād-āṅguṣṭha	Yogādyā	Kṣīrakhaṇḍa
48.	Kālīghāṭa	Dakṣiṇa-pād-āṅguli	Kālikā	Nakuleśa
49.	Vibhāsa	Vāma-gulpha	Bhīmarūpā	Kapālī
50.	Kurukṣetra	Dakṣiṇa-gulpha	Saṃvarī	Saṃvarta
51.	Vindhyaśekhara	Vāma-pād-āṅguli	Vimalā Vindhyavāsinī	Puṇyabhājana

B—Upapīṭhas

1.	Kirīṭakoṇā	Kirīṭa	Bhuvaneśī	Kirīṭin
2.	Keśajāla	Keśa	Umā	Bhūteśa
3.	Vārāṇasī	Kuṇḍala	Viśālākṣī Annapūrṇā	Kālabhairava Viśveśvara
4.	Uttarā	Vāma-gaṇḍ-āṃśa	Uttariṇī	Utsādana
5.	Nalasthāna	Dakṣiṇa-gaṇḍ-āṃśa	Bhrāmarī	Virūpākṣa
6.	Aṭṭahāsa	Oṣṭhāṃśa	Phullarā	Viśvanātha
7.	Samhāra	Dantāṃśa	Śūreśī	Śūreśa
8.	Nīlācala	Ucchiṣṭa	Vimalā	Jagannātha
9.	Ayodhyā	Kaṇṭha-hāra	Annapūrṇā	Harihara
10.	Nandipura	Hār-āṃśa	Nandinī	Nandīśvara
11.	Śrīśaila	Grīv-āṃśa	Sarveśvarī	Carcitānanda
12.	Kālīpīṭha	Siromśa	Caṇḍeśvarī	Caṇḍeśvara
13.	Cakradvīpa	Astra	Cakradhāriṇī	Śūlapāṇi
14.	Yaśora	Pāṇi	Yaśoreśvarī	Pracaṇḍa
15.	Saṭīcala	Karāṃśa	Sunandā	Sunanda
16.	Vṛndāvana	Skandhāṃśa	Kumārī	Kumāra
17.	Gaurīśekhara	Vasā	Yugādyā	Bhīma
18.	Nalahāṭī	Śirānālī	Sephālikā	Yogīśa
19.	Sarvaśaila	Kakṣāṃśa	Viśvamātā	Daṇḍapāṇi
20.	Śoṇa	Nitambāṃśa	Bhadrā	Bhadreśvara
21.	Trisrotā (cf. p. 40, Pādāṃśa No. 42)		Pārvatī	Īśvara
22.	Laṅkā	Nūpura	Indrākṣī	Rākṣaseśvara
23.	Kaṭaka	Carmāṃśa	Kaṭakeśvarī	Vāmadeva
24.	Puṇḍra	Loma	Sarvākṣiṇī	Sarva
25.	Tailaṅga	Lomakhaṇḍa	Caṇḍadāyikā	Caṇḍeśa
26.	Śvetabandha	Bhagnāṃśa	Jayā	Mahābhīma [1]

Materials utilized in the Present Edition of the Pīṭhanirṇaya (Mahāpīṭhanirūpaṇa).

The subjoined text of the *Pīṭhanirṇaya* (*Mahāpīṭhanirūpaṇa*) is based upon the following sources.

A—Manuscript No. 196, entitled *Pīṭhanirṇaya* (and probably also *Mahāpīṭhalakṣaṇa*), in the Government Collection of the Royal Asiatic Society of Bengal.

---

[1] I have failed to secure and examine any copy of the *Śivacarita*.

B—Manuscript No. 3400, entitled *Mahāpīṭhanirūpaṇa*, in the Government Collection of the Royal Asiatic Society of Bengal.
C—Manuscript No. 5303, entitled *Mahāpīṭhanirūpaṇa*, in the Government Collection of the Royal Asiatic Society of Bengal.
D—Text entitled *Mahāpīṭhanirūpaṇa*, quoted from the *Tantracūḍāmaṇi* in the *Prāṇatoṣaṇī Tantra*, Vasumatī ed., pp. 234ff.
E—Text entitled *Pīṭhanirṇaya*, quoted from the *Tantracūḍāmaṇi* in the *Śabdakalpadruma*, s.v. *pīṭha*.
F—Text quoted in the *Vācaspatya* by Tārānātha Tarkavācaspati, s.v. *pīṭha*.
G—Manuscript entitled *Pīṭhanirṇaya*, in the Collection of Mr. S. K. Sarasvatī of the Calcutta University. This manuscript, collected from Rajshahi, was copied about the second quarter of the eighteenth century.
H—Manuscript No. 10863, entitled *Pīṭhanirṇaya*, in the Indian Museum Collection of the Royal Asiatic Society of Bengal. As the text found in this manuscript has wide variations it has been quoted in Appendix I—B. Cf. this text with that of the *Śivacarita*.
I—Manuscript No. 402 (Sanskrit), entitled *Pīṭhanirṇaya*, in the Collection of the Vaṅgīya Sāhitya Pariṣat, Calcutta; copied on the 14th Bhādra, Śaka 1760 (1838 A.D.) and B.S. 1245.
AM—The Bengali version of the *Pīṭhanirṇaya* (*Mahāpīṭhanirūpaṇa*) in the Pīṭhamālā section of the *Annadāmaṅgala* by Bhāratacandra, Vaṅgavāsī ed., pp. 43–47.

Text of the Pīṭhanirṇaya or Mahāpīṭhanirūpaṇa.

पौठनिर्णयः (महापीठनिरूपणम्)[1]

[Sections within square brackets are due to later modifications of the text. They have either to be omitted or to be corrected according to indications given in the foot-notes. Vide Appendix I.]

ईश्वर उवाच ।[2]
मातः परात्परे देवि सर्वागमयौश्वरि ।
कथ्यतां मे सर्वपीठशक्तिभैरवदेवताः[3] ॥ १ ॥

---

[1] The section is styled पौठनिर्णयः in AEGHI; but महापौठनिरूपणं in BCD. The expression महापौठलक्षणं also occurs in A.

[2] A—अथ महापौठलक्षणं ॥ श्रीईश्वर उवाच ॥ B—श्रीगुरवे नमः ॥ श्रीईश्वर उवाच ॥ CD—तन्त्रचूडामणौ (चन्द्रचूडामणौ in C) महापीठनिरूपणं यथा । ईश्वर उवाच । E—ईश्वर उवाच । G—श्रीहरिः । ईश्वर उवाच । H—ॐ नमो भगवत्यै ॥ अथ भावचूडामणौ । अथ पीठनिर्णयः । I—ॐ नमः शिवाय । ईश्वर उवाच । Reference to the *Tantracūḍāmaṇi* is found in the colophon of ABEI.

[3] BCDE—शक्तिभैरव°

THE ŚĀKTA PĪṬHAS

देव्युवाच ।[1]
गृहणु वत्स प्रवक्ष्यामि दयालं भक्तवत्सल ।
याभिर्विना न सिध्यन्ति जपसाधनसत्क्रियाः [2] ॥ २ ॥
पञ्चाशदेकपीठानि एवं भैरवदेवताः [3] ।
अङ्गप्रत्यङ्गपातेन विष्णुचक्रक्षतेन च [4] ।
ममाङ्गवपुषो [5] देव हिताय त्वयि कथ्यते ॥ ३ ॥
ब्रह्मरन्ध्रं हिङ्कुलायां [6] भैरवो भीमलोचनः ।
कोट्टरी [7] सा महादेवी त्रिनुगा या दिगम्बरी ॥ ४ ॥

---

[1] A—श्रीपार्वत्युवाच ; G—श्रीदेव्युवाच ।
[2] ABDEI—ᵒसत्क्रियाः ; G—मन्त्रसाधनतत्क्रियाः ; I—याभां विना ।
[3] A—एकपञ्चाशत् पीठं शक्तिभैरवदेवताः ; BCD—एकपञ्चाशतं पीठं शक्तिभैरवदेवताः ; F—एकपञ्चाशत् पीठाः शक्तिभैरवदेवताः । I—पञ्चाशदेकपीठष् ।

AM— तस्याय सतीर देव मिया चक्रपाणि ।
काटिलेन चक्रधारे करि खानि खानि ॥
येखाने येखाने खस पडिल सतीर ।
महापीठ सेइ स्थान पूजित विधिर ॥
करिया एकाग्र चष्ठ काठिला केशव ।
विधाता पूजिला भव चएश्ता भैरव ॥

Although AM refers to 51 Pīṭhas, it actually speaks of 42 and omits Vārāṇasī, Kanyā-śrama, Nalāhāṭī, Kālīpīṭha or Karṇāṭa, Vakreśvara, Aṭṭahāsa, Yaśora (Jessore), Virāṭa-deśa, Nandipura and Laṅkā. This is because AM locates ten Pīṭhas (associated with the ten fingers of Satī's hands) at Prayāga. AM's readings in most cases tally with those of the Śivacarita. Our G text omits all the extra names excepting Vārāṇasī and Kanyāśrama, while AM's original suggested Maṇibandha instead. The original text seems to have had 42 names (with 10 Pīṭhas located in Kāmarūpa) including either Vārāṇasī or Kanyāśrama.

[4] च is omitted in AC. G—चरिचक्र³ ।
[5] A—समान्यपुयो ; B—[समा]ङ्गवपुषा ; CDE—समान्यवपुषी ; F—समास्त वपुषी : G—ममास्त वपुषी देव हिताय:मररच्चसाम् ; I—सामान्यवपुषो देव हिताय देवरच्चसाम् ।
[6] I—चिङ्कुलाडे ।
[7] AGI—कोट्टवी सा महादेवी ; B—क[ह्वरौ] सा महादेवी त्रिनुगा च ; C—कोट्टरीश महादेवी ; D—कोट्टरी सा महादेव ; E—कोट्टरी सा महामाया ; F—कोट्टरीश महादेव ।

AM— हिंकुलाय ब्रह्मरन्ध्रं फेलिल केशव ।
देवता कोट्टरी भीमलोचन भैरव ॥

The words Koṭarī, Koṭarī and Koṭṭarī are found in Sanskrit lexicons in the sense of 'a naked woman'; cf. digambarī (naked) as an epithet of the Indian mother-goddess. Hiṅgulā is modern Hinglaj (lat. 25° N., long. 65° E.) in Baluchistan. The goddess is locally known as Bībī Nānī, probably the same as Nana known from the Kuṣāṇa coins. Nana was the great mother-goddess worshipped in wide regions of Western and Central Asia.

करवीरे[1] चिन्नेनं मे देवी महिषमर्दिनी ।
क्रोधीशो[2] भैरवस्तन
      सुगन्धायाञ्च नासिका[3] ॥ ५ ॥
देवस्त्यम्बकनामा च सुगन्दा तत्र देवता ॥ ६ ॥
काश्मीरे कण्ठदेशेञ्च[4] त्रिसन्ध्येश्वरभैरवः ।
महामाया भगवती गुणातीता वरप्रदा ॥ ७ ॥
ज्वालामुख्यां तथा जिह्वा[5] देव उन्मत्तभैरवः ।
अम्बिका सिद्धिदा गत्री (देवी)[6]
         स्तनं[7] जालन्धरे मम ॥ ८ ॥

---

[1] D (v.l.) EGI—शर्कारारे ।
   AM— शर्करारे निज वक्त्र त्रिमुखभैरव (वैभव) ।
        महिषमर्दिनी देवी क्रोधीश भैरव ॥

Karavīra or Karavīrapura is often identified with Śarkarāra which is supposed to be no other than modern Sukkur, the chief city of the District of that name in Sind. According to the *Kālikā Purāṇa* (chs. 38-39), Karavīrapura was the capital of the Brahmāvarta country (Eastern Punjab) and was situated near the river Dṛṣadvatī; but the city is usually identified with Kolhapur (locally called Karvīr) in the Bombay Presidency.

[2] ABI—क्रोधेशो ।

[3] GI—सुगन्धा नासिका मम ; I—सुगन्धा तत्र देवता ;
    E—क्रोधीशो भैरवस्तन सर्वसिद्धिप्रदायकः ॥
       सुगन्धायां नासिका मे देवस्त्यम्बकभैरवः ।
       सुन्दरी सा महादेवी सुगन्दा तत्र देवता ॥

The elaboration of the text in E seems to be a later modification of the original.

   AM— सुगन्धाय नासिका पडित्र चक्रवर्ता ।
         त्र्यम्बक भैरव तारे सुगन्दा देवता ॥

The Pīṭha is located at Shikārpur (about 13 miles to the north of Barisal in the Buckergunge District) on the Sondha (Sugandhā). The temple of Tryambakeśvara stands at Ponābāliā-Sāmrāil (about 3 miles to the south of Jhālakāṭi) on the same stream.

[4] B—कण्ठदेशं मे ; I—त्रिनेत्रेश्वरभैरवः ।
   AM— काश्मीरेते कण्ठ देवी महामाया ताय ।
         त्रिसन्ध्य-ईश्वर नाम भैरव तथाय ॥

As there is no reference to the celebrated Śāradā (Sardi) and Amaranātha *tīrthas* of Kāshmīr, there seems to be a fantastic element in the description of this Pīṭha.

[5] A—महाजिह्वा देवोन्मत्त° ; B—तथा जिह्वां ; CDEF—महाजिह्वा ; G—महाजिह्वा देवतो° ; I—महाजिह्वा देव उन्मत्तभैरव ।

[6] A—सखी: ।
   AM— ज्वालामुखे जिह्वा तारे अग्नि चनुभव ।
         देवीर अम्बिका नाम उन्मत्त भैरव ॥

This seems to suggest the reading अम्बिका सिद्धिदा देवी । Jvālāmukhī (lat. 31° N., long. 76° E.) lies in the Kangra District of the Punjab.

[7] F—स्तनी ।

THE ŚĀKTA PĪṬHAS

भीषणो भैरवस्तत्र देवी त्रिपुरमालिनी [1] ॥ ९ ॥
ज्वार्दपीठं [2] वैद्यनाथे वैद्यनाथस्तु भैरवः ।
देवता जयदुर्गाख्या
नेपाले जानु मे शिव [3] ॥ १० ॥
कपाली भैरवः श्रीमान् महामाया च देवता ॥ ११ ॥
मानसे दक्षहस्तो [4] मे देवी दाक्षायणी चर (चरः) ।
[अमरो भैरवस्तत्र सर्वसिद्धिप्रदायकः] ॥ १२ ॥
[उत्कले नाभिदेशस्य [5] विराजात्रेत्रमुच्यते] ।
विमला सा महादेवी जगन्नाथस्तु भैरवः ॥ १३ ॥

---

[1] E—त्रिपुरमालिनी ; B—ईशानो भैरवस्तत्र देवी त्रिपुरमालिनी ।
AM— जालन्धरे तांचार पडिल एक खन ।
त्रिपुरमालिनी देवी भैरव भीषण ॥

Jālandhara (lat. 31° N., long. 75° E.) is the chief city of the Jullundur District of the East Punjab. But the Pīṭha is located near Jvālāmukhī.

[2] ACF—हृद्यपीठं ; B—हृद्यं पीठं ; I—देवताख्या जयदुर्गा ।
AM— वैद्यनाथे हृदय भैरव वैद्यनाथ ।
देवी तारे जयदुर्गा सर्वसिद्धि साथ ॥

Vaidyanātha is the same as Deoghar-Vaidyanāthdhām (lat. 86° E., long. 24° N.) in the Santal Parganas District of Bihar.

[3] DE—जानुनी मम ।
AM— नेपाले दक्षिण जङ्घा कपाली भैरव ।
देवी ताय महामाया सदा महोत्सव ॥

The non-mention of Paśupatinātha, the most famous deity in Nepal, in this connection seems to expose the imaginary character of the description.

[4] I—°हस्तं ; ABC—मान्नवे दक्षहस्तं ; F—मान्नवे ; G—दाक्षायणी चरिः ।
AM— चार खंडे जानि तत्त मानसरोवरे ।
देवी दाक्षायणी चर भैरव विदरे ॥

AM suggests the reading चरः and the omission of the second half of the verse. The Mānasa lake (lat. 30° N., long. 81° E.), the source of the river Śatadru (Satlej), is in the Himalayas. Since Ujjayinī, a city in Mālava, is separately mentioned (v. 16), मानसे appears to be the reading intended. But nothing can be said definitely as Ujjayinī in this case may actually represent a village of Bengal. It is, however, to be noted that the celebrated god Mahākāla (Śiva) is not mentioned in connection either with Ujjayinī or with Mālava. Mālava is modern Malwa; but the name often indicated East Malwa of which the ancient capital was Vidiśā (modern Besnagar in the Gwalior State).

[5] ABCF—नाभिदेशस्तु ; I—°देशस्य ।
G— विरजा चोकले ख्याता नाभिमें मम(जय ?) भैरवः ।
गण्डक्या गण्डकी(गण्डकः?) चण्डी जगन्नाथस्तु भैरवः ॥

Although not free from mistake, this probably points to the original reading of verses 13-14. For elaboration of the earlier text as a later trait, cf. p. 44, note 3.

गण्डक्यां¹ गण्डपातस्तु तत्र सिद्धिर्न संग्रयः ।
तत्र सा ² गण्डकी षष्ठी चक्रपाणिस्तु भैरवः ॥ १४ ॥]
बङ्गलायां वामबाङ्गबेङ्गलाख्या च देवता ।
भौवको भैरवस्तत्र ³ सर्वसिद्धिप्रदायकः ॥ १५ ॥
उज्जयिन्यां कूर्परस्थ ⁴ माङ्गल्य-कपिलाम्बरः (मङ्गला कपिलाम्बरः) ।
[भैरवः सिद्धिदः साच्चादेवी मङ्गलचण्डिका] ॥ १६ ॥

AM— उत्कले पट्टिल नाभि मोच यात्रा सेवि ।
जय नामे भैरव विजया नामे देवी ॥

AM suggests the reading विजया सा मत्रादेवी जयनामा तु भैरवः । or
विजया त्कले ख्याता नाभिर्न जयभैरवः ॥

Virajā or Virajākṣetra is identical with modern Jājpur (lat. 20° N., long. 86° E.) in the
Cuttack District of Orissa.

Cf.   ततो वैतरणीं गच्छेत् सर्वपापप्रमोचनीम् ।
         विरजं तीर्थमासाद्य विराजति यथा ग्रहौ ॥

                                    (महाभारत ।३।८४।१४)

The name of the Bhairava in the modified text is apparently borrowed from the god
Jagannātha at Purī and probably hints at an attempt of claiming that deity to be a
manifestation of Śiva.

¹ B—गण्डके गण्डपातस्तु; E—गण्डपातस्तु; I—गण्डक्यां गण्डकी षष्ठी चक्रपाणिस्तु भैरवः ।
  AM— गण्डकीते तानि गण्ड पड़े चक्रपाय ।
       चक्रपाणि भैरव गण्डकी षष्ठी माय ॥

This suggests the reading गण्डक्यां दत्तगण्डस्य । The Gaṇḍakī (modern Gandak) is a
tributary of the Ganges and meets the latter river near Bakhtyarpur in Bihar. The
Pīṭha has been located at Śālagrāma at the source of the Gandak.

² A—सा तत्र ।
³ I—बाङ्गलायां; तौवको भैरवो देवः; D—भैरवो देवः ।
  AM— बाङ्गलाय वामबाङ्ग फेङ्गला केशव ।
       बाङ्गला चण्डिका तारे भौवक भैरव ॥

AM suggests the reading बाङ्गलायां वामबाङ्गबेङ्गलाख्या । The Pīṭha is located at
Ketugrāma near Katwa in the Burdwan District.

⁴ A—उज्जन्यां कर्पर्खेव; B—उज्जन्यां कुर्परस्थापि; G—उज्ज्येयिन्यां कुर्परस्थ माङ्गले (मङ्गला?);
I—तज्जन्यां च कार्पूरं माङ्गले कपिलेश्वर ।
  AM— उज्जानौते कर्पोनि मङ्गलचण्डी देवी ।
       भैरव कपिलाम्बर प्रभ यांरे सेवि ॥

AM seems to refer to Ujāni or Kogrām in the Burdwan District of Bengal, although
Ujjayinī (modern Ujjain) in the early lists of Pīṭhas must be identified with the famous
city in Avanti or West Mālava, now lying in the Gwalior State in India.
Note that the name of the Bhairava is not Mahākāla who is known to have been the
tutelary deity of Ujjayinī. The 12 jyotirliṅgas as enumerated in the Śiva Purāṇa
(I, 38, 17-20) are Somanātha in Saurāṣṭra, Mallikārjuna on the Śrīśaila, Mahākāla
at Ujjayinī, Oṅkāra at Amareśvara, Kedāra in the Himālayas, Bhīmaśaṅkara at Ḍākinī

THE ŚĀKTA PĪṬHAS

चट्टले दच्चबाङ्गर्मे भैरवचन्द्रशेखरः ।
व्यक्तरूपा भगवती भवानी यत्र[1] देवता ।
विशेषतः कलियुगे वसामि चन्द्रशेखरे ॥ १७ ॥
त्रिपुरायां दच्चपादो देवी त्रिपुरसुन्दरी (देवता त्रिपुरा नलः)[2] ।
[भैरवस्त्रिपुरेशश्च[3] सर्वाभीष्टप्रदायकः[4]] ॥ १८ ॥
त्रिखोतायां वामपादो भाभरी भैरवेश्वरः[5] ॥ १९ ॥
योनिपीठं कामगिरौ[6] कामाख्या तत्र देवता ।
यत्रास्ते त्रिगुणातीता रक्तपाषाणरूपिणौ[7] ॥ २० ॥

(at the source of the Bhīmā north-west of Poona), Viśveśvara at Vārāṇasī, Tryambaka on the bank of the Gautamī (Godāvarī) near Nasik, Vaidyanātha at Citābhūmi (Deoghar-Baidyanāthdhām in the Santal Parganas), Nāgeśa at Dārukāvana (Aundh ?), Rāmeśvara at Setubandha, and Ghṛṣṇeśa (Ghuśrīneśa, Ghuśmeśa) at Śivālaya (Ellora near Daulatabad). The original reading of the passage may have been वज्रयिम्यां कूपरेष्ठ महज्ञा कपिक्षाम्बर: with the second line of the verse omitted. Cf. pp. 44, note 3; 45, note 5.

[1] BDEFI—तत्र ।
    AM—
        चट्टग्रामे त्र्यनिपत्तन् चदे त्र्यनुभव ।
        भवानी देवता चन्द्रशेखर भैरव ॥
The Pīṭha is located at the Sītākuṇḍa on the Chandranath hill in the Chittagong District of East Bengal.

[2] D (v.l.) E—देवता त्रिपुरा मला; G—देवता त्रिपुरा मलः ।
    AM—
        दक्षिण चरणस्थानि पड़े त्रिपुराय ।
        नलजा नामे भैरव त्रिपुरा देवी ताय ॥
The original reading was apparently त्रिपुरायां दच्चपादो देवता त्रिपुरा मलः with the second line of the verse omitted (cf. p. 46, note 4). The Pīṭha is located at Radhakishorepur (old Rāṅgāmāṭi or Udaypur) in the Tripurā (Hill Tipperah) State in Bengal. The city of Tripura or Tripurī, mentioned in early literature, has, however, to be identified with modern Tewar near Jubbulpur in the Central Province. The temple of the goddess at Radhakishorepur was built by king Dharmamāṇikya in Śaka 1423 (1501 A.D.).

[3] A—°स्त्रिपुराच्च । See the Śivacarita, AM, and the G text which speak of the Bhairava as Nala (cf. note 2 above).

[4] E—°फलप्रदः ।

[5] DEG—भैरवोऽम्बरः; I—भैरवाम्बरः ।
    AM—
        तिरोताय पड़े वामपद मनोहर ।
        चमरी देवता ताहे भैरव चमर ॥
AM suggests the reading तिरोतायां वामपाइश्चामरी भैरवोऽम्बरः । It is interesting to note that the word tirotā stands for Sanskrit strī in the Assamese language. But AM here follows the Śivacarita passage referring to Trihuta (Sans. Tīrabhukti), modern Tirhut or North Bihar. Trisrotā is of course the modern Tista, a tributary of the Brahmaputra or Yamunā. The Pīṭha is located at Sālbāri in the Jalpaiguri District.

[6] G—कामरूपे ।

[7] AG—व्यक्ता (I—व्यक्त°) पाषाण°; G—°स्त्रिष्वानन्दोत्थ भैरवः; तत्राप्सीत्पाचली यत्र; I—°मास्तान् त्र्यमानन्दाच्च; भक्काष्ठलो भवेद्यत्र ।
    AM—
        महामुद्रा कामरूपे रत्तोद्योग याय ।
        रामानन्द (v.l. रावा°) भैरव कामाख्या देवी ताय ।

यत्रास्ते माधवः साच्चादुमानन्दोऽथ भैरवः ।
सर्वदा विश्वरेदेवी तत्र मुक्तिर्न संप्रयः ॥ २१ ॥
तत्र श्रीभैरवी देवी तत्र च द्येचदेवता[1] ।
प्रचण्डचण्डिका तत्र मातङ्गी त्रिपुराम्बिका[2] ।
वगला कमला तत्र भुवनेश्वरी सधूमिनी[3] ॥ २२ ॥

AM suggests the reading साच्चाद् रामानन्दोऽथ or साच्चाद् रामानन्दोऽथ । The Kāmarūpa Pīṭha has been located near Gauhati in Assam. The homage paid by certain early rulers of Assam to Kāmeśvara and Mahāgaurī (Kāmākhyā) seems to point to the old name of the Bhairava at the Kāmarūpa Pīṭha.

[1] ABCE—मत्स्यदेवता ; D—न द्येचदेवता ; GI—यत्र च भैरवी देवी यत्र मत्स्यदेवता ।
Kāmagiri in Kāmarūpa is represented as the seat of the ten Mahāvidyās whose names are given as Bhairavī, Kāmākhyā (Kṣetradevatā), Pracaṇḍacaṇḍikā (i.e. Chinnamastā; cf. *Tantrasāra*, pp. 802ff.), Mātaṅgī, Tripurā, Ambikā, Vagalā, Bhuvaneśī (Bhuvaneśvarī) and Dhūminī (Dhūmāvatī). The usually recognized names of the Mahāvidyās (a late medieval Śākta adaptation of the Daśāvatāra conception) are however Kālī, Tārā, Ṣoḍaśī, Bhuvaneśvarī, Bhairavī, Chinnamastā, Dhūmāvatī, Vagalā, Mātaṅgī and Kamalā (the *Bṛhaddharma P.*, II, 6, 126, having Sundarī for Kamalā and Bagalāmukhī for Bagalā). Cf.

काली तारा महाविद्या षोडशी भुवनेश्वरी ।
भैरवी छिन्नमस्ता च विद्या धूमावती तथा ।
वगला सिद्धविद्या च मातङ्गी कमलात्मिका ॥

referred to the *Cāmuṇḍā Tantra* in the *Śabdakalpadruma*, s.v., and to the *Muṇḍamālā Tantra* (cf. *Des. Cat. Sans. MSS.*, R.A.S.B., VIII, p. 164) in the *Tantrasāra* (p. 14). Only some of the names are common to the two lists. That, however, there was no unanimity about the names of the ten Mahāvidyās is demonstrated by another list quoted from the *Mālinīvijaya* in the *Tantrasāra* (loc. cit.):

काली नीला महादुर्गा त्वरिता छिन्नमस्तका ।
वाग्वादिनी चान्नपूर्णा तथा प्रत्यङ्गिरा पुनः ॥
कामाख्यावासिनी बाला मातङ्गी त्रैलवासिनी ॥

This list agrees with that of the *Pīṭhanirṇaya* in recognizing Kāmākhyāvāsinī or Kāmākhyā as one of the ten Mahāvidyās. The name Pracaṇḍacaṇḍikā, recognized by the *Pīṭhanirṇaya*, is found in the following list of the ten Mahāvidyās quoted from the *Tantracintāmaṇi* in *Des. Cat. Sans. MSS.*, R.A.S.B., VIII, p. 388: (1) Śyāmā (Kālī), (2) Tārā, (3) Pracaṇḍacaṇḍikā, (4) Śrī (Kamalā), (5) Bhairavī, (6) Mahālakṣmī, (7) Mātaṅgī, (8) Bhuvaneśvarī, (9) Dhūmāvatī, and (10) Vagalā. An interesting list of the Mahāvidyās in the *Guhyātiguhya Tantra* (*Des. Cat.*, p. 206) identifies the manifestations of the mother-goddess with the ten Avatāras of Viṣṇu :

कृष्णमूर्तिः कालिका स्याद् रामभूर्तिस्तारिणी ।
छिन्नमस्ता वशिंषः स्याद् वामनो भुवनेश्वरी ॥
जामदग्न्यः सुन्दरी स्यान्मीनो भूमावती भवेत् ।
बाला(वगला ?) कूर्ममूर्तिः स्याद्रुद्धभद्रश्च भैरवी ॥
महालक्ष्मीर्भवेद्बुद्धो दुर्गा स्यात् कल्किरूपिणी ।
स्वयं भगवती काली कृष्णस्तु भगवान् स्वयं ॥

Cf. Mahālakṣmī and Durgā for Kamalā and Mātaṅgī. The *Tantracintāmaṇi* (*ibid.*, p. 385) also says, कार्षिकाकृष्णयोस्तारारामयोस्वेकरूपता । The *Muṇḍamālā* list of the Mahāvidyās quoted in the *Tantrasāra* is elsewhere (*ibid.*, p. 580) ascribed to the *Viśvasāra* or the *Cāmuṇḍā Tantra*.

[2] ABCF—त्रिपुराम्बिका ; G—यत्र मातङ्गी ; I—°चण्डिका देवी ।
[3] A—सुधामिनी ; F—सभूमिनी ; G—यत्र भुवनेश्वरी सुधूमिनी ; I—यत्र ; सुधामिनी ।

एतानि परपीठानि[1] ग्रंसन्ति वरभैरवाः[2] ।
[एवं तु[3] देवताः सर्वा एवं तु[4] दश भैरवाः[5] ॥ २३ ॥
सर्वत्र विरला चार्चं[6] कामरूपे मुहे मुहे ।
गौरीशिखरमारुह्य पुनर्जन्म न विद्यते[7] ॥ २४ ॥
करतोयां समारभ्य[8] यावद्दिक्करवासिनीम्[9] ।
त्रतयोजनविस्तीर्णा[10] त्रिकोणा सर्वसिद्धिदम् ।
देवा मरणमिच्छन्ति[11] किं पुनर्मानवादयः[12] ॥ २५ ॥]
भूतधात्री (क्षीरग्रामे) महामाया (°देव) भैरवः क्षीरखण्डकः[13] ।
युगाद्या सा[14] महामाया दक्षाङ्गुष्ठं पदो मम ॥ २६ ॥

---

[1] ACDF—नव°; EGI—वर° ।
[2] ADE—मरभैरव; BF—नवभैरवाः ।
[3] A—वै; DEGI—ता । The whole line is omitted in C.
[4] ADEGI—ते ।
[5] ABC read verse 28 after verse 23. F omits the second line of verse 23 as well as verses 24-25. I reads verse 28 between verses 23 and 24, and verse 25 between verses 27 and 29.
[6] B—देवौ; I—कामरूवे ।
[7] A reads verse 26 after verse 24.
[8] A—समारभ्य; I—समाराद्य ।
[9] I—°वासिनौ; BDE—यावच्छिखरवासिनीम् । The seat of Dikkaravāsinī is located in the *Kālikā Purāṇa* in the eastern part of Kāmarūpa which is the Gauhāti region of Assam. See *supra*, pp. 13, note 1; 17, note 3.
[10] C—°विस्तारं ।
[11] A—°मिच्छन्ति; I—मरणमिच्छन्ति ।
[12] G—पुनर्मानुवादयः । C adds here: इति कामरूपमाहात्म्यम् । It is probable that some of the verses in the description of the Kāmarūpa Pīṭha were a later addition. F reads verses 26-27 after verse 28.
[13] AFG—क्षीरकप्ठकः; I—क्षीरखण्डक ।
AM— क्षीरग्रामे दानिपार चन्द्रछवैभव ।
युगाद्या देवता क्षीरखण्डक भैरव ॥
AM suggests the reading
क्षीरग्रामे महादेव भैरवः क्षीरखण्डकः ।
युगाद्या सा महामाया दक्षाङ्गुष्ठं पदो मम ॥

The Pīṭha is located at Khīragrām near Katwa in the Burdwan District. Cf. note 14 *infra*. B has for verses 26-27:
भूतधात्रौ महामाया वामपदाङ्गुष्ठौ मम ।
नकुलीशः काञ्चीपीठे दक्षपदाङ्गुष्ठौ मम ।

[14] A—युगाद्या सा महामाया दक्षाङ्गुष्पदे; F—युगाद्या सा महादेव दक्षाङ्गु°; BCDE— युगाद्यायां महादेव; G—युगाद्या सा महादेवी दक्षाङ्गुष्ठे; I—महादेवी दक्षांमुष्पदे ।

The *Caṇḍīmaṅgala* mentions the goddess as Yogādyā and connects Kṣīragrāma with Satī's back. For the goddess Yogādyā at Kṣīragrāma, see also *Des. Cat. Vernacular MSS. in the collection of the R.A.S.B.*, IX (Bengali MSS.), pp. 317-18 (Nos. 318, 5372).

नकुलीशः कालीपीठे¹ दक्षपादाङ्गुली च मे² ।
³[सर्वसिद्धिकरौ देवी कालिका तत्र देवता] ॥ २७ ॥
व्यङ्कुलीटन्दं⁴ दृष्टस्य प्रयागे ललिता भवः⁵ ।
जयन्त्यां वामजङ्घा⁶ च जयन्ती क्रमदीश्वरः ॥ २८ ॥
भुवनेश्यो सिद्धिरूपा (सिद्धरूपः) किरीटस्या⁷ किरीटतः
(किरीटाख्ये किरीटकः) ।
[देवता विमला शाम्भी संवर्ती भैरवस्तथा] ॥ २९ ॥

¹ ABDE—कालि°; G—नकुलीशः काम्यपीठे च ।
   AM— कालीघाटे चारिटि चइलि ङानि पार ।
   नकुलेश भैरव कालिका देवी तार ॥

G explains काम्यपीठे as कालीघाटख्याते while AM suggests the reading मकुलेशः कालीघटे ।
Cf. verse 49 below (p. 56). The Pīṭha is located at Kālīghāṭ in the southern suburb of Calcutta. Cf. the description of the Pīṭha in the Śivacarita (p. 41 above). The original text seems to refer to Kālīpīṭha indicating 'the Pīṭha which is the resort of Kālī'. The name of the Pīṭhadevī was possibly not mentioned separately.

² ABCDEG—°पादाङ्गुली मे; I—°पादाङ्गुलीषु च ।
³ This line is omitted in ABCGI. It was interpolated to provide separate mention of the goddess at the Pīṭha.
⁴ A—व्यङ्कुलीत्वन्दं; B—वह्वन्दे तु; F—वह्वस्यैव; GI—वङ्कुलीषु च ।
   AM— प्रयागंदे दुवातेर वह्नली सरस ।
   तावाते भैरव दश महाविद्या दश ॥

It seems that the manuscript consulted by Bhāratacandra read verses 22-23 after verse 28 and, therefore, the ten Mahāvidyās, associated in the text with Kāmarūpa, were transferred to Prayāga. It was also easy to connect the ten Mahāvidyās with the ten fingers of Satī's hands that are said to have fallen at Prayāga (modern Allahabad). The Śivacarita speaks of the Bhairava as Veṇimādhava whose temple stands at the confluence of the Ganges and the Jumna.

⁵ I—भवेत्; ABC—भव ।
⁶ G—°जङ्घा मे; I—जयन्त्यां वामजङ्घायां;
   AM— जयन्ताय वामजङ्घा पेडिल केशव ।
   जयन्ती देवता क्रमदीश्वर भैरव ॥

The Pīṭha is located at Kalajor-Bāurbhog in the Sylhet District of East Pakistan. Gait says (History of Assam, p. 268), 'There is a spot in the Faljur Pargana where part of Satī's left leg is said to have fallen, and here human victims were immolated yearly on the ninth day (mahānavamī) of the Durgā Pūjā. Similar sacrifices were also offered on special occasions, such as the birth of a son in the royal family, or the fulfilment of some request made to the gods. Frequently the victims were self-chosen, in which case, for some time previous to the sacrifice, they enjoyed the privilege of doing whatever they pleased without let or hindrance. Sometimes, however, the supply of voluntary victims ran short, and then strangers were kidnapped for the purpose from foreign territory.'

⁷ AI—किरीटाख्या; B—किरीटस्या किरीटिनो; G—किरीटाखं किरीटकः ।
   AM— किरीटकोषाय पड़े किरीट सुरूप ।
   भुवनेश्यो देवता भैरव सिद्धरूप ॥

AM suggests the reading सिद्धरूपः and the omission of the following line (cf. p. 47, note 2). The Pīṭha is located at Vaṭanagar near Lālbāg in the Murshidabad District.

THE ŚĀKTA PĪṬHAS

[वाराणस्यां विशालाक्षी देवता कालभैरवः ।
मणिकर्णीति विख्याता कुण्डलं च मम श्रुतेः[1] ॥ ३० ॥
कन्याश्रमे च[2] एषं मे[3] निमिषो भैरवस्तथा] ।
सर्वार्थी देवता तत्र[4]

कुसच्छेने च गुल्फतः[5] ॥ ३१ ॥

स्थाणुनांम्रा च सावित्री देवता
मणिवेदके[6] ।
मणिबन्धे[7] च गायत्री सर्वानन्दस्तु भैरवः ॥ ३२ ॥

[1] A—श्रुतेसंम ; G—मणिकर्षिकेति ; I—श्रुति: । E reads verse 29 after this verse. The reference is to Maṇikarṇikā at Benares in U.P. AM substitutes the fictitious Maṇibandha for Kanyāśrama or Vārāṇasī. Vārāṇaśī, not found in the AM, may have been later inserted in the original text (cf. p. 43, note 3). Śiva omits Kanyāśrama and connects Satī's back with Vaivasvata.

[2] B—तु । The name of the Pīṭha reminds one of Kanyākubja or Kānyakubja (modern Kanoj) in the United Provinces. But Kanyāśrama was well known to Bengali Tantric writers who located it in Eastern India. In a discussion on the places which are not suitable for *dīkṣā* (Tantric initiation), the *Tantrasāra* (Vaṅgavāsī ed.. p. 41) quotes the verse

गयायां भाष्करचेने विरजे चन्द्रपर्वते ।
चट्टले च मतङ्गे च तथा कन्याश्रमेषु च ॥

with the following note: भाष्करचेनं दक्षिणदेशे कोणार्क इति प्रसिद्धम् । विरजे विरजाचेने । चन्द्रपर्वते चन्द्रमेश्वरपर्वते । चट्टले चाटर्मा इति ख्याते । मतङ्गे मतङ्गदेशे । कन्याश्रमचन्द्रमेश्वर-गिरिषमौ पर्वतौ कुमार्याश्रमलेन कामरूपे प्रसिद्धः । The location of Kanyāśrama, in the passage, near the Candraśekhara hill and in Kāmarūpa suggests its identification with Kumārīkuṇḍa in the Chittagong District.

[3] AF—मे प्रष्टं ; G—दष्टिमं ; I—पौठं मे निमेषो ।

[4] G—चात्र ।

[5] AM— कुसच्छेने डानि पार गुल्फ च अनुभव ।
विमक्ता तादाते देवी संवर्ते भैरव ॥

AM apparently reads the second line of verse 29 after verse 31. The Bhairava Sthāṇu has to be associated with Sthāṇvīśvara (modern Thanesar) in the Karnal District of the Punjab.

[6] ABCDI—स्थाणू नाम्नी च सावित्री अश्वनाथस्तु भैरवः ; F—मणिवेदिकदेशतः ; G— स्थाणुनाम्ना सावित्री देवता मानवेदके ।

AM— मणिवेदे मणिवम्भ पठितं तांङार ।
स्थाणु नाम्ने भैरव सावित्री देवौ ताङर ॥

This is because of the textual confusion referred to in note 5 above.

A—मणिरत्ने ; BI—मणिरत्ने ; G—मुनिवने ।
AM— मणिवन्धे वाममणिवम्भ अभिराम ।
सर्वानन्द भैरव गायत्री देवी नाम ॥

This is also due to the textual confusion referred to in note 5 above. Maṇibandha (i.e. wrist) cannot be regarded as the name of a place; cf. the confusion in the *Śivacarita* (p. 40 above).

श्रीग्रैले (श्रीहट्टे) च मम ग्रीवा महालक्ष्मीस्तु[1] देवता ।
भैरवः सम्बरानन्दो[2] देग्रे देग्रे व्यवस्थितः ॥ ३३ ॥
काञ्चीदेग्रे च कङ्कालो[3] भैरवो रक्षनामकः ।
देवता देवगर्भाख्या[4]
नितम्बः कालमाधवे[5] ॥ ३४ ॥
भैरवख्यासिताङ्गश्च देवी काली सुसिद्धिदा[6] ।
दृष्ट्वा दृष्ट्वा[7] नमस्कृत्य[8] मन्त्रसिद्धिमवाप्नुयात् ॥ ३५ ॥
[9][कुजवारे भूततिथौ निग्राद्धँ यस्तु साधकः ।
गत्वा प्रदच्छिणीक्रत्य मन्त्रसिद्धिमवाप्नुयात् ॥ ३६ ॥]

---

[1] G—महामाया; I—महालक्ष्मी च ।
[2] E—शम्बरानन्दो; G—कवः स्थितः ।
AM— श्रीहट्टे पठिल ग्रीवा महालक्ष्मी देवी ।
सर्वानन्द भैरव वैभव यांहा षेवि ॥

AM therefore suggests the readings श्रीहट्टे and सर्वानन्द in places respectively of श्रीग्रैले and सम्बरानन्दो; cf. S'ivacarita (p. 40, Nos. 5, 14). As Śrīparvata, probably identical with Śrīśaila, is separately mentioned in verse 41, the reference in this case may actually be to Śrīhaṭṭa (modern Sylhet) in East Pakistan. The Pīṭha is located at Gotatikar-Jainpur near Sylhet. The expression देग्रे देग्रे is not quite happy.

[3] G—कङ्काली भैरवो रक्षनामतः; I—काञ्चिदेग्रे च कङ्कालि भैरवो रक्षनामतः ।
[4] A—वेदगर्भाख्या ।
AM— काञ्चीदेग्रे पठिल कांकालि अभिराम ।
देवगर्भा देवता भैरव रक्ष नाम ॥

Kāñcī, mentioned in the early lists, certainly stands for modern Conjeeveram in the Chingleput District of the Madras Presidency. The Pīṭha in this case, however, is usually located on the Kopāi near Bolpur in the Birbhum District of Bengal.

[5] A—नितम्बं; B—नितम्बं कालमागधे; I—नितम्बकालिमाधवे ।
AM— नितम्बेर अर्द्ध कालमाधवे ताँहार ।
अषिताङ्ग भैरव देवता काली तार ॥

[6] E—च सुसिद्दा; G—भैरवोऽचिताङ्गश्च ।
[7] A—दष्टादष्टा; G—दृष्टादृष्टा ।
[8] ABEGI—महादेव ।
[9] This verse is omitted in CF and may be a later interpolation.

THE ŚĀKTA PĪṬHAS

श्रोणाख्या[1] भद्रसेनस्तु नर्मदाख्ये[2] नितम्बकः ।
रामगिरौ[3] स्नानाच्च[4] श्रिवानी चण्डभैरवः ॥ २७ ॥
[वृन्दावने केशजालमुमा[5] नाम्नी च[6] देवता] ।
[भूतेश्रो भैरवस्तच्च सर्वसिद्धिप्रदायकः] ॥ २८ ॥
संहाराख्य[7] ऊर्द्ध्वदन्तो[8] देवी (°नले) नारायणी शुचौ ।
अधोदन्तो[9] महाशब्दो वाराही पद्ममागरे ॥ २९ ॥

---

[1] AFG—श्रोणाख्ये ; I—श्रेणाख्ये ; B—श्रोणभद्रे भद्रसेनो ।
AM— नितम्बर चार खंडे पड़े नर्मदाय ।
   भद्रसेन भैरव श्रोणाच्यै देवी ताय ॥

AM suggests the reading श्रोणाच्यै भद्रसेनस्तु । There is some doubt whether the Pīṭha has to be located on the Sone or on the Narmada.

[2] BCD—नर्मदाख्या नितम्बके ; F—नर्मदाख्या नितम्बकम् ; G—नर्मदाख्ये नितम्बके ; I—नम्बदाचे नितम्बके ।

[3] B—राजगिरौ ; G—रामाकिन्यां ; I—रामगिर्य्यां । Rāmagiri is modern Ramtek near Nagpur in the Central Province. There is also a tradition identifying Rāmagir with the Chitrakūṭa in Bundelkhand.

[4] AB—तथा नासा ; CDF—तथा बाला ; I—स्वनान्यच्च ।
AM— चार स्नान पड़े तांर रामगिरि स्थाने ।
   शिवानी देवता चण्ड भैरव सेखाने ॥

Note that the nose of Satī is associated in verse 5 (p. 44 above) with Sugandhā.

[5] B—°जालान् ; CD—°जालु ; EF—°जाली ; G—उमानाम्नौ केशजाले भूतेश: परभैरव: (with the second line of the verse omitted)
I— वृन्दावने केशजाले कृष्णनाथस्तु भैरव: ।
   कात्यायनी तव देवी सर्वसिद्धिप्रदायिनी ॥
AM— केशजाल नाम स्थाने पड़े तांर केश ।
   उमा नामे देवी तारे भैरव भूतेश ॥

It seems that the original reading was उमावने केशजालं भूतेश: परभैरव: ॥ Umāvana was a name of Devīkoṭṭa ; cf. style of v. 27 (supra, p. 50, notes 1 and 3). AM supports the reading in G. In the modified text there is reference to the fanciful Śākta claim on the celebrated Vaiṣṇava tīrtha near Mathurā (Muttra) in the United Provinces (cf. Kṛṣṇa referred to in the I text). Keśajāla was sometimes regarded as the name of the Pīṭha owing to confusion ; cf. the case of Maṇibandha in verse 32. See the confusion in the Śivacarita.

[6] A—नाम्नौति ।

[7] ABI—संहाराख्ये ।
AM— ऊर्द्ध दन्तपांतिर अनले इरल धाम ।
   संहार भैरव देवी नारायणी नाम ॥

AM suggests the reading संहाराख्य ऊर्द्ध्वदन्तोऽनले । The Śivacarita regards Saṃhāra as the name of an Upapīṭha ; cf. ABI.

[8] ACFGI—ऊर्द्ध्वदन्ते ।

[9] ACFGI—अधोदन्ते ।

करतोयातटे तस्यं (कर्णे) वामे[1] वामनभैरवः ।
अपर्णा देवता यत्र ब्रह्मरूपाकरोद्भवा[2] ॥ ४० ॥
श्रीपर्वते दत्तगुल्फ(कर्णे)स्थन[3] श्रीसुन्दरी परा ।
सर्वसिद्धीश्वरी[4] सर्वा सुन्दरानन्दभैरवः[5] ॥ ४१ ॥
कपालिनी (कपाली च) भीमरूपा वामगुल्फो[6] विभाषके ।
[7] [भैरवस्तु महादेव सर्वानन्दः शुभप्रदः] ॥ ४२ ॥

AM— पञ्चसागरेते पद्मे अधोदंसार ।
महाभद्र भैरव वाराही देवी तांर ।

Pañcasāgara seems to indicate the oceans, the traditional number of which was, however, four or seven. The reference may also be to the five Kuṇḍas near Hardwar.

[1] E—तन्यात् वन्हि°; G—गुल्फं; I—तस्प ।
  AM— करतोयातटे पद्मे वामकर्णे तांर ।
       वामेष भैरव देवी अपर्णा तांदार ॥

AM suggests the reading कर्णे वामे वामभैरवः । The Karatoyā is a sacred river of northern Bengal. The Pīṭha is located at Bhavānīpur in the Bogra District. G has a note reading भवानीपुरख्याते ।

[2] A—°करोद्भवः; I—तत्र । The last word of the verse is not quite satisfactory.

[3] ACI—गुल्फं; E—तस्प; FG—गुल्फं तत्र ।
  AM— श्रीपर्वते दानि कर्णे फेलिक्लेन षदि ।
       भैरव सुन्दरानन्द देवता सुन्दरी ॥

AM suggests the reading दत्तकर्णस्तत्र । Śrīparvata is the same as the Śrīśaila in the Nallamalur range to the south of the Krishna. But the non-mention of Mallikārjuna (Śiva) and of Devī Bhramarāmbā on the Śrīśaila shows that the description is probably fantastic. As two other places are associated with Satī's gulpha (verses 31 and 42), AM possibly suggests the correct reading of the verse.

[4] ABGI—°सिंदेश्वरी; E—°सिद्धिकरौ ।

[5] CDF—सुनन्द।नन्द° ।

[6] C—गुल्फं; DI°—गुल्फे; B—गुल्फा; F—गुल्फविभागतः; G—कपालिनी क्रोधरूपा वामगुल्फे विभाषके ।
  AM— विभाषेते वाम गुल्फ फेलिह्ला केशव ।
       भीमरूपा देवी तांदे कपाली भैरव ॥

AM suggests the reading कपाली च भीमरूपा and the omission of the second line of the verse (cf. p. 50, note 7). The Pīṭha is located near Tamluk in the Midnapur District.

[7] This line is omitted in ABE and may be a later interpolation. Cf. p. 50, notes 3 and 7.

THE ŚĀKTA PĪṬHAS

उदरध्व (अधरध्व) प्रभासे मे [1] चन्द्रभागा यशस्विनी ।
वक्रतुण्डो भैरव-
स्वोर्द्धोष्टो भैरवपर्वते [2] ॥ ४३ ॥
अवन्ती [3] च महादेवी लम्बकर्णस्तु भैरवः ॥ ४४ ॥
चिबुके [4] भामरी देवी विक्रताक्षो [5] जते स्थले (जनस्थाने) [6] ।
गण्डो गोदावरीतीरे विश्वेशो (विश्वेश्वो) विश्वमाटका [7] ॥ ४५ ॥

---

[1] A—प्रभासमे; BCDE—प्रभासे; G—अधरध्व प्रभासे मे चन्द्राभासा; I—अधरध्व ।

AM— प्रभासे अधर देवी चन्द्रभागा तार्ये ।

वक्रतुण्ड भैरव प्रत्यच्चरूप यार्ये ॥

AM suggests the reading अधरध्व प्रभासे; of. verse 52 below. Prabhāsa or Somnath is a famous holy place in southern Kathiawar.

[2] B—स्वोष्ठो भैरवपर्वते; A—अर्द्धिष्ठि भौरवपर्वते; G—तुष्ट भैरवपर्वते; I—तुष्टी भैरव° ।

AM— भैरव पर्वते स्वोष्ठ पड़े चक्रघाय ।

लघकर्ण भैरव अवन्ती देवी माय ॥

AM suggests the reading लघकर्णस्तु भैरवः । The Devī's name seems to refer the Pīṭha to West Malwa.

[3] ABCDFI—अवन्त्यां ।

[4] ABC—चिबके ।

[5] ABFG—विक्रताक्षा; I—विक्ताक्ष; C—किकुभाक्षा; D—विक्रभाची । Probably विक्रताक्षी is intended.

[6] AM— जनस्थाने चिबुक पड़िल अभिराम ।

विक्रताच भैरव भामरी देवी नाम ॥

AM suggests the reading विक्रताक्षी जनस्थाने । Janasthāna, celebrated in the *Rāmāyaṇa*, lay in the upper Godavari valley in the present Nasik region of the Bombay Presidency. CDF read after this verse: भैरवः सर्वसिद्धी अस्तत्र सिद्धिरनुत्तमा apparently because the reading विक्रताक्षा invited a name of the Bhairava at the Pīṭha.

[7] I—मण्डे;

AM— गोदावरी तीरे पड़े बाम गण्डस्थानि ।

विश्वेश भैरव विश्वमाटका भवानी ॥

AM suggests the reading विश्वेशो विश्वमाटका which shows that verse 46 is probably an interpolation. The reading विश्वेश्वो necessitated the fabrication of the name of the Bhairava at the Pīṭha. The two lines of verse 46 appear to have been inserted by two different hands. Cf. p. 56, note 8.

[दक्षपाणिभैरवस्तु¹ वामगण्डे तु² राकिणी ।
³भैरवो वत्सनाभस्तु तत्र सिद्धिर्न संशयः⁴ ॥ ४६ ॥]
रत्नावल्यां (रत्नवत्यां) दक्षस्कन्धः कुमारो भैरवः शिवः⁵ ।
मिथिलायामुमा देवी⁶ वामस्कन्धो⁷ मद्योदरः⁸ ॥ ४७ ॥
⁹[नलाट्टायां नलापातो योगीशो¹⁰ भैरवस्तथा ।
तत्र सा कालिका देवी सर्वसिद्धिप्रदायिका¹¹ ॥ ४८ ॥
¹²कालीघाटे मुखपातः क्रोधीशो¹³ भैरवस्तथा ।
देवता जयदुर्गाख्या नानाभोगप्रदायिनी ॥ ४९ ॥

---

¹ A—दक्षपाणि ; G—भैरवस्तु वामगण्डे च । Rākiṇī is the same as Raṅkiṇī ; cf. *supra*, p. 33 and note 1.

² I—च । For the right cheek, see verse 14 (p. 46) above.

³ D(v.l.)E read in place of this line: कुमारो भैरवो वत्स सर्वशैलाग्रकोपरि । The reference to Sarvaśaila (literally, all hills) is no doubt fanciful; cf. Pañcasāgara.

⁴ B—वत्सनाभस्तु तत्र सिद्धिमवाप्नुयात् ; GI—वत्सामि भैरवो वत्स सर्वशैलाग्रगोमिथः (I—°गोविषः) ।

⁵ G—रत्नवत्यां दक्षस्कन्धः कुमारो भैरवी शिवा । I—रत्नावल्यां दक्षिणस्कन्धः कुमारी भैरवी शिव ।

AM— रत्नावली स्थाने दानि खस्थ अभिराम ।
कुमार भैरव नाहे देवी शिवा नाम ॥

AM suggests the reading कुमारो भैरवी शिवा as in G. A city called Ratnavatī is mentioned in the *Kāvyamīmāṁsā*; but probably Khanakul-Krishnanagar, on the river Ratnākara (Kānānadī) in the Hooghly District and famous for its temple of Ghaṇṭeśvara Śiva, is indicated. Cf. also the Pramodā *tīrtha* at the confluence of the Vāgmatī and the Ratnāvalī in Nepal.

⁶ A—माक्षी ; CFI—मद्रादेवी ; G—मिथिलायां वामस्कन्धी मद्रादेवी मद्योदरी ।

AM— मिथिलाय वामस्कन्ध देवी मद्रादेवी ।
मद्योदर भैरव सर्वार्थ यारि सेवि ॥

AM supports the reading in G with मद्योदरः for मद्योदरी । Mithilā has been identified with Janakpur in the Nepalese Tarai.

⁷ ABE—स्कान्धी : CFI—स्कन्धे ।

⁸ D—मद्योदरी । I reads after this line भैरवो वत्सनाभस्तु तत्र सिद्धिर्न संशयः (*vide* verse 46).

⁹ The following eight verses are not found in G (and the AM original) and were apparently interpolated.

¹⁰ EI—योगेशो । The Pīṭha is located at Nalahati in the Birbhum District of West Bengal. The word *nalā* is a Bengali corruption of Sanskrit *nalaka* (any long bone).

¹¹ B—तत्र सिद्धिर्न संशयः ।

¹² Verse 49 is omitted in I. DEF have in place of this line: कर्णाटे चैव कर्णा (v.l. कर्णं) मे क्षभीव (v.l. त्वभीव) नाम भैरवः । Cf. verse 27 (p. 50) above. This Kālī Pīṭha is located at Juranpur near Katwa in the Burdwan District. The Pīṭha was not mentioned in the original text.

¹³ D (v.l.)—क्रोधेशो ; B—क्रोधश ।

THE ŚĀKTA PĪṬHAS

वक्रेश्वरे मनःपातो वक्रनाथश्च भैरवः । [1]
नदी पापहरा तत्र देवी महिषमर्दिनी ॥ ५० ॥
यशोरे पाणिपद्मश्च देवता यशोरेश्वरी ।
चण्डश्च [2] भैरवो यत्र तत्र सिद्धिर्न संशयः [3] ॥ ५१ ॥
अट्टहासे चोष्ठपातो देवी सा फुल्लरा स्मृता ।
विश्वेशो [4] भैरवस्तत्र सर्वाभीष्टप्रदायकः ॥ ५२ ॥
त्वारपातो नन्दिपुरे भैरवो नन्दिकेश्वरः ।
नन्दिनी सा महादेवी तत्र सिद्धिमवाप्नुयात् [5] ॥ ५३ ॥
लङ्कायां नूपुरश्चैव भैरवो राक्षसेश्वरः । [6]
इन्द्राक्षी देवता तत्र इन्द्रेणोपासिता पुरा ॥ ५४ ॥
विराटदेशमध्ये तु [7] पादाङ्गुलिनिपातनम् ।
भैरवस्ताम्रताख्यश्च [8] देवी तत्राम्बिका स्मृता ॥ ५५ ॥ [9]]

---

[1] I—मुण्डपातं । The Pīṭha, which had no mention in the original text, is located near Dubrajpur in the Birbhum District. The *Śivacarita* separately mentions Vakreśvara and Vakranātha, which, however, appear to be the same place.

[2] A—चण्डश्च; BF—चण्डश्च भैरवस्तत्र; I—चण्डेशो भैरवो देवस्तत्र ।

[3] I—सिद्धिर्वाप्नुयात्; BE—तत्र सिद्धिमवाप्नुयात्; CF—यत्र सिद्धिमवाप्नुयात् । The Yaśora Pīṭha is located at Īśvarīpur (about 25 miles from the Hasanabad Railway Station) in the Khulna District and not actually at Jessore.

[4] C—विश्नेशो । The Pīṭh, which was not mentioned in the original text, is located near Lābhpur in the Birbhum District.

[5] BCDEFI—सिद्धिर्न संशयः । The Pīṭha is located near Sainthia in the Birbhum District.

[6] I—नन्दिकेश्वरः । The name of the Bhairava suggests that this Laṅkā is identical with Ceylon, although the author may have had no knowledge of the Ceylonese *tīrthas*. Laṅkā (literally, an island) was not referred to in the original text.

[7] A—विराट मध्यदेशे तु; I—°निपातनं । The ancient Virāṭa or Matsya country lay in the Jaipur-Alwar-Bharatpur region of Rajputana; but late medieval writers often placed a Virāṭa country in northern Bengal (cf. *I.C.*, VIII, pp. 53-54). This Pīṭha had no place in the original text.

[8] AE—श्यमताख्यश्च; I—भैरवोऽम्रताख्यश्च ।

[9] D (v.l.) EF add after this verse:
मगधे (v.l. मागधे) दक्षजङ्घा मे बोमकेशश्च भैरवः ।
सर्वानन्दमयी (v.l. °करी) देवी सर्वकाम(v.l. सर्वानन्द)फलप्रदा ॥

This verse was fabricated by one who could not find out all the 51 Pīṭhas owing to errors in the manuscripts consulted; cf. the case of Karṇāta (p. 56, note 12).

एतास्ते कथिताः पञ्च पीठनाथाधिदेवताः[1] ।
चेदाधिपं[2] विना देव पूजयेत् पीठदेवताम्[3] ।
भैरवैर्ह्रियते सर्वं जपपूजादिसाधनम्[4] ॥ ५६ ॥
व्याख्या भैरवं पीठे पीठशक्तिष्व् ह्रङ्कर[5] ।
प्राणनाथ न सिध्येत्[6] कल्पकोटिजपादिभिः ॥ ५७ ॥
न देयं परशिष्याय[7] निन्दकाय दुरात्मने ।
शठाय क्रूरकार्याय[8] दत्वा ब्रह्ममवाप्नुयात् ।
दद्याच्छान्ताय[9] शिष्याय मन्त्रौ मन्त्रार्थसिद्धये ॥ ५८ ॥ [10]

---

[1] A—पीठनाथादि°; G—एतत्ते कथितं वत्स पीठनाथादि°; I—एतत्ते कथित ।
[2] D—चेदाधौषं; G—चेदाधौषं विना यस्तु; I—चेदाधौषं विना देवि ।
[3] CDF—पूजयेदन्य° ।
[4] G—जपपूजादिकं षमम्; I—भैरवे हृदयः सर्वं ।
[5] BCDE—पीठं; A—भैरवपीठं; G—पीठं पीठशक्ति; I—व्याख्या भैरवं पीठं ।
[6] A—सिध्यन्ति; B—सिद्धे तु; CEG—सिध्येत्; I—सिद्धेत ।
[7] A—°शिष्येभ्यो; I—देया ।
[8] B—क्रूरकर्माय; EG—वञ्चकायेदं; I—वञ्चकायेत्यं ।
[9] A—दद्यात् शान्ताय शिष्याय;
EI—दद्यात् शान्ताय शिष्याय नैष्ठिकाय श्रुचौ प्रिये (I—धिरे) ।
साधंकाय कुलीनाय मन्त्रौ मन्त्रार्थसिद्धये ॥

G supports the reading of E with शिष्याय शान्ताय for शान्ताय शिष्याय and शुचि for शुचौ Here is an attempt to make a complete verse in the *anuṣṭubh* out of a half verse. Similar cases are also noticed elsewhere in the text. Cf. pp. 44, note 3; 45, note 5, etc.

[10] Colophon: A—इति तन्त्रचूडामणौ पार्वतीशिवसंवादे एकपञ्चाशद्विद्यान्यक्तौ पीठनिर्णयः समाप्तः; B—इति तन्त्रचूडामणौ शिवपार्वतीसंवादे महापीठनिरूपणं समाप्तं; C—goes on to quote some verses of the *Mahānīlatantra*; E—इति तन्त्रचूडामणौ शिवपार्वतीसंवादे एकपञ्चाशद् विद्यान्यक्तौ पीठनिर्णयः समाप्तः । G—इति चन्द्रचूडामणितन्त्रे (cf. p. 42, note 2 पार्वतीशिवसंवादे विद्यान्यक्तौ पीठनिर्णयः समाप्तः । श्रीदुर्गा । श्रीरमानाथशर्मणः पुस्तकमिदम् । H—इति श्रोभावचूडामणौ षट्कर्मसाधनविधौ पीठनिर्णयः पटलः । I—इति तन्त्रचूडामणौ विद्यान्यक्तौ (विद्या°) पीठनिर्णयं समाप्तं ॥ ॐ नमः परमदेवतायै । प्रभवस्तु प्रकाब्दाः १७।६० (१७६०) सन १२।४५ (१२४५) साल तारिख १४ भाद्रस्य श्रीकाली॰ॽरदेवशर्मणः खाद्दरं पुस्तकम् ॥ श्रीश्रीविश्वेश्वराय नमः । श्रीश्रीदुर्गा ।

Cf. AM— एकमत ना चय पुराण मत यत ।
च्याभि कवि मन्त्रचूडामणि तन्त्र मत ॥

It has been noted above that the *Tripurā Rājamālā* says about a verse of our text: शिववाक्य पीठमाना सन्स्वर प्रमाण । See p. 4, note 1. Note also that Bhāratacandra was aware of the differences of opinion about the Pīṭhas.

APPENDIX I

A

Probable Original Text of the Pīṭhanirṇaya (Mahāpīṭha-nirūpaṇa) Reconstructed on the Basis of Manuscript G and the Annadāmaṅgala.

ईश्वर उवाच ।

मातः परात्परे देवि सर्वज्ञानमयीश्वरि ।
कथ्यतां मे सर्वपीठग्रन्थिभैरवदेवताः ॥ १ ॥

देव्युवाच ।

शृणु वत्स प्रवक्ष्यामि दयाल भक्तवत्सल ।
याभिर्विना न सिध्यन्ति जपसाधनसत्क्रियाः ॥ २ ॥
पञ्चाशदेकपीठानि एवं भैरवदेवताः ।
व्यङ्गप्रत्यङ्गपातेन विष्णुचक्रक्षतेन च ॥ ३ ॥
ममाद्यवपुषो देव हिताय त्वयि कथ्यते ।
ब्रह्मारन्ध्रं हिङ्गुलायां [१] भैरवो भीमलोचनः ॥ ४ ॥
कोट्टरी सा महादेवी त्रिगुणा या दिगम्बरी ।
शर्करारे [२] त्रिनेत्रं मे देवी महिषमर्दिनी ॥ ५ ॥
क्रोधीशो भैरवस्तत्र

सुगन्धायाञ्च [३] नासिका ।
देवस्त्र्यम्बकनामा च सुनन्दा तत्र देवता ॥ ६ ॥
काश्मीरे [४] कण्ठदेशश्च त्रिसन्ध्येश्वरभैरवः ।
महामाया भगवती गुणातीता वरप्रदा ॥ ७ ॥
ज्वालामुख्यां [५] तथा जिह्वा देव उन्मत्तभैरवः ।
अम्बिका सिद्धिदा देवी

स्तनं जालन्धरे [६] भम ॥ ८ ॥
भीषणो भैरवस्तत्र देवी त्रिपुरमालिनी ।
हार्दपीठं वैद्यनाथे [७] वैद्यनाथस्तु भैरवः ॥ ९ ॥
देवता जयदुर्गाख्या

नेपाले [८] जानु मे शिव ।
कपाली भैरवः श्रीमान् महामाया च देवता ॥ १० ॥
मानसे [९] दत्तहस्तो मे देवी दाक्षायणी चरः ।
विरजा ओड्रे [१०] ख्याता नाभिर्मे जयभैरवः ॥ ११ ॥
गङ्गाख्यां [११] गङ्गसङ्गाद्रौ जगन्नाथस्तु भैरवः ।
बङ्गलायां [१२] वामबाङ्गं बङ्गलाख्या च देवता ॥ १२ ॥

भौषको भैरवस्तन्न सर्वसिद्धिप्रदायकः ।
उज्जयिन्यां [११] कूर्परश्च मङ्गला कपिलाम्बरः ॥ १३ ॥
चट्टले [१४] दत्तबाङ्गर्मे भैरवश्चन्द्रशेखरः ।
व्यक्तरूपा भगवती भवानी तत्र देवता ॥ १४ ॥
विशेषतः कलियुगे वसामि चन्द्रशेखरे ।
त्रिपुरायां [१५] दत्तपादो देवता त्रिपुरा नलः ॥ १५ ॥
त्रिखोतायां [१६] वामपादो भामरी भैरवोम्बरः ।
योनिपीठं कामरूपे [१७-२६] कामाख्या तत्र देवता ॥ १६ ॥
यत्रास्ते त्रिगुणातीता व्यक्ता पाषाणरूपिणी ।
यत्रास्ते माधवः साक्षाच्छिवानन्दोऽथ भैरवः ॥ १७ ॥
तत्र श्रीभैरवो देवी तत्र च क्षेत्रदेवता ।
प्रचण्डचण्डिका तत्र मातङ्गी त्रिपुराम्बिका ॥ १८ ॥
वगला कमला तत्र भुवनेश्वरी सधूमिनी ।
एतानि दशपीठानि शंसन्ति दशभैरवाः ॥ १९ ॥
चौर्ग्रामे [२०] सदाशिव भैरवः चौरकाठकः ।
युगाद्या सा महामाया दत्ताङ्कुष्ठं पदो मम ॥ २० ॥
नकुलीग्रः कालीपीठे [२१] दत्तपादाङ्गुलीषु मे ।
अङ्गुलीषु च हस्तस्य प्रयागे [२८] ललिता भवः ॥ २१ ॥
जयन्त्यां [२०] वामजङ्घा च जयन्ती क्रमदीश्वरः ।
भुवनेश्वरी सिद्धिरूपः किरीटाख्ये [२१] किरीटकः ॥ २२ ॥
कन्याश्रमे [२२] च एतं मे निमिषो भैरवस्तथा ।
सर्वाणी देवता तत्र
                    कुरक्षेत्रे [२३] च गुप्ततः ॥ २३ ॥
स्थाणुनार्ह्वा च सावित्री देवता
                              मणिवेदके [२४] ।
मणिबन्धे च गायत्री सर्वानन्दस्तु भैरवः ॥ २४ ॥
श्रीचट्टे [२५] च मम ग्रीवा महालक्ष्मीस्तु देवता ।
भैरवः सम्बरानन्दो देशे देशे व्यवस्थितः ॥ २५ ॥
काञ्चीदेशे [२६] च कङ्कालो भैरवो रुरुनामकः ।
देवता देवगर्भाख्या
                  नितम्बः कालमाधवे [२७] ॥ २६ ॥
भैरवोऽत्रासिताङ्गश्च देवी काली सुसिद्धिदा ।
दृष्ट्वा दृष्ट्वा नमस्कृत्य मन्त्रसिद्धिमवाप्नुयात् ॥ २७ ॥

योगाख्या भद्रसेनस्तु नर्मदाख्ये २७ नितम्बकः ।
रामगिरौ २८ खगानाञ्च त्रिवेणौ चण्डभैरवः ॥ २८ ॥
उमावने ४० केशजालं भूतेशः परभैरवः ।
संहाराख्य ऊर्द्ध्वदन्तेऽनले ४१ नारायणी शुचौ ॥ २९ ॥
अधोदन्ते मच्छाहृद्रो वाराहो पञ्चसागरे ४२ ।
करतोयातटे ४३ कर्णे वामे वामनभैरवः ॥ ३० ॥
अपर्णा देवता तत्र ब्रह्मरूपाकरोद्भवा ।
श्रीपर्वते ४४ दक्षकर्णस्तत्र श्रीसुन्दरी परा ॥ ३१ ॥
सर्वसिद्धीश्वरी देवी सुन्दरानन्दभैरवः ।
कपालौ च भौमरूपा वामगुल्फो विभाषके ४५ ॥ ३२ ॥
अधरख्य प्रभासे ४६ मे चन्द्रभागा यद्दक्षिणौ ।
वक्रतुण्डो भैरवश्च

                ओष्ठो भैरवपर्वते ४७ ॥ ३३ ॥
अवन्ती च मच्छादेवी लम्बकर्णस्तु भैरवः ।
चिवुके भामरी देवी विक्षताख्यो जनस्थाने ४८ ॥ ३४ ॥
गण्डो गोदावरीतीरे ४९ विश्वेशो विश्वमातृका ।
रत्नवत्यां ५० दक्षस्कन्धः कुमारो भैरवो ग्रिवा ॥ ३५ ॥
मिथिलायां ५१ मच्छादेवी वामस्कन्धो महोदरः ।
एतास्ते कथिताः पुत्र पीठनाथाधिदेवताः ॥ ३६ ॥
क्षेत्राद्यौघं विना देव पूजयेत्पीठदेवताम् ।
भैरवैर्क्रियते सर्वं जपपूजादिसाधनम् ॥ ३७ ॥
अज्ञात्वा भैरवं पीठे पीठशक्तिञ्च शाङ्करि ।
प्राङ्नाथं न सिध्येत्तु कल्पकोटिजपादिभिः ॥ ३८ ॥
न देयं परशिष्याय निन्दकाय दुरात्मने ।
शठाय क्रूरकार्याय दत्वा मृत्युमवाप्नुयात् ॥ ३९ ॥
दद्याच्छान्ताय शिष्याय मन्त्रौ मन्त्रार्थसिद्धये ॥ ४० ॥

B

Modified Text of the Pīṭhanirṇaya as found in Manuscript H (with slight emendation of the faulty language of the original)

श्रीशिव उवाच ।
षट्कर्मसाधनं देवि कस्मिन् स्थाने प्रशस्तकम् ।
मातः परावरे नित्ये सर्वज्ञानमहेश्वरि ॥
कथ्यतां मे सर्वपीठं तथा षट्कर्मसाधनम् ।
शक्तिभैरवदेवस्य साधूनां हितकाम्यया ॥

श्रीदेव्युवाच ।

घृणु वत्स प्रवच्यामि दयाळ भक्तवत्सल ।
यानि विना न सिध्यन्ति जपसाधनसत्क्रियाः ॥
पञ्चाग्रदेकपीठानि चैवं भैरवदेवताः ।
प्रधानं पीठकं देव यथा भैरवदेवताः ॥
यच्च साधनं प्रशस्तं तथा षट्कर्म भैरव ॥
गङ्गाद्याः सततं सर्वाः समुद्राश्च तथा नदाः ।
सर्वतीर्थानि सर्वत्र ममाङ्गे घृणु भैरव ॥
व्यक्तप्रत्यक्पातेन विष्णुचक्रात्ततेन च ।
ममास्य वपुषो देव हिताय च न्वृणां घृणु ॥
ब्रह्मरन्ध्रं चिकुलायां भैरवो भीमलोचनः ।
कुटवी सा महाकाली त्रिगुणा या दिगम्बरी ॥
भ्रूङ्ग्यां दक्षनेत्रं मे देवी महिषमर्दिनी ।
क्रोधौघ्रो भैरवस्तत्र सुगन्धनामकाननः ॥
ताराद्यायां वामनेत्रं ताराख्या तारिणी परा ।
उन्मत्तो भैरवस्तत्र सर्वलक्ष्णसंयुतः ॥
मानसे दक्षचक्षो मे तत्र दाक्षायणी चरः ॥
विजये उत्कले ख्याते नाभिमें अम्बभैरवः ।
सोऽयञ्च सिद्धिदः साक्षाद् देवी मङ्गलचण्डिका ॥
सदने दक्षकूर्पे (?) मे भैरवखड्गसंज्ञकः ।
व्यक्तरूपा भगवती भवानी यत्र देवता ॥
सुगन्ध (?) नासिका यत्र देवस्त्र्यम्बकभैरवः ।
आनन्दा देवता तत्र सर्वसिद्धिप्रदायिनी ॥
काश्मीरे कण्ठदेश्च चिसन्येश्वरभैरवः ।
महामाया भगवती गुणातीता वरप्रदा ॥
ज्वालामुख्यां तथा जिह्वा भैरवो वटुकेश्वरः ।
अम्बिका सिद्धिदा गात्री स्तने जालन्धरे मम ॥
भीषणो भैरवस्तत्र देवी त्रिपुरमालिनी ॥
वामस्तनं वक्त्रेश्वरे भैरवश्चन्द्रशेखरः ।
देवता भैरवी तत्र सर्वपीठेषु नायिका ॥
नासा मे नवखण्डे च वैद्यनाथश्च भैरवः ।
देवता दुर्गाख्या च सा सर्वसिद्धिप्रदायिनी ॥
नेपाले जयदुर्गाख्या तत्र वै तालुकं ग्रिव ।
कपाली भैरवस्तत्र महामारी च देवता ॥

विश्लेषतः कलियुगे वसामि चन्द्रशेखरे ॥
त्रिपुरायां दक्षपादो देवी त्रिपुरसुन्दरी ।
भैरवस्त्रिपुरो देवः सर्वसम्पत्प्रदायकः ॥
चिखोतायां वामपादो देवता भ्रामरी स्वयम् ।
योनिपीठं कामगिरौ कामाख्या देवता स्वयम् ॥
यच्चास्ते त्रिगुणात्मिका व्यक्तपाषाणरूपिणी ।
यच्च श्रीभैरवी देवी यच्च मत्तनदेवता ॥
प्रचण्डचण्डिका चैव मातङ्गी त्रिपुरात्मिका ।
बगला कमला तत्र भवानी हरनायिका ॥
महाकाली स्वयं तत्र भद्रकाली तथापरा ।
सर्वशक्तिः स्वयं तत्र सर्वभैरवदेवताः ॥
महाकालः स्वयं तत्र सर्वदेवसमन्वितः ।
सर्वत्र विरला चाहं कामरूपे गृहे गृहे ॥
एतानि वरपीठानि प्रशंसन्ति च भैरवाः ।
एषां ते देवताः सर्वास्तथा क्षेत्राधिदेवताः ॥
अङ्गुलीषु च सर्वेषु प्रयागे ललिता स्वयम् ॥
कुरुक्षेत्रे तथा देवा भैरवाः पुण्यभाजनाः ।
क्षेत्रेष्वन्यो देवता तत्र सर्वपापविनाशिनी ॥
विन्ध्यशेखरमासाद्य पतिता चाङ्गुली मम ।
सर्वेशो भैरवो नामा तत्र तिष्ठति नित्यशः ॥
जयन्त्यां वामजङ्घा मे जयन्ती कुसुमेश्वरी ।
कीकि कीकिश्वरी देवी भैरवो रूद्रनामकः ॥
मेखले[1] मेखली देवी वामाङ्गुली प्रभेदतः ।
[तत्र च भैरवखड्गनामकः स महाबलः] ॥
गौरीशिखरमारुह्य पुनर्जन्म न विद्यते ।
तत्राहं भवता सार्द्धं वसामि नियतं शिव ॥
भूतधात्री महादेवी भैरवः क्षीरखण्डभाक् ।
युगाद्या सा महाविद्या विख्याता भुवनत्रये ॥
नकुलीशः कालीघाटे कालिका तत्र देवता ।
तत्र मे पतिता वत्स केशा मस्तकसंयुताः ॥

---

[1] It is tempting to suggest the emendation मेकले referring to the old Mekala country about the Amarkantak hills. But the author may have actually had in his mind Mekhliganj in the Cooch Bihar State in North Bengal. Cf. Mekhalā of the Rudrayāmala list quoted above (p. 18).

करतोयां समारभ्य यावदिक्षरवासिनीम् ।
ब्रतयोजनविस्तीर्णं योनिचक्रं महेश्वर ।
देवा मर्त्यामिच्छन्ति किं पुनर्मानुषादयः ॥
भुवनेश्यौ सिद्धिरूपा किरीटाख्यायां किरीटिका ।
देवेश्वो भैरवस्तत्र सर्वमङ्गलदायकः ॥
पुष्करायामाभरणां देवता विमला च वै ।
संवर्त्तो भैरवो देव सर्वदेवनमस्कृतः ॥
वाराणस्यां विशालाच्यौ देवता कालभैरवः ।
तत्र मे पतितं लिङ्गं (?) खयमेव सदाश्रिव ।
मणिकर्णिकेति विख्याता कुब्जङ्खे च मम श्रुतेः ॥
अयोध्यायाञ्च मे द्वारो भैरवो हरिश्चरात्मकः ।
तत्र सा देवता पूर्णा महालक्ष्मीः सुखप्रदा ॥
कल्पास्तु मे (कन्याश्रमे?) कात्यायनी वामदेवश्च भैरवः ।
तत्र मे पतितं धर्म नमोऽसो नाम एव च ॥
कुमारी देवता तत्र सर्वाप्याः सर्वं भैरवः ।
तत्र मे पतितं रोम तस्माद् भैरवदेवता ॥
ख्याननामा च सावित्री देवता मणिवेदका (°वेदके?) ।
मणिबन्धे च गायत्री सर्वानन्दश्च भैरवः ॥
श्रीशैले च मम ग्रीवा महालक्ष्मीश्च देवता ।
भैरवः संभ्रतानन्दो देशे देशे व्यवस्थितः ॥
काञ्ची देशे च कङ्कालो भैरवो मदनः खयम् ।
तत्र मे पतिते देव नितम्बे देववल्लभ ॥
देवता वेदगर्भाख्या माधवो भैरवः खयम् ।
तत्र मे पतिता विद्या तथा च कालमाधवे ॥
भैरवः शृङ्गनामा च देवी कालो सुसिद्धिदा ।
मणिद्वीपे महाबाह्यो पतितं मे सुवक्षकम् ।
दृष्ट्वा स्मृत्वा महादेव मन्त्रसिद्धिमवाप्नुयात् ॥
कुजवारे भूततिथौ निश्यार्द्धे यस्तु साधकः ।
नत्वा प्रदक्षिणीकृत्य मन्त्रसिद्धिमवाप्नुयात् ॥
सोमाख्ये भद्रसेनश्च तत्र भद्रा च देवता ।
वामपार्श्वे शुभाख्या च नर्त्तकी दक्षभैरवः ॥
उमानाम्नी केशपाश्ने भूतेशः पूर्णभैरवः ।
संहाराख्ये चोर्द्धदन्तो देवी नारायणी शुचौ ॥

अघोदन्तो महाबध्न वाराणसि सप्तसागरः (°सागरे ?)¹ ।
करतोयातटे ग्राम्या तत्र वामनभैरवः ।
अपर्णा देवता तत्र सर्वेश्वो भैरवः खयम् ॥
श्रीपर्वते नूपुरश्च सुन्दरी तत्र देवता ।
सुन्दरो भैरवो देव योगिनीवल्लभप्रभुः ॥
सिद्धेश्वरी महाविद्या समुद्रो भैरवः खयम् ।
दन्तावक्रौषु मे देव जाता भैरवदेवताः ॥
प्रभासे घन्टिकां देव तत्र कपालिनी परा ।
भैरवः सर्वदेवश्च सर्वभैरवनायकः ॥
गोदावरीमहातीर्थे हरिद्वारे च विश्वसे ।
वक्रेश्वो भैरवस्तत्र भैरवी देवता खयम् ॥
ओष्ठं वैवखते तीर्थे हरिता चिपुटा तथा ।
भैरवः सोमहन्ता च सर्वदेवौ तथापरा ॥
चिवुके डामरौ (भामरौ) देवौ विकटाख्या जले स्थले
गङ्ग गर्गा सुपर्वा च विश्वेश्वो विश्वमातृका ।
दण्डपाणिभैरवश्च वामगण्डे च शाकिनी ॥
ग्रौलखण्डस्याखण्डे मे सर्वभौतिकदेवताः ।
रत्नावल्यां स्कन्धदेशः कुमारो भैरवः खयम् ॥
देवता च प्रिया देवी भैरवश्च खयं प्रियः ॥
मिथिलायां वामदेशे उग्रदेवी महोदरी ।
सेतुबन्धे महाभौमो भैरवो देवता जया ।
लोमखण्डे च देवेश्च स्तैलाङ्गे (तैलङ्गे ?) चण्डनायिका ।
चण्डेश्वो भैरवस्तत्र नित्यं तत्र वसाम्यहम् ॥
भैरवो दौर्गन्दर्गौ च चक्रपाणिश्च भैरवः ।
चोन्नवती महादेवी सर्वसम्पत्प्रदायिनी ॥
पृथिव्यां यानि तीर्थानि याश्च भैरवदेवताः ।
पर्वतेषु ह्रासानेषु गङ्गासागरसङ्गमे ॥
वैद्यावौ सा महादेवी माघवो भैरवः खयम् ।
महाकायो महायोगो भैरवः सर्वविघ्नहृत् (°हृत् ?) ॥
काल्यौ नीलाचलछेन्नं तथा च भुवनेश्वरः ।
विमला विरजा राधा जगन्नाथश्च भैरवः ।
तत्र मे पतितं देव उच्छिष्टं शुष्टिता तथा ।
भुवनेश्वो भैरवस्तत्र वसामि च तया सदा (त्वया सह ?) ॥

---

¹ Note the attempt to correct पत्त into सप्त. See *supra*, p. 53, note 9.

उच्छिष्टचण्डालिनी देवी सर्वपीठेश्वरी परा ।
चक्रद्वीपे मूलपात्रि(?)देवता चक्रधारिणी ।
तत्र मे पतितश्चाक्षं तेन जातो मद्योरगः ॥
एतत्ते कथितं देव पीठनाथादिदेवतम् ।
स्वेच्छाधीयं विना देव पूजयेत् पीठदेवताम् ।
भैरवीरहितं सर्वं जपसाधनकं क्रियाः (?) ।
अद्यात्वा भैरवं पीठं प्रतिष्ठ कुलभैरवम् ।
प्राणनाथ न सिध्यन्ति कल्पकोटिजपादिभिः ।
न देयं परशिष्याय निन्दिताय दुरात्मने ।
प्रठाय वञ्चकायाञ्च दत्वा ब्रह्मवपुयात् ॥
देयं शिष्याय शान्ताय नैष्ठिकाय ममाज्यया ।
एषु स्थानेषु देवेश षट्कर्मसाधनं चरेत् ॥
साधकाय कुलीनाय मन्त्री मन्त्रार्थसिद्धये ।
दद्याच्चेव मद्वादेव अन्यथा पतनं भवेत् ॥

APPENDIX II

Puranic Text containing 108 Names of the Mother-goddess.

नामाष्टोत्तरशतम्

Mts = Matsya Purāṇa: *a* Veṅkaṭeśvara Press ed.; *b* Ānandāśrama ed.; *c* Vaṅgavāsī ed. (ch. 13, verses 26–53).
DBh = Devībhāgavata, Vaṅgavāsī ed. (Bk. VII, ch. 30, verses 55–83).
Pdm = Padma Purāṇa-Sṛṣṭikhaṇḍa, Vaṅgavāsī ed. (ch. 17, verses 184–211).
Skd = Skanda Purāṇa-Āvantyakhaṇḍa, Vaṅgavāsī ed. (Revākhaṇḍa, ch. 98, verses 64–92).

[1] वाराणस्यां विशालाक्षी नैमिषे लिङ्गधारिणी [2] ।

---

[1] Pdm begins the section with the additional line: सावित्री पुष्करे नाम तीर्थानां प्रवरे प्रभे and reads कर्षिके for पुष्करे in verse 4.

It is interesting to note that a number of the holy places mentioned here are also known from the *Viṣṇusaṃhitā* (ch. 85) as *tīrthas* suitable for performing funerary rites. The list of 54 in the *Viṣṇusaṃhitā* includes: Puṣkara, Gayāśīrṣa, Akṣayavaṭa, Amarakaṇṭaka, Varāhaparvata, Narmadātīra, Yamunātīra, Gaṅgā, Kuśāvarta, Binduka, Nīlaparvata, Kanakhala, Kubjāmra, Bhṛgutuṅga, Kedāra, Mahālaya, Naḍantikā, Sugandhā, Sākambharī, Phalgutīrtha, Mahāgaṅga, Trihalikāgrāma, Kumāradhārā, Prabhāsa, Sarasvatī, Gaṅgādvāra, Prayāga, Gaṅgāsāgarasaṅgama, Naimiṣāraṇya, Vārāṇasī, Agastyāśrama, Kaṇvāśrama, Kauśikī, Sarayūtīra, Soṇajyotiṣāsaṅgama, Śrīparvata, Kālodaka, Uttarāmānasa, Vaḍavā, Mataṅgavāpī, Saptārṣa, Viṣṇupada, Svargamārgapada, Godāvarī, Gomatī, Vetravatī, Vipāśā, Vitastā, Śatadrutīra, Candrabhāgā, Irāvatī, Sindhutīra, Dakṣiṇa-Pañcanada and Ausaja. Cf. the *Prāṇatoṣaṇī* lists quoted above, pp. 25, note 3; 28, note 2. Note also the long list of *Pitṛtīrthas* or *Śrāddhatīrthas* in the *Padma Purāṇa*, Sṛṣṭikhaṇḍa, ch. 11. For an important but later list of Śākta *tīrthas*, see *DBh*, VII, 38, 5–30.

[2] DBh—गौरीमुखनिवासिनी ।
श्वेते वै नैमिषारण्ये प्रोक्ता सा लिङ्गधारिणी ॥
The elaboration (cf. p. 58, note 9) points to later modification of the original text.

THE ŚĀKTA PĪṬHAS

प्रयागे ललिता देवी[1] कामाक्षी[2] गन्धमादने ॥ १ ॥
मानसे कुमुदा नाम विश्वकाया तथाम्बरे[3] ।
गोमन्ते गोमती नाम मन्दरे कामचारिणी ॥ २ ॥
मदोत्कटा चैत्ररथे जयन्ती हस्तिनापुरे[4] ।
कान्यकुब्जे तथा गौरी रम्भा मलयपर्वते[5] ॥ ३ ॥
एकाम्बके[6] कौर्त्तिमती विश्वा[7] विश्वेश्वरे[8] विदुः ।
पुष्करे पुरुहूतेति केदारे मार्गदायिनी[9] ॥ ४ ॥
नन्दा[10] हिमवतः पृष्ठे गोकर्णे भद्रकर्णिका[11] ।
स्थाण्वीश्वरे[12] भवानी तु विल्वके[13] विल्वपत्रिका ॥ ५ ॥
श्रीशैले माधवी नाम[14] भद्रा भद्रेश्वरे[15] तथा ।
जया वराहशैले तु[16] कमला कमलालये ॥ ६ ॥
रुद्रकोट्यां[17] रुद्राणी काली कालञ्जरे गिरौ[18] ।
[19]मङ्गालिङ्गे तु कपिला मर्कोटे[20] मुकुटेश्वरी ॥ ७ ॥

---

[1] DBh—प्रोक्ता ।
[2] DBh—कामुकी ; Pdm, Skd—कामुका ।
[3] Skd—°परे ; DBh—प्रोक्ता दक्षिणे चोत्तरे तथा ।
विश्वकामा भगवती विश्वकामप्रपूरिणी ॥ (Cf. p. 66, note 2.)
[4] Skd—जयन्ती दक्षिणे पुरे ।
[5] DBh—गौरी प्रोक्ता कान्यकुब्जे रम्भा तु मलयाचले ।
[6] Mts ab—एकाम्भे ; DBh—एकाम्रपीठे सम्प्रोक्ता देवी सा कौर्त्तिमत्यपि ।
विश्वे विश्वेश्वरौ प्राङ्गः पुरहूतात्र पुष्करे ।
केदारपीठे सम्प्रोक्ता देवी सन्मार्गदायिनी ॥ (Cf. note 3 above; also p. 66, note 2.)
[7] Pdm—विश्वा ।
[8] Pdm (v.l.)—विश्वेश्वरी ।
[9] Pdm—कर्णिके पूरहूतेति केदारे मार्गदायिका । Skd—पुरहूता च ।
[10] DBh—मन्दा ; Skd—हिमवतः पृष्ठे ।
[11] Pdm—भद्रकाञ्चिका ।
[12] Mts, DBh, Skd—स्थानेश्वरे ।
[13] Mts ab—विल्वले. Cf. विन्दुक in the Viṣṇusaṃhitā.
[14] Pdm—देवी ; DBh—प्रोक्ता ।
[15] Mts c—भरेश्वरे ; Skd—भद्रे भद्रेश्वरीति च ।
[16] DBh—वराहशैले तु जया ।
[17] Pdm—रुद्रकोट्यान् ; DBh—रुद्राणी रुद्रकोट्यान् ; Skd—रुद्रकोट्यान् कल्याणी ।
[18] Skd, Pdm, Dbh—तथा ।
[19] DBh reads this line after the following line.
[20] Skd, DBh—माकोट ; Pdm—कर्कोटे भद्रलेश्वरी ।

घालयामे[1] मङ्गादेवी शिवलिङ्गे जलप्रिया ।
मायापुर्यां कुमारी तु सन्ताने ललिता तथा ॥ ८ ॥
[2] उत्पलाच्छौ[3] सङ्खाच्छे[4] कमलाच्छे[4] महोत्पला ।
गङ्गायां[5] मञ्जुला नाम[6] विमला पुरुषोत्तमे ॥ ९ ॥
विपाशायाममोघाच्छी पाटला पुष्पवर्द्धने[7] ।
नारायणी सुपार्श्वे तु त्रिकूटे[8] भद्रसुन्दरी[9] ॥ १० ॥
विपुले विपुला नाम[10] कल्याणी मानसाचले[11] ।
कोटवी कोटितीर्थे तु[12] सुगन्धा माधवे वने[13] ॥ ११ ॥
गोदाश्रमे[14] त्रिसन्ध्या तु गङ्गाद्वारे रतिप्रिया[15] ।
शिवकुण्डे[16] शिवानन्दा[17] नन्दिनी देविकातटे ॥ १२ ॥
रुक्मिणी द्वारवत्यान्तु राधा वृन्दावने वने[18] ।
देवकी मथुरायान्तु पाताले परमेश्वरी ॥ १३ ॥
चित्रकूटे तथा सीता विन्ध्ये विन्ध्यनिवासिनी[19] ।
[20] सह्याद्रावेकवीरा तु हरिश्चन्द्रे[21] तु चन्द्रिका ॥ १४ ॥

---

[1] Skd—शालिग्रामे ।
[2] DBh reads this line after the following line.
[3] Pdm—उत्पलाख्या ।
[4] Skd, Pdm, DBh—शिरखाच्छे ।
    Cf. गोवर्धनं हरिश्चन्द्रं पुरुषन्द्रं प्रथूदकम् ।
    सङ्खाच्छं शिरखाच्छं तथा च कङ्कटी नदी ॥ पद्मपुराण । सृष्टिखण्ड । ११ । ४२
[5] Pdm, DBh—गयायां; Skd—गयायां विमला नाम मङ्गला पुरुषोत्तमे ।
[6] DBh—प्रोक्ता ।
[7] Pdm—पुष्पवर्द्धने । The accounts of Hiuen Tsang appear to support this form of the name.
[8] Mts—विकूटे ।
[9] DBh—भद्र° ।
[10] DBh—देवी ।
[11] Skd, Mts, DBh—मलयाचले । After this line DBh reads the last line of verse 14 and the first of verse 15.
[12] Skd—°तीर्थेषु ।
[13] Pdm—माधवी°; Skd—गन्धमादने (cf. verse 1). Cf. सुगन्धा in the *V.S.*
[14] Pdm—गोदावर्यां; Mts *a* (v.l.)—कुञ्जाचले. Cf. कुञ्जाच in the *V.S.*
[15] Pdm—हरिप्रिया ।
[16] DBh—शिवकुण्डे; Skd—शिवखण्डे ।
[17] Mts *a* (v.l.)—सुनन्दा तु; *b* (v.l.), DBh—शुभानन्दा; Skd—सुभानन्दा ।
[18] Pdm—तथा ।
[19] Mts—विन्ध्याधिवासिनी ।
[20] DBh reads this line after the following one.
[21] Mts *a* (v.l.)—हरसंचन्द्रे; Skd—चण्डिका । For the name हरिश्चन्द्र, see *Padma Purāṇa*, Sṛṣṭikhaṇḍa, ch. 11, v. 42 quoted in note 4 above.

THE ŚĀKTA PĪṬHAS

रमण्या रामतीर्थे तु यमुनायां मृगावती ।
करवीरे महालक्ष्मीरुमादेवी [1] विनायके ॥ १५ ॥
अरोगा [2] वैद्यनाथे तु महाकाले महेश्वरी ।
अभयेत्युष्णतीर्थे तु [3] नाम्रता विन्ध्यकन्दरे ॥ १६ ॥
माण्डव्ये [4] माण्डवी नाम स्वाहा माहेश्वरे [5] पुरे ।
छागलाण्डे [6] प्रचण्डा तु चण्डिकामरकण्टके [7] ॥ १७ ॥
सोमेश्वरे वरारोहा प्रभासे पुष्करावती ।
देवमाता [8] सरस्वत्यां पारावारतटे माता [9] ॥ १८ ॥
महालये महाभागा [10] पयोष्ण्यां पिङ्गलेश्वरी ।
सिंहिका कृतशौचे तु कार्तिकेये यशस्करी [11] ॥ १९ ॥
उत्पलावर्तके लोला सुभद्रा श्रोणसङ्गमे [12] ।
माता सिद्धपुरे [13] लक्ष्मीरनङ्गा [14] भरताश्रमे ॥ २० ॥
जालन्धरे विश्वमुखी तारा किष्किन्ध्यपर्वते [15] ।
देवदारुवने पुष्टिर्मेधा काश्मीरमण्डले ॥ २१ ॥
भीमादेवी हिमाद्रौ तु [16] तुष्टिर्विश्वेश्वरे [17] तथा ।
कपालमोचने शुद्धिर्माता [18] कायावरोहणे ॥ २२ ॥

---

[1] Skd—रूपादेवी ।
[2] Mts b (v.l.), DBh, Skd—आरोग्या ।
[3] Skd—°तीर्थे तु स्वौ या ; Pdm—पुष्पतीर्थे तु नाम्रता ; DBh—नितम्बा विन्ध्य° ।
[4] DBh—माण्डवे ; Skd—माण्डुकीनाम ।
[5] Skd—महेश्वरे ; DBh—माहेश्वरी° ।
[6] DBh—छगलण्डे ; Skd—छागलिङ्गे ; Pdm—वेगले तु प्रचण्डाच ।
[7] Mts—मकरन्दके ; b (v.l.)—मरकण्डे ।
[8] Skd—वेदमाता ।
[9] Pdm—पारापारे तटे स्थिता ; DBh—पारावारतटे भृता ; Skd—पारा पारातटे स्थिते ।
[10] Pdm—महापद्मा ।
[11] Pdm—तु भङ्करी ; DBh—°वतिशङ्करी ; Skd—कार्तिके चैव भाङ्करी ।
[12] Pdm—सिन्धुसङ्गमे ।
[13] DBh—सिद्धवने ; Skd—सिद्धघटे ; Pdm—उमा सिद्धवने ।
[14] Pdm, DBh—लक्ष्मीरनङ्गा ; Skd—लक्ष्मीसरङ्गा ।
[15] Skd—किष्किन्ध्य° ।
[16] Pdm—च ।
[17] DBh—तुष्टिर्विश्वेश्वरी ; Mts—पुष्टिर्विश्वेश्वरे ; Skd—पुष्टिर्विश्वेश्वरे ।
[18] Pdm—शुद्धा माता ।

ब्रह्मोद्वारे ध्वनिर्नाम[1] श्रुतिः पिण्डारके तथा ।
काला[2] तु चन्द्रभागायामच्छोदे ग्रिवकारिणी[3] ॥ २३ ॥
वेणायाममृता नाम[4] बदर्यांसुवैश्यो तथा ।
औषधी[5] कोत्तरकुरौ कुश्रद्वीपे कुश्रोदका ॥ २४ ॥
मन्मथा हेमकूटे तु मुकुटे[6] सत्यवादिनी ।
अश्वत्थे वन्दनीया[7] तु निधिर्वैश्रवणालये ॥ २५ ॥
गायत्री वेदवदने पार्वती ग्रिवसन्निधौ ।
देवलोके[8] तथेन्द्राणी ब्रह्मास्येषु[9] सरस्वती ॥ २६ ॥
सूर्यबिम्बे प्रभा नाम मातृणां वैष्णवी मता ।
अरुन्धती सतीनान्तु रामासु च तिलोत्तमा ॥
चित्ते[10] ब्रह्मकला नाम शक्तिः सर्वशरीरिणाम् ॥ २७ ॥[11]
एतदुद्देश्यतः[12] प्रोक्तं नामाष्टशतमुत्तमम् ।
अष्टोत्तरञ्च तीर्थानां शतमेतदुदाहृतम् ॥ २८ ॥

APPENDIX III
Evolution of the Dakṣayajña Story.

दक्षयज्ञकथामूलम्
(a) प्रविष्ट यस्य वीरकर्मनिष्ठादनुष्ठितं नु नर्यो अपौहृत् ।
पुनस्तदा आहृति यत् कनाया दुहितुरा अनुभूतमनर्वा ॥

---

[1] Mts a—धरा नाम ।
[2] DBh—कक्षा ।
[3] DBh—ग्रिवभारिणी; Pdm—सिद्धिदायिनी; Skd—शक्तिभारिणी ।
[4] Pdm—देवी ।
[5] Mts b—औषधी; DBh—औषधिकोत्तर° । Cf. औषज in the *V.S.*
[6] DBh, Pdm, Skd—कुमुदे ।
[7] Skd—वन्दिनीका ।
[8] DBh—वेदलोके ।
[9] Pdm, Skd—ब्रह्मास्ये तु ।
[10] Pdm—चित्रे ।
[11] Skd adds after this line: भूतेश्वरौ भृगुस्नेहे भर्गो सौभाग्यसुन्दरी ।
[12] Pdm—एतन्मया मया;
    DBh—इमान्यष्टशतानि स्युः पीठानि जनमेजय ।
    तत्संख्याकास्ततोऽन्यानि देवस्य परिकीर्तिताः ॥
    सतौ देवश्रभूतानि पीठानि सन्ति तानि च ।
    अन्यान्यपि प्रसिद्धानि तानि मुख्यानि भूतले ॥

मध्या यत्कार्त्वेमभवदमोकि कामं छखाने पितरि युवत्याम्।
मनाग्येतो जहतुर्वियन्ता सानौ निषिक्तं सुक्कतस्य योनौ॥
पिता यत् खां दुहितरमधिष्कान् क्षया रेतः संजग्मानो निषिञ्चत्।
खाधोऽजनयन् ब्रह्म देवा वास्तोष्पतिं व्रतपां निरतच्नन्॥
(ऋग्वेद, १०।६१।५-७)

(b) प्रजापतिर्ह वै खां दुहितरमभिदध्यौ दिवं वोषसं वा मिथुन्येनया स्यामिति। तां सम्भूव। तद्वै देवानामाग आस य इत्यं खां दुहितरमस्माकं खसारं करोतीति। ते ह देवा ऊचुः। योऽयं देवः पशूनामीष्टेऽतिसंधं वा अयं चरति य इत्यं खां दुहितरमस्माकं खसारं करोति विध्येममिति। तं रुद्रोऽभ्यायत्य विव्याध। तस्य सामि रेतः प्रचस्कन्द। तथैवनं तदास। तस्मादेत-दृषिणाभ्यनूक्तम्। पिता यत्खां दुहितरमधिष्कान् क्षया रेतः संजग्मानो निषिञ्च-दिति। तदाप्निमाहतमित्युक्थं तस्मिंस्तदाख्यायते यथा तदेव रेतः प्राजनयन्। तेषां तदा देवानां क्रोधो वैदघ्र प्रजापतिमभिज्यंस्तस्य तं ग्रास्यं निरक्कन्तन्। स वै यच्च एव प्रजापतिः। ते होचुः। उपग्रानीत यदेदं नामुयासत्कनीयो ह्या ऋतेर्यदेदं स्यादिति। ते होचुः। भगायेनद्दच्ह्याित आसीनाय परिहरत तद्रूगः प्रष्णिष्यति तद्यथाकृतमेवं भविष्यतीति। तद्भगाय दच्ह्याित आसीनाय पर्याञ्जक्रुः। तद्भगोऽवेच्यां पश्चे। तस्याच्श्नी निर्ददाह। तथैवनं तदास। तस्मादाङ्गरन्धो भगइति। ते होचुः। नो ह्वेवाञ्ञ्रामत्पूष्णऽश्नवत् परिहरतेति। तत्पूष्णो पर्याञ्जक्रुः। तत्पूषा प्राश्न। तस्य दतो निर्ज्जघान। तथैवनं तदास। तस्मादाङ्गरदन्तकः पूषेति। ***(श्रतपथब्राह्मण-माध्यन्दिनशाखा। १।७।४। १-७।

(c) प्रजापतिर्वे खां दुहितरमभ्यध्यायद्दिवमित्यन्य आङ्गरुषसमित्यन्ये। तामृष्यो भूत्वा रोहितं भूतामभ्येत्। तं देवा अपश्यन् न ह्वतं वै प्रजापतिः करोतीति। ते तमैच्छन्य एनमारिष्यन्थेतमन्योन्यस्मिन्नाविन्दन्। तेषां या एव घोरतमास्तन्वासंसा एकधा समभरंस्ताः। संभ्रता एष देवोऽभवत्तद्स्यै तद्भूतवन्नाम भवति है स योऽस्य तदेवं नाम वेद। तं देवा अब्रुवन्नयं वै प्रजापतिरक्र्तमकरिमं विध्येति। स तथेव्यब्रवीत् स वै वो वरं वृणा इति वृणीष्वेति। स एतमेव वरमवृणीत पशूनामाधिपत्यम्। तदस्यैतत्पशुमन्नाम पशुमान् भवति योऽस्य तदेवं नाम वेद। तमभ्यायव्याविध्यत्। स विद्ध ऊर्ध्व उदप्रपतत्मेतं मृग इत्याचक्षते। य उ एव मृगव्याधः स उ एव स या रोहित्सा रोहिणी य एवैयुस्त्रिकाड्डा स एवेषु- त्रिकाड्डा। तदा इदं प्रजापते रेतः सिक्तमधावत्तत्सरोऽभवत्। ते देवा अब्रुवन् मेदं प्रजापते रेतो दुषदिति। यदब्रुवन् मेदं प्रजापते रेतो दुषदिति तन्मादुषम- भवत्। ***(ऐतरेयब्राह्मण। ३।३३)

(d) प्रजापतिर्वै खड्गं यज्ञादनिरजयत्। सोऽक्रामयत मेऽयमखा आहुतिः समृद्ध्यै यो मा यज्ञादग्निरमाच्छीदिति। स यज्ञमभ्यायव्याविध्य तदाविद्धं निरक्रन्तत्। तत् प्राग्निचमभवत्तदुदयज्ञसद्रूगाय पर्यंचरंस्तन्नतौच्छेत्। तस्य चक्षुः परापतत्क्माादाङ्ररन्धो वै भग इत्यपिहितं नेच्छेद्यमिच्छृति तत् सविचे पर्यंचरंस्तत्व्यरृच्छाव् तस्य पाणी प्रतिच्छेद तक्क्ष्मे हिरण्मयौ प्रद्यदधुसुक्त्माद्भिरण्यपाणिरिति खुतस्तत् पूष्णो पर्यंचरंस्तत् प्राश्नात्तस्य दन्ताः परोप्यन्त तक्ष्मादाङ्ररदन्तकः पूषा पेष्टभाजन इति। *** (गोपथब्राह्मण। २।९)।

(e) कस्यचित्त्वथ कालस्य दत्तनामा प्रजापतिः।
पूर्वोक्तेन विधानेन यज्ञमाणोऽन्वपद्यत ।
ततस्तस्य मखं देवाः सर्वे ब्रह्मपुरोगमाः ।
गमनाय समागम्य बुद्धिमापेदिरे तदा ।
ते विमानैर्मेघाभानो ज्वलनार्कसमप्रभैः ।
देवस्यानुमते गच्छन् गङ्गाद्वारमिति श्रुतिः ।
प्रक्षिता देवता दृष्ट्वा शैलराजसुता तदा ।
उवाच वचनं साध्वी देवं पशुपतिं पतिम् ।
भगवन् क्व नु यान्त्येते देवाः ब्रह्मपुरोगमाः ।
ब्रूहि तत्त्वेन तत्त्वज्ञ संशयो मे महानयम् ।

महेश्वर उवाच ।

दक्षो नाम महाभागे प्रजानां पतिसत्तमः ।
अश्वमेधेन यजते तत्र यान्ति दिवौकसः ।

उमोवाच ।

यज्ञमेतं महादेव किमर्थं नाधिगच्छसि ।
केन वा प्रतिषेधेन गमनं ते न विद्यते ।

महेश्वर उवाच ।

सुरैरेव महाभागे पूर्वमेतदनुष्ठितम् ।
यज्ञेषु सर्वेषु मम न भाग उपकल्पितः ।
पूर्वोपायोपपन्नेन मार्गेण वरवर्णिनि ।
न मे सुराः प्रयच्छन्ति भागं यज्ञस्य धर्मतः ।

उमोवाच ।

भगवन् सर्वभूतेषु प्रभावाभ्यधिको गुणैः ।
अजय्यश्चाप्यदृश्यश्च तेजसा यज्ञसा श्रिया
अनेन ते महाभाग प्रतिषेधेन भागतः ।
अतीव दुःखमुत्पन्नं वेपथुश्च ममानघ ।

भौम्य उवाच ॥
एवमुक्ता तु सा देवी तदा पशुपतिं पतिम् ।
तुष्णीम्भूताभवद्राजन् दह्यमानेन चेतसा ॥
अथ देव्या मतं ज्ञात्वा हृद्गतं यज्ञिकौर्षितम् ।
स समाज्ञापयामास तिष्ठ त्वमिति नन्दिनम् ॥
ततो योगबलं ज्ञात्वा सर्वयोगेश्वरेश्वरः ।
तं यर्ज्ञं स महातेजा भौमैरनुचरैस्तदा ॥
सहसा घातयामास देवदेवः पिशाकहृत् ॥ ***
(महाभारत ।१२।२८३।१९-२२) ।

(f) *** केचिदभञ्जुः प्रागवंग्रं पब्रौघ्राला तथापरे ।
सद आग्नीध्राञ्चाच्च तद्दिहारं महानसम् ।
वह्वजुर्यज्ञपात्राणि तज्जेकेऽस्मौननाघ्नयन् ।
कुण्डेष्वमूचयन् केचिद्दिभिदुर्वेदिमेखलाः ॥
अवाघन्त मुनीनन्ये एके पन्नौरतर्जयन् ।
अपरे जगृङ्र्देवान् प्रत्यासन्नान् पलायितान् ॥
भृगुं बबन्ध मणिमान् वीरभद्रः प्रजापतिम् ।
चण्डेग्रः पूषर्णां देवं भगं नन्दीश्वरोऽग्रहीत् ॥
सर्वे एवर्तिजो दृष्ट्वा सदस्याः सदिवौकसः ।
तैरर्ध्यमानाः सुभ्रग्रां ग्रावभिर्नैकधाद्रवन् ॥
जुह्वतः स्रुवहस्तस्य श्मश्रूणि भगवान् भवः ।
भगोलुंलुचे सदसि योऽहसत् श्मश्रु दर्शयन् ॥
भगस्य नेत्रे भगवान् पातितस्य रुषा भुवि ।
उज्जहार सदःस्थोऽक्ष्णा यः शपन्तमसूसुचत् ॥
पूष्णो ह्यपातयद्दन्तान् कलिङ्गस्य यथा बलः ।
शप्यमाने गरिमणि योऽहसद्दर्शयन् दतः ॥ ***
(भागवतपुराण ।४।५।१४-२१)

(g) *** वीरभद्रोऽपि दौष्मात्मा ब्रह्मस्खैवोद्धतं करम् ।
व्यस्तम्भयदहौष्मात्मा तथान्येषां दिवौकसाम् ॥
भगस्य नेत्रे चोत्पाट्य करजाग्रेण लौलया ।
निहत्य मुष्टिना दन्तान् पूष्णश्चैवमपातयत् ॥
तथा चन्द्रमसं देवं पादाङ्गुष्ठेन लीलया ।
धर्षयामास बलवान् क्षयमाणो गणेश्वरः ॥
वह्नेर्हस्तद्वयं छित्त्वा जिह्वामुत्पाट्य लीलया ।
जघान मूर्ध्नि पादेन मुनीनपि मुनीश्वरः ॥
तथा विष्णुं सगरुडं समायान्तं महाबलः ।
विद्याघ निग्रहितैर्बाणैः स्तम्भयित्वा सुदर्शनम् ॥ ***
(कूर्मपुराण ।१।१५।६०-६४) ।

APPENDIX IV

Date of the *Tantrasāra*.

The celebrated Tantric encyclopedia entitled *Tantrasāra*, composed or rather compiled by the great Bengali leader of Tantric thought named Kṛṣṇānanda, is well known to all students of the Tantra literature. In the colophons added to some of the chapters of the *Tantrasāra* the author calls himself 'Mahāmahopādhyāya-Kṛṣṇānanda-Vāgīśa-Bhaṭṭācārya'; but later writers usually refer to him as Kṛṣṇānanda Āgamavāgīśa. *Vāgīśa* seems to have been an abbreviated form of *Āgamavāgīśa*. The late Mr. N. N. Vasu gave the following description of the family, to which Kṛṣṇānanda Āgamavāgīśa, author of the *Tantrasāra*, belonged, in the *Vārendra-Brāhmaṇa-Vivaraṇa* Volume of his *Vaṅger Jātīya Itihāsa* (in Bengali): 'This family is known in the community of the Vārendra Brāhmaṇas as the Kāśyapa-gotrīya Maitras of Maṇḍalajānī. It originally flourished at Āgameśvarī-talā at Śrīdhāma-Navadvīpa; but later, owing to an expansion of the family, its members scattered themselves over different parts of Bengal. A branch of the family still lives at Śrīdhāma and is devoted to the worship of the goddess Āgameśvarī' (p. 157). A number of traditions about Kṛṣṇānanda's religious life have also been quoted in the work. In connection with the date of Kṛṣṇānanda Āgamavāgīśa, Mr. Vasu says (*loc. cit.*), 'Kṛṣṇānanda, Śrīcaitanya and Raghunātha Śiromaṇi were co-students at the Catuṣpāṭhī of the same Guru at Navadvīpa. At first Kṛṣṇānanda and Caitanya were great friends; but dissension separated them when Caitanya preferred to worship Kṛṣṇa according to the principle known as the Sakhī-bhāva. Kṛṣṇānanda requested his friend not to take up the new course, but was insulted; and from that time they began to preach the Śākta and Vaiṣṇava doctrines separately. Kṛṣṇānanda attained perfection with the Śakti-mantra and conceived and popularized the form of the image of the goddess Kālī.[1] Before this, Kālī was usually worshipped at a Ghaṭa. The Ghaṭa established for the purpose of worshipping the goddess by Kṛṣṇānanda at the temple of Āgameśvarī at Navadvīpa still exists and a large number of Śāktas flock to it for worshipping Mahāmāyā.' The story narrated by Mr. Vasu invites comments. In the first place, we know that Kṛṣṇānanda began his work with an adoration to Lord Kṛṣṇa, identified with Viṣṇu (*Tantrasāra*, Vaṅgavāsī edition, p. 1):

नत्वा कृष्णपदद्वन्द्वं ब्रह्मादिसुरपूजितम् ।
गुरुश्च ज्ञानदातारं कृष्णानन्देन धीमता ॥

---

[1] According to a tradition recorded by Vasu, Kṛṣṇānanda was ordered by the goddess Kālī in a dream to popularize the form of her image. On being questioned as to how the form could be realized, the goddess replied that it would be revealed to the devotee the next morning. Early next day when Kṛṣṇānanda came out of his house, he found a young cowherdess engaged in preparing cowdung cakes. She was standing in the *ālīḍha* pose (with the right knee thrown to front and the left leg firm behind in a slanting position) and had a large ball of cowdung in her left hand and a small one in the right, upraised to be set on a wall in the form of a cake. On the sudden consciousness of her being noticed by Kṛṣṇānanda the woman felt very much ashamed and pressed her tongue, that lolled, with her teeth (cf. Bengali লজ্জায় জিভ কাটা which gives an expression to the feeling of shame). The appearance of the cowherdess as seen by Kṛṣṇānanda that morning was popularized by him as the form of the image of Dakṣiṇa-Kālī. Kṛṣṇānanda began to worship small images of this type made of mud by himself every day to be immersed early next morning in the waters of the Ganges. Later the king of Navadvīpa introduced the worship of large images of the same type on the newmoon of the month of Kārttika.

This seems to show that Kṛṣṇānanda Āgamavāgīśa was not initiated into the Śakti-mantra, but was a Tāntric devotee who received his initiation into the Vaiṣṇava formula.[1] In the Śyāmā or Kālī section of the *Tantrasāra*, the author quotes the opinions of various Tantra works, but does not express any special view of his own (cf. *op. cit.*, p. 472ff; also Pūrṇānanda's *Śyāmārahasya*, ed. R. N. Chatterji, pp. 11-12).

In the second place, it is extremely difficult to regard Kṛṣṇānanda Āgamavāgīśa as a co-student of the celebrated Vaiṣṇava saint Caitanya of Navadvīpa and the great Bengali logician Raghunātha Śiromaṇi. Caitanya was born on the full-moon day of Phālguna in Śaka 1407, corresponding to the 18th February, 1486 A.D., and died at the age of 48 on the seventh *tithi* of the bright half of Āṣāḍha in Śaka 1455 (1533 A.D.). *Vide* D. C. Sen, *Vaṅgabhāṣā O Sāhitya*, 5th edition, pp. 256, 266; R. G. Bhandarkar's Collected Works, Vol. IV, pp. 118-19. According to the *History of Indian Logic* (pp. 463-65) by S. C. Vidyabhushan, Raghunātha Śiromaṇi flourished between 1477 and 1547 A.D., although recent writers on the subject suggest that the Śiromaṇi was born about 1460-65 A.D., composed his famous *Tattvacintāmaṇidīdhiti* about 1490-1500 A.D. and was therefore about a generation earlier than Caitanya (cf. *V.S.P.P.*, Vol. L, p. 13; LIII, pp. 1, 3). If, therefore, the story narrated by Mr. Vasu has to be believed, we have to assume that Kṛṣṇānanda was born about 1480 A.D. and died sometime about the middle of the sixteenth century. There is, however, evidence to show that the *Tantrasāra* was composed several years after 1577 A.D.

The great Tantric teacher Pūrṇānanda Paramahaṃsa, who was an inhabitant of the 'Mymensing District of Bengal (cf. Introduction to the Calcutta Sanskrit Series edition of the *Śrītattvacintāmaṇi*), wrote his famous work entitled *Śrītattvacintāmaṇi* in the Śaka year 1499 corresponding to 1577 A.D. This is clear from the following passage of the work:

श्रीमत्परमहंस-परिव्राजक-श्रीगुरु-ब्रह्मानन्द-मुखारविन्द-निस्यन्दमान-परमरहस्याति-रहस्य-निगममकरन्द-सन्दोहतुन्दिलानन्दः श्रीपूर्णानन्दपरमहंसः श्रीतत्त्वचिन्तामणिं चतुर्दशप्रमताधिकनवनवतिप्रकाशैर्वितनोति ।

The *Śrītattvacintāmaṇi* by Pūrṇānanda has been quoted by Kṛṣṇānanda Āgamavāgīśa in his *Tantrasāra* (p. 155). Now even if Pūrṇānanda and Kṛṣṇānanda were contemporaries, it is difficult to believe that in that age, when there was little facility of communication, Kṛṣṇāna) da of Navadvīpa in the Nadia District could have information about the work of Pūrṇānanda of Mymensing and secure a copy of it immediately after its composition. The *Tantrasāra* thus does not appear to have been composed much earlier than *circa* 1600 A.D. If, under the circumstances, it is conjectured that the *Tantrasāra* was written by Kṛṣṇānanda when he was more than hundred years old, the story of Kṛṣṇānanda, Caitanya and Raghunātha Śiromaṇi having been co-students under the same Guru may not be altogether impossible. But such a suggestion, if not wholly absurd, is certainly rather improbable. It can hardly be accepted without any corroborative evidence. The *Tantrasāra*

---

[1] That Kṛṣṇānanda was not anti-Vaiṣṇava is even admitted by a tradition recorded by Vasu, according to which Śākta Kṛṣṇānanda had a brother named Sahasrākṣa who was a Vaiṣṇava. One day a number of bananas, preserved by Kṛṣṇānanda with a view to offering them to the goddess Āgameśvarī (Kālī), was, during his absence, dedicated by Sahasrākṣa to his own tutelary deity, the god Kṛṣṇa-Viṣṇu. At this Kṛṣṇānanda became very much annoyed. But when at night the Āgamavāgīśa was worshipping the goddess, he and his Vaiṣṇava brother, who happened to be near him, noticed with surprise that the goddess had Gopāla (child Kṛṣṇa) on her lap and was feeding him with bananas like a mother. Thereafter the two brothers realized that there was really no difference between the Vaiṣṇava and Śākta forms of worship.

also quotes Rāghava Bhaṭṭa (loc. cit., p. 16 et passim), who wrote the *Padārthādarśa* commentary on the *Śaradātilaka* and flourished in 1493-94 A.D., and the *Tantrakaumudī* (loc. cit., p. 374) composed by the Maithila Devanātha at the court of king Malladeva Naranārāyaṇa of Kamta (1555-87 A.D.; cf. *Pravāsī*, 1354 B.S., pp. 507-08).

In the preface to the *Kālīkhaṇḍa* or Section I of the *Śaktisaṅgama Tantra*, published in the Gaekwad Oriental Series, Dr. B. Bhattacharya has made an attempt to determine the date of the composition of the *Śaktisaṅgama* and has incidentally discussed the date of the *Tantrasāra* by Kṛṣṇānanda Āgamavāgīśa. Dr. Bhattacharya says that Kṛṣṇānanda, author of the *Tantrasāra*, was a disciple of Pūrṇānanda Paramahaṃsa, author of the *Śrītattvacintāmaṇi*. As the preceptor, i.e. Pūrṇānanda, wrote his work in 1577 A.D., the disciple, i.e. Kṛṣṇānanda, in Dr. Bhattacharya's opinion, may have composed his *Tantrasāra* about thirty years later, that is to say, about 1607 A.D. Unfortunately however the suggestion that the author of the *Tantrasāra* was a disciple of that of the *Śrītattvacintāmaṇi* is absolutely unwarranted.

It is well known that Tantric devotees regard the Guru or preceptor as equal or even superior to all the gods as an object of veneration. Kṛṣṇānanda himself quotes the following verse in praise of the Guru from the *Jñānārṇava Tantra* in his *Tantrasāra* (p. 2):

गुरुः पिता गुरुर्माता गुरुर्देवो गुरुर्गतिः ।
शिवे रुष्टे गुरुस्त्राता गुरौ रुष्टे न कश्चन ॥

In this connection, the attention of scholars may be drawn to the views of various Tantra works quoted in the Guru-śiṣya-Prakaraṇa of the *Prāṇatoṣaṇī Tantra* (Vasumatī edition, pp. 91-103), especially to the following citations from the *Guru Tantra* and the *Guptasādhana Tantra* (cf. *ibid.*, pp. 94-95):

न गुरोरधिकं ज्ञानं न गुरोरधिकं तपः ।
न गुरोरधिकं मन्त्रो न गुरोरधिकं फलम् ॥
न गुरोरधिका देवी न गुरोरधिकः शिवः ।
न गुरोरधिका मूर्तिर्न गुरोरधिको जपः ॥

(गुरुतत्त्व)

गुरुर्ब्रह्मा गुरुर्विष्णुर्गुरुर्देवो महेश्वरः ।
गुरुस्तीर्थं गुरुर्यज्ञो गुरुर्दानं गुरुर्जपः ॥
गुरुरभिगुरुः सूर्यः सर्वं गुरुमयं जगत् ॥

(गुरुसाधनतत्त्व)

The section from Pūrṇānanda's *Śrītattvacintāmaṇi* quoted above, in which the author introduces himself as a disciple of another Tantrācārya named Brahmānanda Paramahaṃsa, demonstrates very clearly how much respectfully a Tantric devotee is expected to refer to his Guru. In his *Śyāmārahasya* Pūrṇānanda refers to himself as श्रीगुरुपादपद्मपरामोदान्तलन्ध्राजित: पूर्णानन्दगिरिः । There is a distinct injunction as regards the mention of one's preceptor in the *Kulārṇava Tantra* from which the following verses have been quoted in the *Prāṇatoṣaṇī Tantra* (p. 103):

श्रीगुरुं कुलजास्त्राणि पूजास्थानानि यानि च ।
भक्त्या श्रीपूर्वकं देवि प्रणम्य च प्रकीर्तयेत् ॥
गुरुं नाम्ना न भाषेत स्वपकारजावृते प्रिये ।
श्रीनाथदेवखामीति विवादे साधने वदेत् ॥

It is very interesting to note in this connection that the following lines of the *Tantrasāra* (p. 489) attributes a particular view to Pūrṇānanda Paramahaṃsa and refutes it categorically:

पूर्णानन्दमतेन लक्ष्यजपे पुरश्चरणं; तत् सन्दिग्धमतं; नागातन्त्रे लक्ष्यत्रयद्ध्र्मानात्
लक्ष्यत्रयेनैव पुरश्चरणं सिद्धमिति ।[1]

If Pūrṇānanda had been the preceptor of the author of the *Tantrasāra*, he would not certainly have been mentioned in the above passage merely as *Pūrṇānanda* but would have been called at least *Śrī-Pūrṇānanda* (if living).[2] This non-reverential reference to the author of the *Śrītattvacintāmaṇi* in the *Tantrasāra* shows beyond doubt that Kṛṣṇānanda Āgamavāgīśa was not a disciple of Pūrṇānanda Paramahaṃsa.

On the title page as well as in the introduction (p. 21) of the Vasumatī edition of the *Prāṇatoṣaṇī Tantra*, its author Rāmatoṣaṇa Vidyālaṅkāra is represented as the *vṛddhaprapautra* or great-great-grandson of Kṛṣṇānanda Āgamavāgīśa author of the *Tantrasāra*. Curiously enough the book itself proves clearly that the statement is wrong. Vasu's statement (*loc. cit.*) that the author of the book represents himself as the grandson of Sātu Ācārya seems also to be wrong. It is well known to the students of Tantra literature that Rāmatoṣaṇa's work was prepared and published under the patronage of Bābu Prāṇakṛṣṇa Viśvāsa of Khardaha near Calcutta, who was a great patron of Śāstric learning. The author calls his work a *latā* (*vallī*, etc.) or creeper styled *Prāṇa-toṣaṇī* wherein parts of the names of both himself and his patron were cleverly accommodated. In a large number of passages in the work, Rāmatoṣaṇa refers to his indebtedness to Prāṇakṛṣṇa as well as to the latter's qualities, laudable activities and family relations. In many passages he also speaks of himself and his family. The following passage (p. 147):

श्रीप्राणकृष्णख्यातिरस्य निर्देशवतीं
मैनेयवंशाङ्कुलाश्रितचक्रवर्तीं । etc.

says that Rāmatoṣaṇa Vidyālaṅkāra belonged to a Vaṃśaja (non-Kulīn) family of the Maitreyas of the Vārendra Brāhmaṇa community. Elsewhere (p. 77) he refers to his father Kṛṣṇamaṅgala Vidyāvāgīśa and his mother Gaṅgādevī:

कृष्णमङ्गलविद्यावागीशसूनुः सतां मुदे
गङ्गादेवीसुतोऽकार्षीदृग्मकाव्यं द्वितीयकम् ॥

---

[1] Cf. *ibid.*, p. 488: अस्य पुरश्चरणं लक्ष्यजपः पूर्णानन्दमतेन । The reference is to Ch. v of Pūrṇānanda's *Syāmārahasya* which was composed later than his *Śrītattvacintāmaṇi* (1577 A.D.). The mention of Pūrṇānanda and the *Śrītattvacintāmaṇi* is noticed in the old and complete manuscripts of the *Tantrasāra* including one said to be copied in 1658 A.D. (probably during the author's lifetime).

[2] Sometimes the Guru's name (if he was dead) was mentioned without honorific expressions when he was clearly said to have been one's preceptor: cf. *tripurānandena mad-guruṇā vyākhyātam* in Brahmānanda's *Tārārahasya*.

In another passage (p. 105) Rāmatoṣaṇa speaks of his elder brother Rāmalocana Vidyābhūṣaṇa who is said to have been the author of a commentary on the *Vāstuyāga* entitled *Vāstuyāgapradīpikā*; cf.

मद्यजरामलोचनविद्याभूषणकृत-वास्तुयागप्रदीपिकाहृतहयन्नौर्षप्रराचे, etc.

There are several passages referring to Kṛṣṇānanda Āgamavāgīśa, author of the *Tantrasāra*, as a distinguished member of the family to which Rāmatoṣaṇa belonged; cf.

अस्मद्रोष्ठीगरिष्ठकृष्णानन्दागमवागीशेन खङ्गततन्त्रसारे सर्वं लिखितम् (p. 104);

अस्मद्रोष्ठीगरिष्ठकृष्णानन्दागमवागीशेन खङ्गततन्त्रसारग्रन्थे लिखिता (p. 143).

It is evident that the Āgamavāgīśa was an ancestor of the author of the *Prāṇatoṣaṇī Tantra*. Fortunately, however, there are some sections of the work which clearly define the relationship between Kṛṣṇānanda and Rāmatoṣaṇa and says that the former was the latter's *atyativṛddhaprapitāmaha*, i.e. great-grandfather's great-grandfather; cf.

अस्मदत्यतिवृद्धप्रपितामह-कृष्णानन्दागमवागीशेन तन्त्रसारे लिखिते (p. 116);

अस्मदत्यतिवृद्धप्रपितामह-सहृदयगोष्ठीगरिष्ठ-कृष्णानन्दागमवागीश-भट्टाचार्यैः खङ्गततन्त्रसारे लिखितम् (p. 75).

Rāmatoṣaṇa was therefore the *atyativṛddhaprapautra*, i.e. great-grandson's great-grandson, of Kṛṣṇānanda Āgamavāgīśa Bhaṭṭācarya and certainly not the latter's *vṛddhaprapautra* or great-grandson as asserted by the editor of the Vasumatī edition of the *Prāṇatoṣaṇī Tantra*. There is moreover a detailed genealogy in the work (p. 146) which makes the relation between the author of the *Prāṇatoṣaṇī* and that of the *Tantrasāra* absolutely clear.

Cf. श्रीमान् श्रीमान् भुवनविदिततन्त्रसारस्य कर्ता
कृष्णानन्दोऽजनि भुवि नवद्वीपदेशप्रदीपः ।
काश्यौनाथोऽभवदिह सुतस्तस्य सारावलीज्ञात्
विद्वान् मान्योऽजनि तदनुजो विश्वनाथाग्र्ययोऽतः ॥
गोपालो निर्यञ्जतियग्रक्षौ मधोः सुदनाचा (सुदनख्या)-
भूतौ पुत्रौ मधुसुत इतः कालिदासः प्रसिद्धः ।
तत्पुत्रोऽभूद्भुवरपरो नाथ एकान्तबुद्धि-
स्तत्सूनुस्त्वामेवदिह सुधीमंङ्कृणः कृष्णापूर्वं ॥
श्रीकृष्णामङ्कसुतो नववह्निकायाः
श्रीरामतोषण इदं कृतवान् द्वितीयम् । etc.

From the above details as well as those quoted before, the following genealogy of the Maitra or Maitreya family, to which Kṛṣṇānanda and Rāmatoṣaṇa belonged, may be prepared and offered in a tabular form:

THE ŚĀKTA PĪṬHAS

In the *Vārendra-Brāhmaṇa-Vivaraṇa* (p. 161) by the late Mr. N. N. Vasu there is a genealogical table of the Maitras of Maṇḍalajānī which slightly differs from the one quoted above. Although the details supplied by Rāmatoṣaṇa in his *Prāṇatoṣaṇī* appear to be authoritative, it has been suggested (*Pravāsī*, B.S. 1354, p. 506) that the *Sārāvalī* and the *Nirṇaya* have been wrongly ascribed to Kāśīnātha and Gopāla respectively. Another mistake of Rāmatoṣaṇa has been pointed out by quoting the following verse of Gopāla-Pañcānana's *Tantradīpikā* (MS.):

आगमवागीशपौत्रेण हरिनाथस्य सूनुना ।
श्रीगोपालेन विप्रेण कृतेयं तन्त्रदीपिका ॥ (*loc. cit.*)

which is said to be supported by the *Kulapañjikās*. It will not be out of place to quote the corresponding portion of Mr. Vasu's table (said to be quoted from Yādava Cakravartin's *Kulaśāstradīpikā*) for easy reference and to point to the interesting fact that most of the names in the family exhibit Vaiṣṇava influence none of them being typically Śākta.

It will be seen that Kṛṣṇānanda, author of the *Tantrasāra*, was the seventh in ascent from Rāmatoṣaṇa, author of the *Prāṇatoṣaṇī*, in the family. If, as is usual, a period of twenty-five years is counted for each generation, Kṛṣṇānanda has to be placed about 150 years before the time of Rāmatoṣaṇa. The date of the composition of the *Prāṇatoṣaṇī* is given in the work (p. 3) as: प्राके नेत्रयुगादिकाम्बुपिमिते ज्स्तौते ज्स्ह्यायात्निन्यौ, that is to say, the *akṣayā tithi* (probably the *akṣaya-tṛtīyā* or the third *tithi* of the bright half of Vaiśākha) in the Śaka year 1742 (1820 A.D.). That the book was printed and published shortly before the 29th of Kārttika of the Bengali San 1231, corresponding to the 13th of November, 1824, is known from the *Samācāradarpaṇa* of that date cited by B. N. Banerji in his *Saṃvādapatre Sekāler Kathā*, Vol. I, p. 60.[1] If then Rāmatoṣaṇa composed his *Prāṇatoṣaṇī* in 1820 A.D., it seems that his seventh ancestor Kṛṣṇānanda wrote his *Tantrasāra* about 1670 A.D.

In the preface to the Vaṅgavāsī edition of the *Tantrasāra*, the late Pandit Pañcānana Tarkaratna says that amongst various manuscripts of the work utilized in preparing the text of the above edition, one belonging to Pandit Haripada Smṛtitīrtha, Professor of the Mulajor Sanskrit College, was found to have been copied in Śaka 1580 which would correspond to 1658 A.D. A recent note published in the *Pravāsī*, B.S. 1354, pp. 506–08, speaks of certain manuscripts of the *Tantrasāra* believed to be copied in Śaka 1601 (1679 A.D.), Śaka 1568 (1646 A.D.) and Śaka 1554 (1632 A.D.). These dates can be accepted only after careful examination. I had the opportunity of examining only the third of these manuscripts in the library of the Vaṅgīya Sāhitya Pariṣat and find that the third figure of the year supposed to be Śaka 1554 is extremely doubtful. In any case, however, there is no doubt that the *Tantrasāra* was composed by the great Kṛṣṇānanda Āgamavāgīśa Bhaṭṭācārya sometime in the seventeenth century. It may not be improbable that Kṛṣṇānanda flourished in *circa* 1595–1675 A.D. and composed the *Tantrasāra* in the earlier part of his life.

APPENDIX V

An Index of Pīṭhas.

'Ain = 'Ain-i-Akbarī; Ānanda = Ānandārṇava Tantra; Aṣṭādaśa = Aṣṭādaśapīṭha; Caṇḍī = Caṇḍīmaṅgala; Hevajra = Hevajra Tantra; Jñāna = Jñānārṇava Tantra; Kālikā = Kālikā Purāṇa; Kubjikā = Kubjikā Tantra; Nāma = Nāmāṣṭottaraśata (Appendix I); Nīla = Bṛhan-Nīlatantra; Pīṭha = Pīṭhanirṇaya or Mahāpīṭhanirūpaṇa (text edited above, pp. 42-58, with notes); Prāṇa = Prāṇatoṣaṇī Tantra; Rudra = Rudrayāmala; Sādhana = Sādhanamālā; Śiva = Śivacarita. The names of the Devī's limbs, the Devī and the Bhairava have been mentioned, in cases where they are indicated, in order to show the uncertainty of the traditions about them.

A

Abdhisaṅgama—Nīla, Prāṇa (Jyotirmayī). See Sāgarasaṅgama.

Acchoda—Nāma (Śivakāriṇī, Śivadhāriṇī, Siddhidāyinī, Śaktidhāriṇī); modern Achchhavat in Kashmir.

---

[1] Cf. *ibid.*, Vol. II, pp. 802-03 where the year of publication of the *Prāṇatoṣaṇī* is given as 1823 A.D. on the authority of the *Friend of India*, Vol. III, No. 11. The *Saṃvādpatre Sekōler Kathā*, Vol. I (2nd ed.), p. 486, gives the year of its composition as Śaka 1743; but the word *netra* indicates 'two' (not 'three') according to Sanskrit lexicons.

Ādipīṭha—Nīla.
Aditipura—Nīla.
Ādinātha—Nīla.
Āditya—Nīla.
Adrikūṭa—Nīla, Prāṇa (Rudrāṇī—Mahāyogin).
Ādyantapura—Nīla.
Agastyāśrama—Nīla, Prāṇa (Mahāvidyā, Mattamedhā); one of the many places especially in Southern India associated with Agastya's name; probably Agastipuri near Nasik.
Aila, Aileyakavana—Prāṇa, Nīla.
Airāvatī—See Irāvatī.
Akampa—Nīla.
Akṣayagrīva—Kubjikā (v.l. Hayagrīva); probably a mistake for Akṣayavaṭa.
Akṣayavaṭa—Nīla, Prāṇa (Akṣayā); the sacred banyan tree located at many *tīrthas*, notably at Prayāga or Allahabad in U.P. and at Gayā in Bihar.
Ālāpura—Aṣṭādaśa (Yugalā); possibly a mistake for Elāpura.
Amala—Nāma (v.l. Malaya); cf. Anala.
Amarakaṇṭaka—Nāma (v.l. Makarandaka, Marakaṅkaṭa—Caṇḍī); Nīla, Prāṇa (Amareśī); the source of the Sone and Narmada in the Eastern C.P.
Amaraparvata, Kanakāmaraparvata—Nīla; same as Meru.
Amareśa—Nīla, Prāṇa (Caṇḍī, Maheśvarī—Kuśatuṅgāra); on the south bank of the Narmada, opposite Onkarnath, and to the north-west of Khandwa.
Ambara—Nāma (Viśvakāyā, Viśvakāmā); modern Amber in the Jaipur State, Rajputana.
Ambikā—Kubjikā; Nīla; may be Ambikā-Kālnā in the Burdwan District.
Ambujapura—Nīla.
Āmrakeśvara—See Āmrātakeśvara.
Āmrātakapura—Nīla, Prāṇa (Sūkṣmā—Sūkṣma); Nīla (Surūpeśā). See Āmrātakeśvara, Āmrakeśvara.
Āmrātakeśvara—Jñāna. See Āmrātakapura.
Amṛtakauśika—Nīla, Prāṇa (Kauśikā). See Kauśikā.
Anala—Pīṭha (v.l. Śuci); Śiva (Mahāpīṭha; Ūrdhvadanta—Nārāyaṇī—Saṃkrūra); cf. the name of the Nala lake in the Ahmadabad region.
Ānanda—Nīla. See under *Nandataṭa*.
Anantapura—Nīla.
Aṅga—Rudra; east Bihar.
Animāpura—Nīla.
Aniruddhapura—Nīla.
Annapūrṇā—Nīla.
Antarvedī—Rudra; the Ganges-Jumna Doab between Prayāga and Haridvāra.
Araṇya—See Vareṇya.
Arbuda—Jñāna; Nīla (Kātyāyanī); Mount Abu in the Sirohi State, Rajputana.
Ardhanālaka—Kubjikā (v.l. Vardhamānaka).
Āryāvarta—Prāṇa (Mahāryā). For the Tantric Āryāvarta in the eastern U.P., see *I.C.*, VIII, p. 57.
Asurāntakapura—Nīla.
Aśusiddhipura—Nīla.
Aśvamedhapura—Nīla.

Aśvaprada—Nīla, Prāṇa; probably the Asvakranta hill near Gauhati in Assam.
Aśvatīrtha—Nīla, Prāṇa; at the confluence of the Gaṅgā and Kālīnadī near Kanauj.
Aśvattha—Nāma (Vandanīyā).
Aṭṭahāsa—Jñāna; Nīla (Bhīmākālī); Pīṭha (Oṣṭha—Phullarā—Viśveśa); Śiva (Upapīṭha; Oṣṭhāṃśa—Phullarā—Viśvanātha); Nīla, Prāṇa (Cāmuṇḍā); Prāṇa (Mahānandā—Mahānanda); near Labhpur in the Birbhum District, Bengal.
Aujasa, Aurasa—Nīla, Prāṇa (Vīryadā); fictitious; but cf. Ausaja in *Viṣṇu S*.
Avanti—Nīla, Prāṇa (Atipāvanī); the same as Ujjayinī or the country round it.
Avantyāśrama—Nīla, Prāṇa; probably mistake for Agastyāśrama.
Avimukta—Nīla, Prāṇa (Viśālākṣī—Mahādeva); same as Vārāṇasī, Kāśī.
Ayodhyā—Rudra; Kubjikā; Nīla, Prāṇa (Bhavānī); Śiva (Upapīṭha; Kaṇṭhahāra—Annapūrṇā—Harihara); modern Ajodhya in the Fyzabad District, U.P.

B

Badarī—Kubjikā; Nāma (Urvaśī); Nīla, Prāṇa (Śrīvidyā); same as Badarikāśrama (Badrinath in Gahrwal, U.P.) in the Himalayas.
Bāhudā—Nīla, Prāṇa (Anantā); identified with the Dhumela or Burha-Rapti, a tributary of the Rapti in Oudh.
Bahulā—Pīṭha (v.l. Bāhulā; Vāmabāhu—Bahulā, Bāhulā—Bhīruka): Śiva (Mahāpīṭha;—Vāmabāhu—Bahulā—Bhīruka); located at Ketugram near Katwa in the Burdwan District, Bengal.
Bālidāṅgā—Caṇḍī (Dakṣiṇahasta—Rājeśvarī); in the Hooghly District, Bengal.
Balipura—Nīla (Allā); may be the same as Mahābalipura or Mamallapuram (Chingleput District), 30 miles to the south of Madras.
Beṇā—Nāma (Amṛtā); the Beṇā (tributary of the Krishnā), the Pengaṅgā or the Waingaṅgā. See Veṇā.
Bhadra—Nāma (v.l. Bhadreśvara); Nīla, Prāṇa (v.l. Bhadrāśva;—Bhadrakarṇikā). See Bhadreśvara. Bhadrāśva is a mythical division of the Jambudvīpa.
Bhadrakāleśvara—Nīla, Prāṇa (Mahābhadrā, Bhadrakālī).
Bhadrakarṇa—Nīla, Prāṇa (Bhadrakarṇikā—Mahādeva); identified with Karṇapura or Karnali on the south bank of the Narmada.
Bhadreśvara—Nāma (v.l. Bhadra;—Bhadrā, Bhadreśvarī); Nīla, Prāṇa (Rāmā); possibly Bhadreswar in the Hooghly District.
Bhairava—Nīla, Prāṇa (Bhairavī—Bhairava). See Bhairavaparvata.
Bhairavaparvata—Pīṭha (v.l. Bhīruparvata;—Oṣṭha, Ūrdhvoṣṭha—Avantī—Lambakarṇa, Namrakarṇa). See Bhairava; probably in West Malwa.
Bharatāśrama—Nāma (Aṅganā, Anaṅgā, Taraṅgā); Nīla, Prāṇa (Bhagavatī).
Bhīma—Nīla, Prāṇa (Bhīmeśvarī—Bhīmeśvara). See Bhīmā under *Himādri*. The *tīrtha* may also be connected with the Bhīmā, a tributary of the Krishna.
Bhīruparvata—See Bhairavaparvata.
Bhṛgu, Bhṛgupurī—Jñāna; Nīla (v.l. Guptapura;—Vrajeśvarī); identified with Balia in U.P. Bhṛgupura was also the name of Broach (Tawney, *Prab. Cint.*, trans., p. 136).
Bhṛgutuṅga—Nīla, Prāṇa; a mountain in Nepal.
Bījāpur—'Ain (Tuljā Bhavānī, Turjā Bhavānī); probably same as Pūrṇagiri. The shrine of Bhavānī actually stands at Tuljapur near Osmanabad in the Hyderabad State.

Bilva, Bilvaka—See Vilvala.
Brahmaśiras—Nīla, Prāṇa (Brahmāṇī).
Brahmāsya—Nāma; fictitious.
Brahmāvarta—Nīla, Prāna (Vrajeśvarī); in the eastern Punjab.

C

Caitraratha—Nāma (Madotkaṭā).
Cakradvīpa—Śiva (Upapīṭha;—Astra—Cakradhāriṇī—Śūlapāṇi); possibly one of the several Cakratīrthas.
Candanaparvata—Nīla (Mahānandā).
Caṇḍapura, Caṇḍīpura—Nīla (Pracaṇḍā).
Candrabhāgā—Nāma (Kālā, Kalā); Nīla, Prāṇa (Candrabhāgā); river Chenab in the Punjab.
Candrapura—Jñāna; Nīla (Sītā or Asitā); possibly Chanda in C.P.
Candrāsthira—Jñāna (v.l. Caraṣthira, Carasthita).
Carasthira—See Candrāsthira.
Carasthita—See Candrāsthira.
Caṭṭagrāma—Śiva (Mahāpīṭha; Dakṣiṇahastārddha—Bhavānī—Candraśekhara). See Caṭṭala.
Caṭṭala—Pīṭha (Dakṣiṇabāhu—Bhavānī—Candraśekhara). See Caṭṭagrāma; in the Chittagong District of East Bengal.
Cauhāra—Jñāna; mentioned in the short list but not in the long one; possibly a wrong reading.
Chāgalaṇḍa—See Chāgaliṅga.
Chāgalāṇḍa—See Chāgaliṅga.
Chāgaliṅga—Nāma (v.l. Chāgalāṇḍa, Chagalaṇḍa;—Pracaṇḍā); Prāṇa (Balipriyā).
Chāyāchatrapura—Jñāna.
Chāyāpura—Nīla; a mistake for Chāyāchatrapura.
Citrakūṭa—Nāma (Sītā); in Bundelkhand, or less probably Chitor (Mewar).
Citta—Nāma; fictitious.

D

Dakṣa-Pañcanada—Nīla, Prāṇa (Dakṣiṇā). See Pañcanada. *Dakṣa* (from Sans. *dakṣiṇa*) means 'south'.
Dārukeśa—v.l. Āmrātaka. Cf. the Dvarakeswar river running through the Bankura District.
Dehalikā—Nīla, Prāṇa (Amba); possibly modern Delhi. But cf. Trihalikāgrāma of the *Viṣṇusaṃhitā*.
Devadāruvana—Nāma (Puṣṭi); in the region of Badrinath in the Himalayas, or modern Aundh in the Deccan.
Devakoṭa—Same as Devīkoṭṭa.
Devakoṭṭa—Same as Devīkoṭṭa.
Devakūṭa—Jñāna. Same as Devīkoṭṭa.
Devaloka—Nāma; fictitious.
Devidaikoṭha—Rudra. See Devīkoṭṭa.
Devikātaṭa—Nāma (Nandinī); river Devikā is the modern Deeg in the Punjab.
Devikoṭa—See Devīkoṭṭa.
Devīkoṭṭa—Jñāna; Kālikā (Pada—Mahābhāgā); Nīla (Akhileśvarī); modern Bangarh in the Dinajpur District, Bengal. Same as Devakoṭṭa, Devakoṭa, Devakūṭa, Devīkoṭa, Devīkūṭa, Devidaikoṭha.
Devīkūṭa—Kālikā; see Devīkoṭṭa.
Drāviḍa—Nīla, Prāṇa (Sarasvatī); the Tamil country in southern India.
Durgā—Nīla, Prāṇa; a tributary of the Sabarmati in Gujarat.

Dvāravatī—Nāma (Rukmiṇī); Nīla, Prāṇa; modern Dwarka in northwestern Kathiawar.

E

Ekāgra—v.l. Ekāmra.
Ekāmra—Jñāna; Nāma (Kīrtimatī); Nīla (Ekā); modern Bhuvaneśvara in Orissa.
Elāpura—Jñāna; Nīla, Prāṇa (Vīrā); Nīla (Mahāsampat); modern Ellora in the Hyderabad State.

G

Gaṇakṣetra—Nīla, Prāṇa (Maṅgalā—Prapitāmaha); probably the same as Gaṇeśvara.
Gaṇḍaka—Same as Gaṇḍakī.
Gaṇḍakī—Pīṭha (Gaṇḍa—Gaṇḍakī—Cakrapāṇi); Śiva (Mahāpīṭha; details as in Pīṭha); river Gaṇḍakī is a tributary of the Ganges which it meets near Bakhtyarpur in the Patna District, Bihar.
Gandhamādana—Nāma (Kāmākṣī, Kāmukī, Kāmukā); a Himalayan peak at Badarikāśrama. In *Nāma*, verse 11, we have Gandhamādana as a v.l. for Mādhavavana, Mādhavīvana.
Gaṇeśvara—Prāṇa, Nīla.
Gaṅgā—Nāma (v.l. Gayā;—Maṅgalā); Nīla, Prāṇa (Śivāmṛtā); the sacred river Ganges.
Gaṅgādvāra—Nāma (Ratipriyā, Haripriyā); Nīla, Prāṇa (Nārāyaṇī, Vaiṣṇavī); the same as Haridvāra, the place where the Ganges enters the plain from the Himalayas.
Gaṅgārāmācala—v.l. Gaṅgāvāmācala.
Gaṅgāsāgara—Nīla, Prāṇa; near the Sāgar islands where the Bhāgīrathī enters the Bay of Bengal.
Gaṅgāvāmācala—Nīla, Prāṇa (Śivā); v.l. Gaṅgāvāṭācala; Gaṅgārāmācala.
Gaṅgāvāṭācala—v.l. Gaṅgāvāmācala.
Gaṅgāvilva—Prāṇa, Nīla.
Gaṅgodbheda—Prāṇa, Nīla.
Gargoccheda—Nīla, Prāṇa (v.l. Gaṅgodbheda).
Gauḍa—Rudra; in a narrow sense the Murshidabad District with the southern part of the present Maldah District; in a wider sense the western half or the whole of Bengal.
Gaurīśekhara—Śiva (Upapīṭha; Vasā—Yugādyā—Bhīma). Cf. Gaurīśikhara in Kāmarūpa (Pīṭha).
Gautameśvara—Nīla, Prāṇa; possibly one of the places called Gautamāśrama.
Gayā—Nāma (v.l. Gaṅgā;—Maṅgalā); Nīla, Prāṇa (Gayeśvarī); Aṣṭādaśa (Māṅgalyakoṭikā); the celebrated city in Bihar.
Ghaṇṭākarṇa—Kubjikā.
Ghāṭaśilā—Caṇḍī (Vāmapada—Rukmiṇī; actually *Raṅkiṇī*); a place between Kharagpur and Tatanagar or Jamshedpur on the Bengal-Nagpur Railway.
Giri—Tantrasāra; part of the name Merugiri wrongly regarded as a separate name.
Godāśrama—Nāma (v.l. Godāvarī, Kubjāmraka;—Trisandhyā). See Godāvarī.
Godāvarī, Godāvarītīra—Kubjikā; Pīṭha (Vāmagaṇḍa—Viśveśī, Rākiṇī—Viśveśa, Daṇḍapāṇi, Vatsanābha); Śiva (Mahāpīṭha;—Vāmagaṇḍa—Viśvamātṛkā—Viśveśa); Nīla, Prāṇa (Gaveśvarī); the celebrated river of the Deccan. See Godāśrama, Saptagodāvara.

Gokarṇa—Jñāna; Nāma (Bhadrakarṇikā, Kālikā); Nīla, Prāṇa (Bhadrā—Mahābala); Nīla (Sarvamaṅgalā); modern Gendia about 30 miles from Goa.
Gomanta—Nāma (Gomatī); located in the Goa region.
Gomatī—Nīla, Prāṇa (Vimukti); one of the many rivers of this name.
Gorakṣacāriṇī—See Gorakṣakāriṇī; cf. the tīrtha called Gorakṣa on the Gomanta. Another Gorakṣa is the town of Gorkha, 53 miles to the west of Katmandu in Nepal. Cf. also Gorakhpur in U.P.
Gorakṣakāriṇī—Kubjikā (v.l. Gorakṣacāriṇī).
Govardhana—Kubjikā; Nīla, Prāṇa (Ambikā); near Nasik in the Bombay Presidency.

H

Haṃsatīrtha—Nīla, Prāṇa; possibly connected with Haṃsamārga (probably Haṃsadvāra or the Niti Pass in Kumaon; identified with modern Hunza and Nagar; cf. *JUPHS*, XVII, pp. 48-49) in the Himalayas.
Haratīrtha—Nīla, Prāṇa (Gavīśvarī); probably the same as Harakṣetra or Bhuvanesvar.
Haridrā—Nīla; may be the same as Haridvāra.
Haridvāra—Śiva (Mahāpīṭha:—Jaṭhara—Bhairavī—Vakra); Prāṇa, Nīla. See Gaṅgādvāra.
Hariścandra—Nāma (v.l. Harmacandra;—Candrikā); Nīla, Prāṇa (Subheśvarī).
Hārīta—Nīla, Prāṇa (Hariṇākṣī); probably the same as Hārītāśrama near Udaipur in Rajputana.
Harmacandra—Nāma (v.l. Hariścandra)
Haroccheda, Harodbheda—Prāṇa, Nīla.
Hastināpura—Jñāna; Nāma (Jayantī); Nīla (Rājeśvarī Mahālakṣmī); in the Meerut District, U.P.
Hayagrīva—Kubjikā (v.l. Akṣayagrīva).
Hayakṣetra—Aṣṭādaśa; probably the same as Hayagrīva.
Hemakūṭa—Nāma (Manmathā); the Varṣaparvata lying to the north of the Kimpuruṣavarṣa that is situated to the north of the Himavat and the Bhāratavarṣa; apparently a part of the northern Himalayas.
Himādri—Nāma (Bhīmā); cf. Bhīmāsthāna near Shahbazgarhi (Peshawar District) of the Mahābhārata. See Himālaya, Himavat.
Himālaya—Nīla (Pārvatī). See Himavat, Himādri.
Himavat—Nāma (Nandā, Mandā). The Nandāsthāna is different from the Bhīmāsthāna and is no doubt the same as the celebrated Nandādevī peak in the Garhwal District, U.P. See Himādri, Himālaya.
Hiṅglāja—Caṇḍī (Nābhi; the Devīnāma is doubtful); same as Hiṅgulā; on the Aghor or Hingool river in Baluchistan.
Hiṅgulā, Hiṅgulāṭa—Kubjikā; Rudra; Pīṭha (Brahmarandhra—Koṭṭarī, Koṭṭavī, Koṭṭarīśā—Bhīmalocana); Śiva (Mahāpīṭha;—Brahmarandhra—Koṭṭarī—Bhīmalocana); Prāṇa; same as Hiṅglāja (Hinglaj) in Baluchistan where the goddess is locally called Bībī Nānī.
Hiraṇyākṣa—Nāma (v.l. Kamalākṣa;—Mahotpalā).
Hiraṇyapura—Jñāna; Nīla (Suvarṇā); modern Herdoun or Hindaun in the Jaipur State, about 70 miles from Agra.
Hṛṣīkeśa—Kubjikā; on the Ganges, about 24 miles to the north of Hardwar on the way to Badrinath.

I

Ilānta—Nīla.
Ilodayagiri—Nīla.

Indirāpura—Nīla.
Indrānandapura—Nīla.
Indrāṇī—Nīla.
Indranīla—Nīla, Prāṇa (Mahākānti); cf. the Himalayan peak Indrakīla mentioned in the *Kāvyamīmāṃsā*.
Indriśvara, Indrīśvarīpura—Nīla.
Indumatī—Nīla, Prāṇa (Pūrṇimā).
Indupura—Nīla.
Induvatīpura—Nīla. Same as Indumatī.
Induvijayapura—Nīla.
Irāvatī—Nīla, Prāṇa (Ī); river Rāvī in the Punjab.
Īśāna—Nīla.
Īśānyaiśapura—Nīla.
Iṣṭhanābha—Nīla, Prāṇa (Svāyambhuvā—Svayambhū).
Iṣṭapura—Nīla.
Īśvara—Nīla.
Īśvarayoga—Nīla.

J

Jāhnavīsaṅgama—Nīla, Prāṇa (Tṛpti, Svadhā); Jāhnavī is another name of the Ganges, while *Saṅgama* indicates a confluence. But the confluence referred to here cannot be determined.
Jāhnavītaṭa—Nīla (Vijayā). Jāhnavī is another name of the Gaṅgā.
Jājpur—See Yājapura (Jahājapura in the *Aṣṭādaśa*), Yāgapura, Virajā, Utkala; in the Cuttack District, Orissa. See also Nabhigayā.
Jālandhara—Hevajra; Kālikā (in the north;—Caṇḍī—Mahādeva); Kālikā (Stanadvaya;—Caṇḍī); Rudra; Jñāna; Kubjikā; Nāma (Viśvamukhī); Nīla (Nāgarī, Jvālāmukhī), Pīṭha (Stana—Tripuramālinī, Tripuranāśinī—Bhīṣana); Śiva (Mahāpīṭha;—Vāmastana—Tripuramālinī—Bhīṣaṇa); in the Punjab. 'Ain speaks of the goddess at Nagarkot-Kangra as Jālandharī which is the same as Jvālāmukhī. The *Ānandārṇava* gives the name of the Pīṭha as Jālandhra. The Jālandhara Pīṭha is now located near Jvālāmukhī.
Jālandharagiri—Same as Jālandhara.
Jālandhra—See Jālandhara.
Jālaśaila—Same as Jālandhara.
Jaleśvara—Jñāna; in the Balasore District, Orissa.
Janasthāna—Śiva (Mahāpīṭha) and Pīṭha (Civuka—Bhrāmarī—Vikṛta, Vikṛtākṣa); on the Godāvarī in the Nasik region of the Bombay Presidency. V.l. Jalasthala.
Japyeśvara—Nīla, Prāṇa (Triśūlinī—Triśūlin); probably the same as Jalpeśvara in the Jalpaiguri District, Bengal.
Jayanta—Nīla, Prāṇa (Jayantī); probably the same as Jayantī.
Jayantā—Same as Jayantī.
Jayantī—Śiva (Mahāpīṭha) and Pīṭha (Vāmajaṅghā—Jayantī—Kramadīśvara); in the Sylhet District, Assam (now East Pakistan) See Jayanta, Jayantā, Jayantikā.
Jayantikā—Jñāna. See Jayantī.
Jayapura—Nīla (Jayā); may be Jaipur in eastern Rajputana.
Jvālā—Aṣṭādaśa (Vaiṣṇavī); possibly Jvālāmukhī is intended.
Jvālāmukhī—Kubjikā; 'Ain; Nīla, Prāṇa; Pīṭha (Jihvā—Siddhidā, Ambikā—Unmatta); Śiva (Mahāpīṭha;—Jihvā—Ambikā—Vaṭakeśvara, Unmatta); in the Kangrah District, Punjab.
Jvalantī—Rudra; probably the same as Jvālāmukhī.
Jyotiḥsara—Prāṇa, Nīla.

K

Kailāsa—Jñāna; Nīla (Bhuvaneśvarī); in the Himalayas.
Kālamādhava—Pīṭha (Nitamba—Kālī—Asitāṅga); Śiva (Mahāpīṭha;—
Vāmanitamba—Kālī—Asitāṅga). See Mādhava.
Kalamb, kubja—Nīla, Prāṇa; represented as a combination of two names.
Kālañjara—Nāma (Kālī); Nīla, Prāṇa (Kālī—Nīlakaṇṭha); in the Banda District, U.P.
Kāleśvara—Jñāna (v.l. Kāmeśvara); cf. Ṣaṭpañcāśaddeśavibhāga, verses 10 and 40 (I. ., VIII, p. 33ff.).
Kālīghāṭa—Pīṭha (Muṇḍa—Jayadurgā—Krodhīśa, Krodheśa); Śiva (Mahāpīṭha;—Dakṣiṇapādāṅguli—Kālī—Nakuleśa). Pīṭha refers to the devasthāna at Juranpur near Katwa (Burdwan District), while Śiva speaks of the more important Kalighat in the southern suburb of Calcutta. For the same confusion see Kālīpīṭha. In the original part of Pīṭha, Kalighat is referred to as Kālīpīṭha. See also Kālīghaṭṭa.
Kālīghaṭṭa—Nīla, Prāṇa (Guhyakālī); Nīla (Kālī); same as Kālīghāṭa
Kaliṅga—Rudra; the Purī-Ganjam region in a narrow sense, but often it indicated the whole coast land down to the Godavari in the south.
Kālīpīṭha—Pīṭha (Dakṣiṇapādāṅguli—Kālī—Nakuleśa, Nakulīśa); Śiva (Upapīṭha;—Śiromśa—Caṇḍeśvarī—Caṇḍeśvara). See Kālīghāṭa, Kālī ghaṭṭa.
Kālīpura—See Kanyāpura.
Kālodaka—Nīla, Prāṇa (Kālī).
Kāmagiri—Pīṭha (in Kāmarūpa;—Mahāmudrā or Yoni—Kālī—Umānanda, Śivānanda, Rāvānanda, Rāmānanda); near Gauhāti in Assam. See Kāmarūpa, which is also called Kubjikā Pīṭha in the Kālikā P.
Kāmakoṭa, Kāmakoṭī, Kāmakoṭṭa—Jñāna; Nīla (Kāmeśvarī).
Kamalā—Kubjikā. See Kamalālaya.
Kamalākṣa—Nāma (v.l. Hiraṇyākṣa).
Kamalālaya—Nīla, Prāṇa (Kamalākṣī—Kamalākṣa).
Kāmarūpa—Hevajra; Nīla, Kālikā (in the east;—Kāmeśvarī—Kāmeśvara; Kālikā (Yoni—Kāmākhyā); Sādhana; 'Ain; Rudra; Jñāna; Kubjikā; Ānandārṇava; Caṇḍī (Madhyadeśa—Kāmarūpa-Kāmākhyā); Pīṭha (see Kāmagiri); Śiva (Mahāpīṭha;—Yoni—Kāmākhyā, Nīlaparvatī—Rāvānanda, Umānanda). Pīṭha associates the Gaurīśikhara with this place, while Kālikā places the sthānas of Dikkaravāsinī and Lalitakāntā in the Kāmarūpa country which corresponds to the Gauhati District of Assam and the adjoining region. The temple of Kāmākhyā stands on the Nīlakūṭa or Nīlaparvata, called the Kāmarupa-parvata by Rājaśekhara in the Kāvyamīmāṃsā. This blue hill is the same as Kāmagiri.
Kāmeśvara—Jñāna (v.l. Kāleśvara); cf. Kāmeśvaranātha at Karon in the Balia District, U.P. Kāmeśvara and Mahāgaurī (Kāmākhyā) were tutelary deities of the ancient kings of Assam (Kāmarūpaśāsanāvalī, Intro., p. 32, n. 2).
Kāmodaka—Nīla, Prāṇa (v.l. Kālodaka).
Kāmrāj—'Ain (Śāradā); in Kashmir. The reference is to modern Sardi.
Kanakāmaraparvata—Same as Meru, Amaraparvata.
Kanakhala—Nīla, Prāṇa (Śraddhā); Prāṇa (Śivogrā—Ugra); near Haridvāra (Hardwar).
Kāñcī—Rudra; Nīla, Praṇa (Kanakakāñcī); Pīṭha (Kaṅkāla—Devagarbhā—Ruru); Śiva (Mahāpīṭha;—Kaṅkāla—Vedagarbhā—Ruru). The earlier references are to modern Conjeeveram in the Chingleput District, Madras; but some late works (composed in Bengal) possibly speak of a locality on the Kopāi in the Birbhum District, Bengal.

Kāñcikāpurī—Aṣṭādaśa. The name is the same as Kāñcī.
Kaṇvāśrama—Nīla, Prāṇa (v.l. Kanyāśrama); possibly one of the several places associated with the name of Kaṇva.
Kānyakubja—Jñāna; Nāma (Gaurī); Nīla (Brahmāṇī); in the Farrukhabad District, U.P.
Kanyāpura—Nīla (v.l. Kālīpura;—Kanyā); see Kaṇvāśrama, Kanyāśrama.
Kanyāśrama—Pīṭha (Pṛshṭha—Sarvāṇī—Nimiṣa); located in eastern India at Kumārīkuṇḍa near the Kumira railway station in the Chittagong District.
Kapālamocana—Nāma (Śuddhi). One of the several places known by this name in different parts of India.
Karatoyātaṭa—Pīṭha (Vāmakarṇa, Talpa—Aparṇā—Vāmana, Vāmeśa); Śiva (Mahāpīṭha;—Vāmakarṇa—Aparṇā—Vāmeśa). The Pīṭha is located at Bhavānīpura near the bank of the Karatoyā in the Bogra District, North Bengal.
Karavīra, Karavīrapura—Nāma (Mahālakṣmī); Pīṭha (v.l. Śarkarāra;— Trinetra—Mahiṣamardinī—Krodhīśa, Krodheśa); Prāṇa (Satī); the capital of Brahmāvarta and on the Dṛṣadvatī in the Eastern Punjab according to the *Kālikā Purāṇa;* but usually identified with Kolhapur (called Karvir) in the South Maratha country.
Karkoṭa—Nāma (v.l. Mākoṭa); modern Karra, about 40 miles north-west of Allahabad; according to local tradition, Satī's hand fell at this place.
Karṇasūtra—Kubjikā. See Karṇatīrtha.
Karṇatīrtha—Nīla, Prāṇa. See Karnasūtra.
Kārttikeya—Nāma (Yaśaskarī, Saṅkarī, Atiśaṅkarī); possibly modern Baijnath near Almora in the Kumaon District, U.P.
Kāśī—Kubjikā; Nīla, Prāṇa (Annapūrṇā); in U.P. Same as Vārāṇasī, Avimukta. Vaṃśīdāsa connects it with Satī's *keśa.*
Kāśmīra (Kāshmīr)—Jñāna; Nāma (Medhā); Aṣṭādaśa (Sarasvatī); 'Ain (see Kāmrāj); Śiva (Mahāpīṭha) and Pīṭha (Kaṇṭha—Mahāmāyā— Trisandya, Trisandhyeśvara).
Kaṭaka—Śiva (Upapīṭha;—Carmāṃśa—Kaṭakeśvarī—Vāmadeva); modern Cuttack in Orissa.
Kaulagiri—Jñāna; same as Kolvagiri.
Kauśikī—Nīla, Prāṇa; river Kosi running through Nepal and Bihar.
Kavarī—Nīla, Prāṇa; same as Kāverī.
Kāverī—Nīla, Prāṇa (Kapileśvarī); river in the Tamil country in Southern India. See Kavarī.
Kāyāvarohaṇa—Nāma (Mātā); also called Kāyāvatāra, associated with the tradition of Nakulīśa, an incarnation of Śiva; same as Kārvān in the Dabhoi Taluk of the Baroda State.
Kedāra—Jñāna; Nāma (Mārgadāyinī); Nīla (Varadā); Prāṇa; in the Himalayas. See Kedāreśvara.
Kedāreśvara—Nīla, Prāṇa (Sanmārgadāyinī). See Kedāra.
Keśajāla—Pīṭha (v.l. Vṛndāvana); Śiva (Upapīṭha;—Keśa—Umā— Bhūteśa). See Vṛndāvana. The name is apparently due to a textual confusion.
Kirīṭa, Kirīṭakoṇā—Pīṭha (Kirīṭa—Bhuvaneśī, Vimalā—Siddhirūpa, Sam- varta); Śiva (Upapīṭha;—Kirīṭa—Bhuvaneśī—Kirīṭin); Prāṇa (Kirī- ṭeśvarī). The *tīrtha* is located at Vaṭanagara near Lālbāg in the Murshidabad District, Bengal.
Kiṣkindhyaparvata—Nāma (Tārā); in the modern Hyderabad State, or modern Kekind in the Jodhpur State.

Kokāmukha—Śiva (Mahāpīṭha;—Kŏk or Kukṣi—Kokeśvarī—Kokeśvara); modern Barāhchhatra (Varāhakṣetra) on the Kauśikī in Nepal.
Kolvagiri—Jñāna; possibly modern Coorg or Koḍagu which means 'steep mountains' (Pargiter, *Mark. Pur.*, trans., p. 364 n.); but more probably it has to be identified with Kolāpura or Kolhapur (*I.C.*, VIII, p. 49). See Kaulagiri, Karavīra, Mahālakṣmī.
Koṭa—Nāma (v.l. Mākoṭa), possibly Koṭatīrtha at Kalanjar.
Koṭimudrā—Rudra; possibly same as Koṭitīrtha.
Koṭitīrtha—Nāma (Koṭavī); one of the several places of this name.
Kṛṣṇabenyā (Kṛṣṇabenvā)—Nīla, Prāṇa (Bhedinī); river Krishna running through the Deccan.
Kṛtaśauca—Nāma (Siṃhikā).
Kṣīragrāma—Kubjikā; Caṇḍī (Pṛṣṭha—Yogādyā); Pīṭha (Dakṣiṇapādāṅguṣṭha—Yugādyā—Kṣīrakhaṇḍa, Kṣīrakaṇṭha); Śiva (Mahāpīṭha;—Dakṣiṇapādāṅguṣṭha—Yogādyā—Kṣīrakhaṇḍa). See Kṣirikā; modern Khirgram near Katwa in the Burdwan District, Bengal.
Kṣīrapura—Nīla (Yugādyā, Kṣīrā); same as Kṣīragrāma.
Kṣīrikā—Jñāna. See Kṣīragrāma.
Kubjāmraka—Nāma (v.l. Godāvarī, Godāśrama); near Hṛṣīkeśa in the Himalayas; the same as Kanakhala according to some authorities.
Kulānta—See Kūpānta.
Kumāra, Kumāradhāma—Nīla, Prāṇa (Kaumarī); possibly the same as Cape Comorin.
Kumuda—Nāma (v.l. Mukuṭa;—Satyavādinī).
Kuñcapaṭṭana—Aṣṭādaśa (Cāmuṇḍā); a mistake for Krauñca° (Banavasi).
Kūpānta—Jñāna (v.l. Kulānta).
Kurukṣetra—Kubjikā; Nīla, Prāṇa (Śivā—Sthāṇu); Prāṇa (Aruṇekṣaṇā, Raṇekṣaṇā); Pīṭha (Dakṣiṇagulpha—Sāvitrī—Sthāṇu); Śiva (Mahāpīṭha;—Dakṣiṇagulpha—Saṃvarī, Vimalā—Saṃvarta); near Thanesar in the eastern Punjab.
Kuśadvīpa—Nāma (Kuśodakā); one of the seven mythical Dvīpas of the world; cf. Kusha, the old Persian name of Ethiopia. See Kuśāvarta.
Kuśāvarta—Nīla, Prāṇa; a tank at Tryambak near Nasik or a Ghat at Hardwar.

L

Lagnikāśrama—Nīla, Prāṇa; possibly a mistake for Nagnikāśrama.
Lakṣmaṇoccheda, Lakṣmaṇodbheda—Prāṇa, Nīla.
Lalitā, Lalitāpura—Nīla, Prāṇa (Lalitā); possibly Lalitpur in the Jhansi District, U.P.
Laṅkā—Aṣṭādaśa (Śaṅkarī); Śiva (Upapīṭha) and Pīṭha (Nūpura—Indrākṣī—Rākṣaseśvara); modern Ceylon, but the *Aṣṭādaśa* makes separate mention of Laṅkā and Siṃhaladvīpa. The word *laṅkā*, means 'an island' and may indicate any island in the sea or a river.
Liṅga—Nīla, Prāṇa (Liṅgavāhinī); Nīla (Bhairavī).

M

Madanta—Nīla, Prāṇa (Madantī).
Madantikā—Nīla, Prāṇa.
Mādhava—Kubjikā. See Mādhavavana, Mādhavīvana, Kālamādhava.
Mādhavavana—Nāma (v.l. Mādhavīvana, Gandhamādana;—Sugandhā); probably the same as Madhuvana or Mathurā. See Mādhava.
Mādhavīvana—See Mādhavavana.
Madhupurī—Rudra; Kubjikā; same as Mathurā (Muttra) in U.P.
Madhurā—Nīla, Prāṇa (Devakī, Mādhavī); same as Mathurā.

Madreśvara—See Bhadreśvara; cf. Madra in the Sialkot region of the Punjab.
Magadha, Māgadha—Rudra; Pīṭha (Dakṣiṇajaṅghā—Sarvānandamayī—Vyomakeśa); modern Patna-Gaya region in South Bihar.
Mahābala—Prāṇa (Prabalā); possibly owing to confusion with Mahāvana.
Mahābodhi—Nīla, Prāṇa (Mahābuddhi); modern Bodhgayā (possibly Bodhigayā) in the Gaya District, Bihar.
Mahāgaṅgā—Nīla, Prāṇa; the river Alakanandā in the Himalayas.
Mahākāla—Nāma (Maheśvarī); Prāṇa (Mahākālī—Mahākāla); cf. god Mahākāla at Ujjain.
Mahākarṇa—Kubjikā.
Mahālakṣmī, Mahālakṣmīpura—Jñāna; Nīla (Ambikā); possibly the same as Kolhapur where stands the great shrine of the goldess Mahālakṣmī. But the *Jñānārṇava* makes a distinction between Kolvagiri and Māhā-lakṣmī. See Karavīra, Kolvagiri.
Mahālaya—Nīla, Prāṇa (Mahābhāgā—Rudra); Nāma (Mahābhāgā, Mahā-padmā); same as Oṅkāranātha or Amareśvara.
Mahāliṅga—Nāma (Kapilā).
Mahānāda—Nīla, Prāṇa (Māheśvarī).
Mahānadī—Nīla, Prāṇa (Mahodayā); the celebrated river running through Orissa.
Mahānala—Prāṇa, Nīla.
Mahāpathapura—Nīla (Māheśvarī); possibly a mistake for Maheśvarapura.
Mahātīrtha—Nīla, Prāṇa (Mahodarī); Nīla, Prāṇa (Haṃseśvarī).
Mahāvana—Nīla, Prāṇa (Bhadrā, Bhadrakālī, Bhadreśvarī); the same as Purāṇa-Gokula, six miles from Mathurā.
Mahāviṣṇupada—Nīla, Prāṇa; possibly the same as Viṣṇupada.
Mahendra, Mahendrapura—Jñāna; Nīla, Prāṇa (Mahāntakā—Mahāntaka); Nīla (Jagadīśvarī); the celebrated peak in the Ganjam District of Orissa. The records of the Gaṅga kings speak of Śiva Gokarṇeśvara on the Mahendra.
Maheśvarapura—Nāma (Svāhā); same as Māhiṣmatī, Māheśvarapura, Māheśvarīpura; modern Maheśvara in the Indore State, C.P.
Māheśvarapura—See Maheśvarapura.
Māheśvarīpura—See Maheśvarapura.
Māhiṣmatī—Kubjikā; modern Maheśvara in the Indore State or less probably Mandhātā in the Nimar District, C.P.
Māhvara—Aṣṭādaśa (Ekavīrakā). See Sahyādri.
Maināka—Nīla, Prāṇa (Akhilavardhinī); one of the several peaks or mountains of this name.
Makarandaka—See Amarakaṇṭaka.
Mākoṭa—Nāma (v.l. Koṭa, Karkoṭa;—Mukuṭeśvarī, Maṅgaleśvarī); Nīla, Prāṇa (Muṇḍakeśvarī—Mahākoṭa).
Mālava—Jñāna (v.l. Mānava); Nīla, Prāṇa (v.l. Malinī;—Raṅgiṇī); Nīla (v.l. Mānava;—Mahāvidyā); Śiva (Mahāpīṭha;—Vāmajānu—Subha-caṇḍī—Tāmra); modern Malwa, the eastern part of which was known as Ākara or Daśārṇa with its capital at Vidiśā, and the western part as Avanti or Apara-Mālava with its capital at Ujjayinī. Cf. Mānava, Mānasa, Malaya.
Malaya—Nāma (Rambhā); Nāma (v.l. Mānasa;—Kalyāṇī); cf. Mānasācala. Malaya has been identified with the southern part of the Western Ghats to the south of the Nilgiri.
Mānava—Jñāna (v.l. Mālava).
Mānasācala—Nāma (v.l. Malayāchala;—Kalyāṇī).

Mānasasarovara—Nāma (Kumudā); Nīla, Prāṇa (Gaurī); Pīṭha (Dakṣiṇahasta—Dākṣāyaṇī—Hara, Amara); Śiva (Mahāpīṭha;—Dakṣiṇahastārdha, Vāmahasta—Dākṣāyaṇī—Hara); the source of the Śatadru (Satlej) in the Himalayas.
Maṇḍaleśvara—Nīla, Prāṇa (Khāṇḍavī—Śaṅkara); Prāṇa (Karavīrā—Acaleśvara).
Mandara—Nāma (Kāmacāriṇī); Prāṇa (Bhuvaneśvarī); the Mandār hill in the Bhagalpur District, Bihar, or a mythical mountain in the Western Sea (Arabian Sea).
Māṇḍavya—Nāma (v.l. Māṇḍava;—Māṇḍavī, Maṇḍukī); same as Māṇḍavyapura (modern Mandor) in the Jodhpur State, Rajputana.
Maṅgalakoṭa, Maṅgalakoṭara (°koṭṭaka)—Nīla, Prāṇa (Maṅgalā); at the junction of the Ajay and Kunur in the Burdwan region.
Maṇibandha—Śiva (Mahāpīṭha;—Vāmamaṇibandha—Gāyatrī—Śaṅkara, Saivāṇa); Pīṭha (see Maṇiveda); the name seems to have been created out of a confused text.
Maṇikarṇikā (at Vārāṇasī)—Pīṭha (Kuṇḍala—Viśālākṣī—Kāla). See Vārāṇasī (modern Benares) in U.P.
Māṇikī—..ṣṭādaśa; probably a wrong reading.
Maṇipura—Kubjikā; possibly a place in the Manipur State in eastern India is indicated.
Maṇiveda—Pīṭha (Maṇibandha—Gāyatrī—Sarvānanda); Śiva (Mahāpīṭha; —Dakṣiṇamaṇibandha—Sāvitrī—Sthāṇu); possibly the same as Maṇipura.
Marakaṅkaṭa—See Amarakaṇṭaka.
Māruteśa, Māruteśvara—Jñāna; Nīla.
Mātaṅga—Nīla, Prāṇa (Mātaṅgī); same as Mātaṅgavāpī, modern Mātaṅgāśrama at Bakraur on the Phalgu, opposite Bodhgaya in the Gaya District, Bihar.
Mātaṅgavāpī—Nīla, Prāṇa; same as Mātaṅga.
Mathurā—Nāma (Devakī). See Madhurā, Madhupurī; modern Muttra in U.P.
Mātṛdarśa—Nīla, Prāṇa (Jaganmātā).
Mātṛgaṇa—Nāma (fictit.ous); Nīla, Prāṇa.
Māyā—Nīla, Prāṇa. See Māyāpurī, Māyāvatī, Māyāpura.
Māyāpura—Jñāna; Nīla (Māyā). See Māyā, Māyāpurī, Māyāvatī; the Haridvāra (Hardwar) region.
Māyāpurī—Nāma (Māyāvatī). See Māyā, Māyāpura, Māyāvatī.
Māyāvatī—Rudra; Kubjikā; same as Māyā, Māyāpura, Māyāpurī, i.e. the Hardwar region.
Meghavana—Nīla, Prāṇa (Meghasvanā).
Mehāra—Sarvānandataraṅgiṇī; a small Pargana in the Tippera District, East Bengal.
Mekhalā—Rudra; Mekalā, capital of Mekaladeśa in the Amarkantak region. Cf. also Mekliganj in the Coch Bihar State, B ngal.
Meru—Tantrasāra; Nīla (v.l. Amaraparvata;—Svargalakṣmī); same as Merugiri.
Merugiri—Jñāna; a mythical mountain; same as the mythical Sumeru, often identified with the Hindukush.
Mithilā—Rudra; Pīṭha (Vāmaskandha—Umā—Mahodara); Śiva (Mahāpīṭha;—Vāmaskandha—Mahādevī—Mahodara); modern Janakpur in the Nepalese Tarai.
Mukuṭa—Nāma (v.l. Kumuda).

Muṇḍapṛṣṭha—Nīla, Prāṇa (Śivā); the Brahmayoni hill at Gayā, particularly its portion containing the Viṣṇupada temple.
Munīśvara—Nīla, Prāṇa (Śuddhabuddhi).

N

Nābhigayā—Same as Gayānābhi or Jājpur (Orissa). Vaṃśīdāsa connects it with Satī's navel.
Nādavaṭa—Prāṇa, Nīla.
Nāgapurī—See Yāgapurī.
Nāgarakoṭa-Kangra—'Ain (Jālandharī, probably the same as Jvālāmukhī); Caṇḍī (Mastaka—Jvālāmukhī); same as Jvālāmukhī.
Nāgarasambhava—Kubjikā. See Nāgarasambhava.
Nāgarasambhava—Same as Nagarasambhava.
Nāgatīrtha—Nīla, Prāṇa (Surasā).
Naimiṣa—Nāma (Liṅgadhāriṇī). See Naimiṣāraṇya.
Naimiṣāraṇya—Nīla, Prāṇa (Prajñā, Liṅgadhāriṇī—Maheśvara); Prāṇa (Sukathā); modern Nimkhar or Nimsar and Misrikh regions in the Sitapur District, U.P. See Naimiṣa.
Naipāla—Same as Nepāla.
Nalāhāṭī—Pīṭha (Nalā—Kālī—Yogeśa, Yogīśa); Śiva (Upapīṭha;—Śirānālī—Śephālikā—Yogīśa); identified with Nalahati in the Birbhum District, Bengal.
Nalasthāna—Śiva (Upapīṭha;—Dakṣiṇagaṇḍāṃśa—Bhrāmarī—Virūpākṣa); probably Nalahati mentioned separately.
Nandapura—Nīla, Prāṇa (Mahānanda); possibly the same as Nandipura.
Nandataṭa—Nīla, Prāṇa (v.l. Nandavaṭa; Mahānanda); possibly a mistake for Nandātaṭa. For an Ānandā Mahāpīṭha, see *Skand P.*, Brahmakhaṇḍa, Dharmāraṇyakhaṇḍa, ch. 37, v. 62.
Nandavaṭa—See Nandataṭa.
Nandipura—Pīṭha (Hāra—Nandinī—Nandikeśvara); Śiva (Upapīṭha;—Hārāṃśa—Nandinī—Nandikeśvara); near Sainthia in the Birbhum District, Bengal.
Nārikela—Kubjikā; cf. Nārikeladvīpa mentioned in literature and such localities as Nārikeldāṅgā (near Calcutta) in Lower Bengal.
Narmadā—Nīla, Prāṇa (Narmadā); Pīṭha (v.l. Sona;—Nitamba—Śonā—Bhadrasena); Śiva (Mahāpīṭha;—Dakṣiṇanitamba—Śoṇākṣī—Bhadrasena); the celebrated river rising from the Amarkantak and falling into the Gulf of Cambay.
Narmadoccheda, Narmadodbheda—Nīla, Prāṇa (Dāruṇā).
Nepāla, Naipāla—Kubjikā; Jñāna; Nīla (Puṇyadā); Pīṭha (Jānu—Mahāmāyā—Kapālī); Śiva (Mahāpīṭha;—Dakṣiṇajaṅghā—Mahāmāyā, Navadurgā—Kapālī); the reference may be to Katmandu, the capital of Nepal.
Nīlācala, Nīlaparvata—Nīla, Prāṇa (Vimalā); Śiva (Upapīṭha;—Ucchiṣṭa—Vimalā—Jagannātha). See Virajā, Utkala. The reference seems to be to the Purī temple (said to be on the Nīla mountain) in Orissa, although; but there was another Nīlaparvata in Kāmarūpa from which Kāmākhyā was called Nīlapārvatī.
Nīlavāhinī—Kubjikā.

O

Oḍḍiyāna—Same as Uḍḍiyāna.
Oḍiyāna—Same as Uḍḍiyāna.
Oḍra—modern Orissa, but sometimes confused with Oḍḍiyāna in the Swat valley.

Oghavatī—Nīla, Prāṇa (Mahāvidyā); the river Apagā (a branch of the Chitang) running by Thanesar and Pehoa in the Eastern Punjab.
Oṅkāra—Nīla (Gāyatrī); Jñāna (possibly v.l. Praṇava); modern Oṅkāreś-vara or Oṅkāranātha, i.e. the island of Mandhata in the Narmadā (32 miles north-west of Khandwa) in the Nimar District, C.P.

P

Pampāsaras—Nīla, Prāṇa (v.l. Pañcāpsaras;—Śāraṅgā); near modern Hampe in the Bellary District, Madras.
Pañcakaṭī—wrong reading for Pañcavaṭī.
Pañcanada—See Dakṣapañcanada.
Pañcāpsaras—Nīla, Prāṇa; located differently by different writers.
Pañcasāgara—Śiva (Mahāpīṭha) and Pīṭha (Adhodanta—Vārāhī—Mahā-rudra); possibly the oceans are indicated, although their traditional number was four or seven. But cf. Pañcatīrtha.
Pañcatīrtha—Nīla, Prāṇa; near Hardwar.
Pañcavaṭī—Nīla, Prāṇa (Tapasvinī). See Janasthāna in which Pañcavaṭī was situated.
Pāṇḍu—Nīla, Prāṇa (Pāṇḍarānanā); possibly the same as the Pāṇḍya country in the southern corner of India.
Parameśvarapura—Nīla (v.l. Śamaneśvarapura).
Pārasya—Nīla (Paramānanda); Persia.
Pūrātaṭa—Nāma (v.l. Pārāvāratīra); Pārā is the same as the Pārvatī in Malwa.
Pārāvāratīra—Nāma (v.l. Pārātaṭa;—Mātā, Pārā, Pāvā).
Pāṭala—Nīla, Prāṇa (Pāṭaleśvarī); possibly Pāṭaliputra (near modern Patna) or Pāṭana (Patna<*Pattuna*) is indicated.
Pātāla—Nāma Parameśvarī); possibly Pāṭala is indicated, but is reminiscent of the region of Patalene, the ancient city and district, located by classical writers about the mouths of the Indus.
Pauṇḍravardhana—Jñāna, Nīla (Suveśā); same as Puṇḍra, Puṇḍravardhana.
Payoṣṇī—Nāma (Piṅgaleśvarī); probably the river Paisuni, a tributary of the Jumna between the Ken and the Tons.
Piṇḍāraka—Nāma (Dhṛti); Prāṇa; 16 miles to the east of Dvārakā in Kathiawar. See Piṇḍārakavana.
Piṇḍārakavana—Nīla, Prāṇa (Dhanyā). See Piṇḍāraka.
Piṅgā—Prāṇa, Nīla.
Piyālamārga—Prāṇa, Nīla.
Prabhāsa—Nāma (Puṣkarāvatī); Nīla, Prāṇa (Īśvarī); Nīla, Prāṇa (Sura-pūjitā); Nīla, Prāṇa (Puṣkarekṣaṇā—Somanātha); Pīṭha (Udara, Adhara—Candrabhāgā—Vakratuṇḍa); Śiva (Mahāpīṭha;—Adhara—Candrabhāgā—Vakratuṇḍa); modern Somnath in the Junagarh State, Kathiawar.
Prabhāsakhaṇḍa—Śiva (Mahāpīṭha;—Marma—Siddhīśvarī—Siddhīśvara); probably in the Prabhāsa region, or one of the other two Prabhāsas near Kurukṣetra or Kauśāmbī.
Pradyumna—Aṣṭādaśa; probably Pandua in the Hooghly District.
Praṇava—possibly the same as Oṅkāra.
Prapā—Nīla, Prāṇa (Pāpanāśinī).
Prasaṅga—Prāṇa, Nīla.
Prayāga—Kubjikā; Jñāna; Rudra; Aṣṭādaśa (Mādhaveśvarī); Nīla (Triveṇī?); Nāma (Lalitā); Pīṭha (Hastāṅguli—Lalitā—Bhava); Śiva (Mahāpīṭha;—Dvi-hast-āṅguli—Kamalā—Veṇīmādhava); modern Allahabad in U.P. The temple of Veṇīmādhava lies at the confluence of the Ganges and the Jumna.

Pṛthūdaka—Nīla, Prāṇa (Mahāvegā); modern Pehoa in the Karnal District, Punjab.
Puṇḍra—Śiva (Upapīṭha;—Loma—Sarvākṣiṇī—Sarva). See Puṇḍravardhana.
Puṇḍravardhana—Nāma (v.l. Puṇyavardhana;—Pāṭalā); same as Puṇḍra, Paundravardhana; identified with modern Mahasthan in the Bogra District, Bengal.
Puṇyādri—Nīla (v.l. Puṣyādri;—Mahāpuṇyā); possibly the same as Pūrṇagiri.
Puṇyavardhana—Same as Puṇḍravardhana. For this form of the name, see Watters, *On Yuan Chwang's Travels in India*, II, p. 185.
Puraścandra—Nīla, Prāṇa (Pureśvarī).
Purasthira—Jñāna (v.l. Purasthita).
Purasthita—Jñāna (v.l. Purasthira).
Pūrṇa—Same as Pūrṇagiri.
Pūrṇagiri—Hevajra; Kālikā (in the south;—Pūrṇeśvarī—Mahānātha); Kālikā (Skandhagrīvā—Pūrṇeśvarī); Sādhana; Jñāna; Rudra; probably located by the 'Ain in the Bijapur region of the Bombay Presidency. Same as Pūrṇa, Pūrṇaśaila. The name may not be unconnected with that of the Pūrṇā (modern Paira), a branch of the Godavari. The *Ānandārṇava* gives the name of the Pīṭha as Pūrṇabhūdhara.
Pūrṇaśaila—Same as Pūrṇagiri.
Puruṣottama—Nāma and Prāṇa (Vimalā); same as Purī in Orissa.
Puṣkara—Nāma (Puruhūtā); Prāṇa (Kamalākṣī); Prāṇa (Purahūtā—Rājagandhi); near Ajmer in Rajputana.
Puṣpatīrtha—Nāma (v.l. Uṣṇatīrtha); possibly connected with the Puṣpagiri in the Malaya range.

R

Rādha, Rādhā—Rudra; Nīla, Prāṇa (Maṅgalacaṇḍī); in a narrow sense, the land watered by the Ajay in the Burdwan District, Bengal.
Rājabolahāṭa—Caṇḍī (Vāmahasta—Viśālalocanī); near Serampur in the Hooghly District, Bengal.
Rājagiri—Pīṭha (v.l. Rāmagiri); possibly a form of Rājagṛha. Cf. Rājaparvata.
Rājagṛha—Jñāna; modern Rajgir in the Gaya District, Bihar.
Rājaparvata—Nīla; probably the same as Rājagiri.
Rāmā—Nāma (fictitious).
Rāmagiri—Kubjikā; Nāma (Trisandhyā); Pīṭha (v.l. Rājagiri;—Stana, Nāsā, Nalā—Śivānī—Caṇḍa); Śiva (Mahāpīṭha;—Dakṣiṇastana—Śivānī —Caṇḍa); possibly modern Ramtek near Nagpur in C.P., or Chitrakūṭa in the Banda District, U.P.
Ramaṇa, Ramaṇaka—Nīla, Prāṇa (Durgā).
Rāmatīrtha—Nāma (Ramaṇā); Nīla, Prāṇa (Mahādhṛti); the ancient Rāmatīrtha in Sūrpāraka (modern Sopara) in the Thana District, Bombay, although in this case Rāmagiri may be indicated.
Rāmeśvara—Nīla, Prāṇa (Prabhā); Prāṇa (Mahāsiddhi); the celebrated Setubandha Rāmeśvara in the Ramnad District, Madras. See Setubandha. Another Rāmeśvara lies at the confluence of the Banas and the Chambal.
Rāmoccheda, Rāmodbheda—Prāṇa, Nīla.
Raṇakhaṇḍa—Śiva (Mahāpīṭha;—Dakṣiṇakaphoni—Bahulākṣī—Mahākāla); possibly the same as Bahulā separately mentioned.
Rāsavṛndāvana—Nīla, Prāṇa (Rādhā). See Vṛndāvana.

Ratnāvalī—Pīṭha (v.l. Ratnavatī;—Dakṣiṇaskanda—Kumārī—Śiva); Śiva (Mahāpīṭha;—Dakṣiṇaskandha—Śivā—Śiva); possibly the same as the city of Ratnavatī mentioned in the *Kāvyamīmāṃsā*, but may also be a locality in Bengal. Ratnāvalī is the name of a sacred tributary of the Vāgmatī in Nepal.
Ratnavatī—See Ratnāvalī.
Ṛṇamocana—Nīla, Prāṇa (Vimukti).
Rudrakoṭī—Nāma (Rudrāṇī, Kalyāṇī); either the *tīrtha* of this name in Kurukṣetra, or that near the source of the Narmadā.

S

Sāgarasaṅgama—Nīla, Prāṇa (Svāhā); possibly the same as Gaṅgāsāgarasaṅgama.
Sahasrākṣa—Nāma (Utpalā, Utpalākṣī)
Sahyādri—Nāma (Ekavīrā).
Śākambharīpura—Nīla, Prāṇa; modern Sambhar near Pushkar.
Śālagrāma—Nāma (Mahādevī); at the source of the river Gaṇḍakī or Gaṇḍak.
Śāligrāma—Same as Śālagrāma.
Śamaneśvarapura—Nīla (v.l. Parameśvarapura;—Mahāvrajeśvarī).
Sambheda—Nīla, Prāṇa (Śubhavāsinī); supposed to be about the mouth of the Indus.
Saṃhāra—Śiva (Upapīṭha;—Dantāṃśa—Śureśī—Śureśa); apparently due to a textual corruption (cf. *Pīṭha*, verse 39 and notes).
Śaṅkhasaṃharaṇa—Prāṇa; same as Śaṅkhoddhāra.
Śaṅkhoddhāra—Nāma (Dhvani, Dharā); the island of Baṭi (Beyt) at the south-western extremity of the Gulf of Cutch.
Santāna—Nāma (Lalitā).
Saptagodāvara—Nīla, Prāṇa (Śrī, Akhileśvarī); at Solangipur, 16 miles from Pithapuram in the Godavari District of the Madras Presidency.
Saptārci—Nīla, Prāṇa; possibly the same as Guptārci at Viṣṇupada, or Saptārṣa (Satara) in the south Maratha country.
Śāradā—Nīla, Prāṇa (Śāradā); modern Sardi in Kashmir.
Sarasvatī—Nāma (Devamātā); Nīla, Prāṇa; river in the eastern Punjab running by Pehoa.
Sarayū, Sarayūtīra—Nīla, Prāṇa (Śāradā); the celebrated river running through Oudh, now called Ghagra or Gogra.
Śarīrin—Nāma (fictitious).
Śarkara—Śiva (Mahāpīṭha;—Trinetra—Mahiṣamardinī—Krodhīśa); same as Sarkarāra.
Śarkarāra—Pīṭha (v.l. Karavīra); identified with Sukkur in Sindh.
Sarvaśaila—Śiva (Upapīṭha;—Kakṣāṃśa—Viśvamātā—Daṇḍapāṇi); a vague reference to 'all hills'.
Ṣaṣṭhīpura—Nīla (Ṣaṣṭhī).
Śatadru—Nīla, Prāṇa (Śatarūpā); river running through the Punjab; now called Satlej.
Satī—Nāma (fictitious).
Satīcala—Śiva (Upapīṭha;—Karāṃśa—Sunandā—Sunanda).
Setubandha—Nīla, Prāṇa (Rāmeśvarī). See Rāmeśvara, Śvetabandha.
Siddhapura—v.l. Siddhavaṭa; either Siddhaur near Barabanki in U.P. or Sidpur about 64 miles from Ahmedabad; but may also be one of the several Siddhāśramas.
Siddhavana—v.l. Siddhavaṭa.

Siddhavaṭa—Nāma (v.l. Siddhavana, Siddhapura;—Mātā Lakṣmī, Umā Lakṣmī).
Siddhitīra—Nīla, Prāṇa (Siddhidā).
Siṃhala, Siṃhaladvīpa—Kubjikā (v.l. Siṃhanāda); Rudra; Aṣṭādaśa; modern Ceylon.
Siṃhanāda—Kubjikā (v.l. Siṃhala).
Sindhusaṅgama—v.l. Soṇasaṃgama. Sindhu is the Indus running through north-western India to the Arabian Sea.
Sirihaṭṭa—See Śrīhaṭṭa.
Śivacaṇḍa—v.l. Śivakuṇḍa.
Śivakuṇḍa—Nāma (v.l. Śivakuñja, Śivacaṇḍa;—Śivānandā, Śubhānandā, Sunandā, Sabhānandā).
Śivakuñja—v.l. Śivakuṇḍa.
Śivaliṅga—Nāma (Jalapriyā).
Śivapīṭha—Nīla, Prāṇa (Jvālāmukhī).
Śivasannidhi—Nāma (fictitious).
Someśvara—Nāma (Varārohā); possibly the same as Somanātha or Prabhāsa in Kathiawar.
Soṇa—Pīṭha (v.l. Narmadā;—Nitambā—Narmadā—Bhadrasena); Śiva (Upapīṭha;—Nitambāṃśa—Bhadrā—Bhadreśvara); Prāṇa (Kaṇakeśvarī); celebrated tributary joining the Ganges near Patna in Bihar.
Soṇasaṅgama—Nāma (v.l. Sindhusaṅgama;—Subhadrā); the reference may be to the Śoṇa-Gaṅgā-Saṅgama near Patna.
Śrīgiri—Nīla, Prāṇa (Śrī); same as Śrīśaila.
Śrīhaṭṭa—Sādhana (v.l. Sirihaṭṭa); Pīṭha (v.l. Śrīśaila); Śiva (Mahāpīṭha;—Grīvā—Mahālakṣmī—Sarvānanda); modern Sylhet in Assam.
Śrīparvata—Pīṭha (Dakṣiṇakarṇa—Sundarī—Sundarānanda, Sunandānanda); Śiva (Mahāpīṭha;—Dakṣiṇakarṇa—Sundarī—Sundarānanda); Prāṇa (Śaṅkarī—Tripurāntaka). See Śrīśaila.
Śrīpīṭha—Jñāna; possibly the same as Śrīhaṭṭa.
Śrīpura—Nīla (Śrīramā); possibly Sirpur in the Raipur District, C.P.
Sthala—Nīla, Prāṇa (Sthalā—Sthala).
Sthāneśvara—Same as Sthāṇvīśvara.
Sthāṇu—meant for Sthāṇvīśvara according to a wrong reading in Prāṇa.
Sthāṇvīśvara—Nāma (Bhavānī); modern Thanesar in the Ambala District, Punjab.
Strīrājya—Rudra; associated with the land of the Nu-wangs in eastern Tibet, who are said to have been ruled by a woman styled Pinchiu. The Strīrājya is usually located in the Kumaon-Garhwal region of the Himalayas. Hiuen Tsang seems to locate a western Strīrājya about Makran (Walters, *op. cit.*, II, p. 257).
Subhadra—Nīla, Prāṇa (Bhavyā); cf. the name Subhadrā applied to the Irawadi.
Suci—Pīṭha (v.l. Anala;—Ūrdhvadanta—Nārāyaṇī—Saṃkrūra, Saṃhāra); cf. Supārśva.
Sugandhā—Śiva (Mahāpīṭha) and Pīṭha (Nāsikā—Sunandā—Tryambaka); Prāṇa; modern Shikarpur on the Sondha (Sugandhā) near Barisal in South Bengal.
Śuklatīrtha, Śukratīrtha—Prāṇa (Śraddhā); near Broach in Gujarat.
Suparṇa—Nīla, Prāṇa (Utpalā—Sahasrākṣa); possibly the source of the Tons (Tamasā), tributary of the Jumna.
Supārśva—Nāma (Nārāyaṇī); cf. Suci.
Svargamārga—Nīla, Prāṇa (Svargadā).

Svargoccheda, Svargodbheda—Nīla, Prāṇa (Mahārātrī).
Śvetabandha—Śiva (Upapīṭha;—Bhagnāṃśa—Jayā—Mahābhīma); apparently a mistake for Setubandha.

T

Tailaṅga—Śiva (Upapīṭha;—Lomakhaṇḍa—Caṇḍadāyikā—Caṇḍeśa); Telengana or the present Telugu speaking area in the Deccan. Dey, *G.D.*, s.v. Triliṅga, said to be first mentioned in Rājaśekhara's *Viddhaśālabhañjikā*.
Tamolipta—Nīla, Prāṇa (Tamoghnī); modern Tamluk in the Midnapur District, Bengal. Other old forms of the name were Tāmralipta, Tāmralipti, Dāmalipta, etc.
Tantra—Nīla, Prāṇa (Gautameśvarī).
Tārā—Śiva (Mahāpīṭha;—Netrāṃśatārā—Tāriṇī—Unmatta); identified with Tarapur near Nalahati in the Birbhum District, Bengal. See Ugratārā.
Tirotā—Pīṭha (v.l. Trisrotā); but it is a corruption of *Trihuta* in *Śiva*, though the latter form itself is a corruption of Sanskrit *Tīrabhukti*.
Tīrthasaṅgama—Nīla, Prāṇa (Saṅgamā).
Traipura—v.l. Tripura.
Trihuta—Śiva (Mahāpīṭha;—Vāmapada—Amarī—Amara); Tirhut (Sanskrit *Tīrabhukti*) indicating the northern part of Bihar. See Tirotā.
Trikūṭa—Nāma (Bhadrasundarī, Rudrasundarī); the mythical peak of Ceylon on which the city of Laṅkā was supposed to have been situated. There was another Trikūṭa in the northern Konkan.
Tripada—Nīla, Prāṇa (Caṇḍā); possibly Tirupati (Tripadī; but really Sans. *Śrīpati*) is indicated.
Tripura—Nīla (Sundarī); probably the same as Tripurā, and not Tewar near Jubbulpore.
Tripurā—Kubjikā; Pīṭha (Dakṣiṇapada—Tripurā, Tripurasundarī—Nala, Tripureśa, Tripurākṣa); Śiva (Dakṣiṇapada—Tripurā—Nala); the Tripurā (Hill Tipperah) State in Bengal. Udayapura or Rāṅgāmāṭi (modern Rādhākiśorapura), old capital of Tripurā, is indicated.
Trisrotā—Jñāna; Pīṭha, (v.l. Tirotā;—Vāmapada—Bhrāmarī, Amarī—Īśvara, Amara); Śiva (Mahāpīṭha;—Dakṣiṇajānu—Caṇḍikā—Sadānanda); Śiva (Upapīṭha;—Padāṃśa—Pārvatī—Īśvara, Bhairaveśvara); the river Tista running through northern Bengal. *Śiva* mentions Trisrotā both as a Mahāpīṭha and as an Upapīṭha.
Triveṇī—Kubjikā; either the Yuktaveṇī near Allahabad or more probably the Muktaveṇī near Calcutta.

U

Uḍḍīnapura—Nīla; probably a mistake for Uḍḍiśa or Uḍḍīyāna.
Uḍḍiśa—Jñāna; same as Oḍra from Sanskrit *Oḍraviṣaya*, Prakrit *Oḍḍaviṣa*, *Oḍḍaïsa*; modern Orissa (*Oḍiṣā*).
Uḍḍīyāna, Uḍḍīyāna—Hevajra; Kālikā (in the west;—Kātyāyanī—Jagannātha); Kālikā (Urudvaya;—Kātyāyanī); Rudra; Jñāna; Kubjikā; land watered by the river Swat in north-western India, but sometimes confused with Oḍra (Orissa).
Uḍiyāna—Same as Uḍḍiyāna.
Ugratārā—Vaṃśīdāsa connects it with Satī's eyes. See Tārā.
Ujānī—Pīṭha (v.l. Ujjayinī, Urjanī, Ujjanī); Śiva (Mahāpīṭha;—Vāmakaphoni—Maṅgalacaṇḍī—Kapilāmbara); modern Kogram in the Burdwan District, Bengal.

Ujjanī—See Ujānī, Ujjayinī.
Ujjayinī—Jñāna; Aṣṭādaśa (Mahākālī); Nīla; Pīṭha (v.l. Ujānī, Ujjanī, Urjanī;—Kūrpara—Maṅgalacaṇḍī—Kapilāmbara); modern Ujjain in the Gwalior State; but see also Ujānī.
Urjanī—See Ujānī, Ujjayinī.
Uṣṇatīrtha—Nāma (v.l. Puṣpatīrtha;—Abhayā).
Utkala—Śiva (Mahāpīṭha;—Nābhi—Vijayā—Jaya); Aṣṭādaśa (Virajā); roughly speaking another name of Oḍra or Orissa. See Virajā.
Utpalāvartaka—Nāma (Lolā); cf. the name of Utpalāvatī, a river (modern Vyapar) in the Tinnevelly District, Madras, and that of Utpalāvata or Utpalāraṇya (modern Bithoor) near Cawnpore, U.P.
Uttarā—Śiva (Upapīṭha;—Vāmagaṇḍāṁśa—Uttariṇī—Utsādana); possibly the Uttaragā or Rāmgaṅgā in Oudh.
Uttarakuru—Nāma (Auṣadhi, Oṣadhi); a Himalayan tract, often supposed to have included the northern part of Garhwal.
Uttaramānasa—Nīla, Prāṇa (Nīlā); the Ganga lake at the foot of the Harmuk peak in Kashmir, or a sacred place at Gayā.

V

Vāgmatī—Kubjikā; river in Nepal, whose junctions with the Maradārikā, Maṇisrohiṇī, Rājamañjarī, Ratnāvalī, Cārumatī, Prabhāvatī and Triveṇī form respectively the Śānta, Śaṅkara, Rājamañjarī, Pramodā, Sulakṣaṇa, Jaya and Gokarṇa *tīrthas*; also old Tista (*Hist. Beng.*, II, p. 10).
Vaidyanātha—Kubjikā; Nāma (Arogā, Ārogyā); Pīṭha (Hṛdaya—Jayadurgā—Vaidyanātha); Śiva (Mahāpīṭha;—Hṛdaya—Jayadurgā, Navadurgā—Vaidyanātha); modern Deoghar-Baidyanāthdhām in the Santal Parganas District, Bihar.
Vaiśravaṇālaya—Nāma (fictitious).
Vaivasvata—Śiva (Mahāpīṭha;—Pṛshṭha—Tripuṭā—Śamanakarman, Nimiṣa).
Vakranātha—Śiva (Mahāpīṭha;—Manas—Pāpaharā—Vakranātha); possibly the same place is referred to in *Śiva* as both Vakreśvara and Vakranātha (cf. double mention of Trisrotā). See Vakreśvara. For *Pāpaharā* as the name or an epithet of the river at Vakreśvara, see *Pīṭha*, v. 50.
Vakreśvara—Pīṭha (Manas—Mahiṣamardinī—Vakranātha); Śiva (Mahāpīṭha;—Dakṣiṇabāhu—Vakreśvarī—Vakreśvara); near Dubrajpur in the Birbhum District, Bengal.
Vāmana—Jñāna; probably Vāmanasthalī (Banthali) near Junagarh, Kathiawar.
Vaṅga—Rudra; originally the land watered by the mouths of the Ganges, but later south-east Bengal.
Varāhaparvata, Varāhaśaila—Nāma (Jayā); Nīla; Prāṇa (Vārāhī); either Baramula in Kashmir, or Barahchhatra in Nepal.
Vārāhī—Kubjikā; cf. Varāhaparvata.
Vārāṇasī—Rudra; Aṣṭādaśa (Viśālākṣī); Nīla; Nāma (Viśālākṣī); Pīṭha (see Maṇikarṇikā); Śiva (Upapīṭha;—Kuṇḍala—Viśālākṣī, Annapūrṇā—Kālabhairava, Viśveśvara); modern Benares in U.P.
Vardhamāna—Kubjikā; possibly Burdwan in Bengal. But see Dey, *G.D.*, s.v.
Vareṇya—Prāṇa (v.l. Araṇya;—Sandhyā—Ūrdhvaretas).
Vaśiṣṭhatīrtha—Nīla, Prāṇa (Arundhatī); on Mount Abu in the Sirohi State, Rajputana, or on Mount Sandhyachal near Gauhati in Assam, or a place near Ayodhya.
Vastrapada—Nīla, Prāṇa (Bhuvaneśvarī—Bhava); possibly a mistake for Vastrāpatha (modern Girnar) in Kathiawar, although the Vastrapā

or Vastrāpada country seems to be located in the Mahābhārata (II, 48, 14; III, 80, 108) in the north-west.
Vastreśvara—Nāma (v.l. Viśvesvara;—Puṣṭi, Tuṣṭi); possibly the same as Vastrāpatha or Girnar in Kathiawar. See Vastrapada.
Vaṭaparvatikā—Nīla, Prāṇa (Pañcavargā); mentioned in a Pāla record and in Vijayarāma Sena's *Tīrthamaṅgala* (second half of the 18th century) and identified with the Vaṭeśvaraparvata situated near Pātharghāṭā in the Patna District, Bihar (*Bhāratavarṣa*, Jyaiṣṭha, B.S. 1350, p. 405).
Vaṭīparvatikā—Wrong reading of Vaṭaparvatikā.
Vedamastaka—Nīla, Prāṇa (Vedamātā); same as Vedaśiras.
Vedaśiras—Nīla, Prāṇa; same as Vedamastaka.
Vedavadana—Nāma (fictitious).
Vedeśa—Nīla, Prāṇa (Vedadā); possibly Vaidiśa or Vidiśā (modern Besnagar in the Gwalior State) is indicated.
Vegala—Nāma (v.l. Chāgaliṅga, Chagalaṇḍa, Chāgalāṇḍa).
Veṇā—See Beṇā.
Veṇumatī—Nīla, Prāṇa (Puṇyā).
Vibhāsa—Pīṭha (Vāmagulpha—Bhīmarūpā—Kapālī, Sarvānanda); Śiva (Mahāpīṭha;—Vāmagulpha—Bhīmarūpā—Kapālī); near Tamluk in the Midnapur District, Bengal.
Vidyāpura—Nīla, Prāṇa (Vidyā); probably the same as Vidyānagara or Vijayanagara (modern Hampe) in the Bellary District, Madras. Vidyānagara was possibly also a name of Rajahmundry or of a place near it in the Godavari District. Another Vidyānagara is supposed to be modern Bijaynagar at the confluence of the Sindh and the Para, 25 miles below Narwar.
Vijayā—Prāṇa, Nīla.
Vijayanta—Nīla, Prāṇa (Aparājitā).
Vilvaka—Nāma (v.l. Vilvala;—Vilvapatrikā); Nīla (Rupiṇī); Prāṇa. See Bilvaka.
Vilvala—See Vilvaka.
Vimalā—Kubjikā.
Vimaleśvara—Nīla, Prāṇa (Viśvā—Viśva); cf. the name of Vimalagiri (modern Palitana), a Jain *tīrtha* in Kathiawar.
Vināyaka—Nāma (Umā, Rūpā); one of the eight Vināyaka *tīrthas* in the Bombay Presidency, viz. Ranjangaon, Margaon, Theur, Lenadri, Ojhar, Pali, Madh and Siddhatek.
Vindhya—Kubjikā; Nāma (Vindhyavāsinī); Jñāna; Śiva (Mahāpīṭha;—Vāmapadāṅguli—Vindhyavāsinī—Puṇyabhājana). The temple of Vindhyavāsinī lies at Bindhyachal near Mirzapur in U.P. See Vindhyakandara, Vindhyagaṅgāsaṅgama.
Vindhyagaṅgāsaṅgama—Nīla, Prāṇa (Vindhyavāsinī). See Vindhya.
Vindhyakandara—Nāma (Amṛtā, Nitambā, Mṛgī); different from Bindhyachal near Mirzapur; cf. Vindhya.
Vipāśā—Nāma (Amoghākṣī); Nīla, Prāṇa (Mahābalā); modern Beas, a tributary of the Sindhu or Indus.
Vipula—Nāma (Vipulā).
Viraja, Virajapura, Virajā, Virajākṣetra in Utkala—Kubjikā; Jñāna; Nīla; Pīṭha (Nābhi—Vimalā, Vijayā—Jagannātha, Jaya); modern Jājpur on the Vaitaraṇī in the Cuttack District, Orissa. See Utkala, Yāgapurī, Jājpur, Yājapura, Nābhigayā.
Virāṭa—Pīṭha (Padāṅguli—Ambikā—Amṛta, Amṛtākṣa). The ancient Virāṭa country lay in the Jaipur-Alwar-Bharatpur region of Rajputana; but another country of that name was placed by late-medieval writers in northern Bengal (*I.C.*, VIII, p. 54).

Viśālā—Nīla, Prāṇa (Viśālā); possibly Viśālā-Badarī or Badarikāśrama in the Himalayas.

Viṣṇupada—Nīla, Prāṇa (Guptārci); Prāṇa (Viṣṇupriyā); probably the hill of that name at Gayā in Bihar. For another Viṣṇupada, see *Sel. Ins.*, I, p. 277.

Viśveśvara—Nāma (Viśvā, Vilvā).

Vṛndāvana—Pīṭha (v.l. Keśajāla;—Keśa—Umā—Bhūteśa); Nāma (Rādhā); modern Brindaban near Mathurā (Muttra) in U.P. See Rāsavṛndāvana.

Vyāghrapura—Nīla, Prāṇa (Hara); possibly the same as Buxar (really Vyāghrasaras) in the Shahabad District, Bihar.

Y

Yāgapurī—Nīla, Prāṇa (v.l. Nāgapurī;—Virajā); same as Virajā, Yājapura, Jājpur, Nābhigayā.

Yājapura—Caṇḍī (Dakṣiṇapada—Virajā). See Virajā, Yāgapurī, Utkala, Jājpur. The Assia range about a mile to the south of Jajpur in the Cuttack District, Orissa, is said to have borne the name Catuṣpīṭha-parvata.

Yamunā—Nāma (Mṛgāvatī); Nīla, Prāṇa (Kālindī); modern Jumna, the principal tributary of the Ganges.

Yaśora—Pīṭha (Pāṇi—Yaśoreśvarī—Caṇḍa); Śiva (Upapīṭha;—Pāṇi—Yaśoreśvarī—Pracaṇḍa); modern Jessore in Bengal, although the Pīṭha is located at Īśvarīpura (Khulna District) not far from Hasanabad in the 24-Parganas District.

Yugādyā—Pīṭha (v.l. Kṣīragrāma).

APPENDIX VI

Śiva and Śakti in the Orthodox Indian Pantheon.

The age covered by the composition of the Ṛgvedic hymns is considerably wide (between *circa* 1400 B.C. and 1000 B.C.). It is therefore no wonder, considering the popularity of the union of Aryan males with non-Aryan females, that the speech as well as the social and religious life of the Aryan peoples began to be modified as early as that age.[1] Attention

---

[1] Cf. 'The ideas of *Karma* and transmigration, the practice of *Yoga*, the religious and philosophical ideas centering round the conception of the divinity as Śiva and Devī and as Viṣṇu, the Hindu ritual of *Pūjā* as opposed to the Vedic ritual of *Homa*—all these and much more in Hindu religion and thought would appear to be non-Aryan in origin; a great deal of Puranic and epic myth, legend and semi-history is pre-Aryan; much of our material culture and social and other usages, e.g. the cultivation of some of our most important plants like rice and some vegetables and fruits like the tamarind and the cocoanut, etc., the use of the betel-leaf in Hindu life and ritual, most of our popular religions, most of our folk crafts, our nautical crafts, our distinctive Hindu dress (the *Dhotī* and the *Sāḍī*), our marriage in some parts of India with the use of vermilion and turmeric—and many other things—would appear to be legacy from our pre-Aryan ancestors' (S. K. Chatterji, *Indo-Aryan and Hindi*, p. 31). 'The Austric tribes of India appear to have belonged to more than one group of the Austro-Asiatic section—to the Kol, to the Khasi and to the Mon-Khmer groups. They were in the neolithic stage of culture and perhaps in India they learned the use of copper and iron. They brought with them a primitive system of agriculture in which a digging stick (**laṅ, laṅg, *liṅ*—various forms of an old word **lak*) was employed to till the hillside. Terrace cultivation of rice on hills, and plains cultivation of the same grain were in all likelihood introduced by them. They brought, as the names from their language would suggest, the cultivation of the cocoanut (*nārikela*), the plantain (*kadala*), the betel vine (*tāmbūla*), the betel-nut (*guvāka*), probably also turmeric (*haridrā*) and ginger (*śṛṅgavera*), and some vegetables like the brinjal (*vātiṅgana*) and the pumpkin (*alābu*). They appear not to have been cattle-breeders—they had no use for milk, but they were the first people to tame the elephant, and to domesticate the fowl. The habit of counting by twenties in some parts of North India (cf. Hindi *koḍī*,

may be drawn in this connection to the borrowing of the cerebral consonantal sounds from non-Aryan speech, to the speedy modification of the Ṛgvedic god Rudra and to the germ of theism, a non-Aryan institution later completely absorbed in Indian (i.e. mixed Aryo-aboriginal) religious life, to be traced possibly in the reference in the Ṛgveda (I, 22, 20) to the Sūris (meaning 'sectarian devotees of the god Viṣṇu' according to later works) as a class favoured by Viṣṇu. It is, however, interesting to note that, while the pre-Aryan Father-god was in the process of amalgamation with Aryan Rudra even in the early Vedic period, the absorption of the pre-Aryan Mother-goddess in the orthodox Indian religious life of later days took a considerably longer period of time.

The objects unearthed at the prehistoric (circa 2750 B.C.) sites of the Indus Valley prove the prevalence of the cult of the Father-god and Mother-goddess among the pre-Aryan peoples of India. The Mohenjodaro people worshipped a male god who may be regarded as the proto-type of Śiva. He is represented as seated in the Yoga posture, surrounded by animals, and has three visible faces with two horns on two sides of a tall head-dress. The ithyphallic (ūrdhva-liṅga) characteristic is also very marked. This apparently explains the later conception of Śiva as a Yogin, styled Paśupati, his Liṅga being specially important and his special attributes being the three eyes and the trident, probably associated respectively with the three faces and the two horns together with the head-dress. Some stone pieces looking exactly like the Śiva-liṅga have actually been discovered at Mohenjodaro. The Liṅga of the Father-god or Creator was worshipped apparently as a symbol not only of creation but also of virility. See Banerjea, *Dev. H. Icon.*, pp. 174ff.

The objects found at Mohenjodaro include many figurines of the Mother-goddess and point to the wide prevalence of her cult. Such figurines, discovered from prehistoric as well as later sites in different parts of India, are usually nude, but wear a peculiar head-dress, a wide girdle and a quantity of jewellery. A prehistoric terracotta seal from Harappa contains a representation of the same goddess who is shown upside down with her legs wide apart and a plant issuing from her womb and with a pair of tigers (cf. the association of the lion with the Indian Mother-goddess) towards the left, standing facing each other. The fundamental idea of the Mother-goddess cult was the belief in a female energy as the source of all creation. The Indus valley people appear to have also worshipped the Yoni as the symbol of this goddess just as they adored the Liṅga of the Father-god. Certain objects discovered at Mohenjodaro have their upper and lower surfaces undulating, while in some others the lower surface is flat but the upper one takes a quatre-foil form. Marshall regards these as representations of the Yoni, the female organ of generation symbolizing motherhood and fecundity. Yoni-rings of later date have been found from other sites. Certain disc-like objects, usually with well-carved decorative designs, have been found at old sites like Taxila and Rajghat and have been associated with the Yoni cult. See *op. cit.*, pp. 183ff.

Bengali *kuḍi*, 'score, twenty' from the Austric) appears to be the relic of an Austro-Asiatic habit. The later Hindu practice of computing time by days of the moon (*tithis*) seems also to be Austric in origin' (*op. cit.*, pp. 30-31). The 'notion of Brahman, the Supreme Spirit beyond the conception of the manifest gods, dwelling in the void by itself and creating the world out of itself, through its will or desire, can be looked upon as an Austric contribution in the evolution of Indian thought' (Chatterji in *Bhārata-kaumudī*, I, p. 206). India's script and architecture and the caste system are also pre-Aryan. For the contributions of the non-Aryans to Indian culture, see also *Pre-Aryan and Pre-Dravidian in India*, ed. P. C. Bagchi, Calcutta, 1929.

The Ṛgveda (VII, 21, 5; X, 99, 3) refers in a deprecatory manner to a class of people called Śiśnadeva. Whether they were Aryan (under the influence of an aboriginal cult) or non-Aryan in origin cannot be determined; but there is no doubt that at least the orthodox section of the Ṛgvedic Aryans disapproved of the phallic cult. The Ṛgvedic Rudra (literally, 'the howling one'), essentially the spirit of stormy clouds, was conceived as discharging brilliant shafts and killing men and cattle with his weapons as well as with diseases (I, 114; VII, 46). The giver of diseases was sometimes also regarded as the healer of them (I, 43, 4, etc.). Rudra's interesting epithet Paśupa (I, 114, 9) seems to point to his rapprochement with the pre-Aryan deity worshipped at Mohenjodaro even as early as the later Ṛgvedic age when some people also spoke of his 'universal sovereignty' (VII, 46, 20). In the Śatarudrīya section of the Yajurveda (Taittirīya, 4, 5, 1; Vājasaneyi, 16), Rudra's benign form is distinguished from his malignant appearance and he is called the heavenly physician, the god lying on the mountains (Giriśa), the wearer of matted hair (Kapardin), and the lord of paths, forests, cattle, forest-tribes and outcasts, thieves and robbers. He is also called Śarva (archer), Bhava (benign), Śambhu (beneficent), Śiva (auspicious) and the wearer of tiger-skin. Thus the conception of a terrible destroyer as quite its opposite resulted from partially an attempt at appeasement by flattery and partially perhaps from his gradual amalgamation with the pre-Aryan Father-god. The Rudras, in the plural, are called Gaṇa (a tribe) and leaders of tribes (Gaṇapati) and of workmen, potters, cartmen, carpenters and Niṣādas who belonged to proto-Australoid forest-tribes. The Atharvaveda (cf. IV, 28; VI, 93, 2; VII, 87, 1; XI, 2, 1; XV, 5) refers to Bhava (called Rājan, the archer and the protector of the Vrātyas or outcasts), Paś ipati, Ugra, Rudra, Mahādeva and Īśāna as distinct forms of the god. Śarva and Bhava, called Bhūtapati and Paśupati, are desired to remove their deadly poison to other places. In the Śūlagava sacrifice mentioned in the Gṛhyasūtras (Āśvalāyana, 4, 9), a bull was sacrificed to appease Rudra outside the limits of a village. This shows that the god was not exactly within the orthodox pantheon apparently owing to his association with non-Aryan tribes. He is called by the names Hara, Mṛḍa, Bhīma and Śaṅkara, and one is directed to adore Rudra at the time of traversing a path and a crossing of four roads, of passing by a heap of dung and a creeping serpent, of being overtaken by a tornado and of coming to a variegated scene, a sacrificial site and an old tree (Hiraṇyakeśin, 1, 5, 16; cf. Pāraskara, III, 15). The Śvetāśvatara Upaniṣad (cf. Chs. III–IV), which is earlier than the Bhagavadgītā (circa third century B.C.) and contains speculations approaching closely the Bhakti cult of later days, calls the god Bhagavat, the Great Soul and also Maheśvara in whose power stands Māyā and Prakṛti. It is also said that, knowing Śiva who is minuter than the minute, the creator and protector of the universe, the one having many forms and the one alone encompassing the world and concealed in all beings, men (Brahmarṣis) become free from all nooses and attain eternal peace. The god is further said to be the one unchangeable principle that existed before creation. The earliest exposition of the Pāśupata doctrine is found in the Atharvaśiras Upaniṣad (cf. R. G. Bhandarkar, Vaiṣṇavism, etc., p. 159) which is, however, not a very ancient work. The Śiva-bhāgavatas of Patañjali's Mahābhāṣya (originally composed in the second century B.C.), under Pāṇini, V, 2, 76, were apparently followers of the Pāśupata-vrata mentioned in this Upaniṣad. Thus the pre-Aryan Father-god, amalgamated with Vedic Rudra, gradually came to be, as Rudra-śiva, a great force in the composite religious life of India long before the birth of Christ, although even in later times often his non-Aryan origin and association were remembered and pointedly mentioned (cf. the legend about the destruction of Dakṣa's sacrifice, *supra*, p. 6). This shows that the influence of Śiva, worshipped by the pre-Aryans, was strong enough to overcome the reluctance of the orthodox Aryan element and to occupy a front seat in the Indo-Aryan pantheon in spite of opposition.

The pre-Aryans appear to have conceived the Mother-goddess as the wife of the Father-god; but, in the Vedic literature, the Mother-goddess is rarely referred to.[1] The *Yajurveda* (cf. *Taittirīya*, I, 8, 6) mentions Ambikā as Rudra's sister. In connection of the Śūlagava sacrifice in honour of Rudra, the *Gṛhyasūtras* speak of the 'wife of Bhava' (*Hiraṇyakaśin*, II, 3, 8) apparently as a subordinate deity. Sometimes Rudrāṇī, Śarvāṇī and Bhavānī are mentioned side by side (*Pāraskara*, III, 8). The *Kena Upaniṣad* gives a story in which Umā Haimavatī (daughter of the Himavat) disclosed the nature of Brahman (probably Śiva) to the gods (cf. R. G. Bhandarkar, *op. cit.*, p. 158). But she is not called Rudraśiva's wife. Ambikā's mention as Rudra's spouse in the interpolated tenth section of the *Taittirīya Āraṇyaka* (X, 18) is of course very late. Thus in the age covered by the Vedic literature, when the non-Aryan Father-god was considerably near the front rank in the orthodox Indian pantheon, the worship of the Mother-goddess does not appear to have been popular with the higher classes of the society. Even if she made any progress towards recognition, that was possibly as a subordinate to her husband Śiva. This may have been due mainly to the fact that the cult of the Mother-goddess as such was originally unknown to the Aryans who were moreover a patrilineal people unlike the matrilineal aboriginals. Even in the early centuries of the Christian era when the Liṅga cult was becoming widely popular among the people of different classes (although the phallic emblems were gradually being made symbolical by removing their earlier realistic character which was apparently disliked by the orthodox) and when the appearance of *Ommo* (*Umā* from the Dravidian *Amma* meaning the universal mother) on the coin of Huviṣka proves that the Mother-goddess cult became an important factor in Indian religious life, Śakti seems to have been subordinated to Śiva by the upper classes of people who moreover practically ignored the worship of *Yoni* as the symbol of the Mother-goddess. Certain *tīrthas* containing Yoni tanks are no doubt mentioned in the *Mahābhārata*; but the worship of *Yoni* is prescribed only in the late-medieval *Tantra* [2] works which were also not favoured universally by all classes of the society. This particular cult was specially disliked by the orthodox upper classes.

The representation of the bull, i.e. Śiva in his theriomorphic form, on an Indo-scythian coin of about the beginning of the Christian era, that of

---

[1] Her influence is slightly noticed in the conception of Vedic Aditi (spirit of the boundless sky), described as the mighty mother of the Ādityas and as associated with Dakṣa. See Macdonell, *Ved. Myth.*, sect. 41. But she is a minor deity of the Vedic pantheon and was gradually forgotten with the development of the Dākṣāyaṇī-Haimavatī conception of the Mother-goddess.

[2] Cf. also the late-medieval work *Bṛhaddharma* P., II, 1, 38·

योनिः साक्षात् भगवती लिङ्गं साक्षात्महेश्वरः ।
तयोस्तु पूजनेन स्यात् सर्वदेवतपूजनम् ॥

Also देवीं वरं भगाभिकाम् (II, 10, 53); देवीं कुर्याद्योन्याकृपां चैव देवीं प्रकीर्तिता (II, 27, 32).
See also सर्वासु खलु नारीषु ममाभिद्धानमुत्तमम् ।
कुमारीषु च सर्वासु युवतीषु विशेषतः ।
तासां योनिं क्षतं दृष्ट्वा प्रणमेत्कामनुस्मरन् ॥ (II, 11, 99-100).

Śiva in his anthropomorphic form such as on the pre-Christian Ujjain coins and on those of Gondophernes and the Kuṣāṇas belonging to the first and second centuries A.D. (the ithyphallic characteristic of Śiva or Harihara being apparent on a coin of Huviṣka), the discovery from all parts of India of innumerable symbolical phallic emblems of Śiva dating from about the beginning of the Gupta age (although certain realistically made Liṅgas such as that of Gudimallam and their representation on coins such as those from Ujjain have been assigned to dates prior to the beginning of the Christian era), the description of an exceptionally large number of Indian rulers of all parts of the country as exclusive devotees of Maheśvara or Śiva in records dating from the first century A.D. (cf. *Sel. Ins.*, I, pp. 125, 331, 387, 394, 419f., etc.), the mention of ten generations of Pāśupata *ācāryas* in a Mathurā inscription of 381 A.D. (*ibid.*, pp. 269ff.) and the evidence of the epics and the Purāṇas show beyond doubt that Śiva's status at least in the early centuries of the Christian era was practically the same as it is today in the religious life of India. See *Dev. H. Icon.*, Chs. IV-V. But the case of Śakti, in spite of her growing popularity with different classes of people as suggested by Huviṣka's coin, seems to have been different. The evidence of certain later sections of the *Mahābhārata* and the *Purāṇas* like the *Mārkaṇḍeya* no doubt shows that the Mother-goddess, conceived as the wife of Śiva, was nearing the front rank about the age of the imperial Guptas. But even in the period following this age we very often find her associated and apparently subordinated to Śiva. Attention may be drawn in this connection to the adoration of Kāmeśvara and Mahāgaurī in the early-medieval records of some kings of Kāmarūpa (*Kāmarūpaśāsanāvalī*, Intro., p. 32) where the most important deity was no doubt Kāmākhyā (Mahāgaurī). Interesting is also Hiuen Tsang's mention of Bhīmādevī of Gandhāra in association with Mahādeva worshipped by the *Tīrthikas* or *Pāśupatas*. It is well known that the Kāpālika sect of the Śaivas worshipped Śakti in association with Śiva (*supra*, p. 10, note 1). It is also to be noted that the Śulkīs of Orissa, although their family-deity was Stambheśvarī, claimed to have been exclusively devoted to Maheśvara (D. R. Bhandarkar, *List*, Nos. 1697-98, 1700). The very name of the goddess shows that she was made out on a *Stambha* indicating a *Liṅga* (such Liṅgas with the representation of Śaktis being found in Eastern India; cf. *Hist. Beng.*, I, p. 452) and was thus subordinate to Śiva. A king of the Bhañja family of Orissa claims to have obtained boons from the goddess Stambheśvarī although he was a worshipper of Viṣṇu personally (*List*, No. 1493). There are similar other references to the worship (usually and especially by the aboriginals) of particular forms of the Mother-goddess; cf. Vindhyavāsinī mentioned in the *Harivaṃśa* (*circa* fourth century A.D.) and Vākpatirāja's *Gauḍavaha* (eighth century). Jālandhara (Jvālāmukhī), Uḍḍiyāna (in the Swat valley), Kāmarūpa, Śrīhaṭṭa and Pūrṇagiri were regarded as the greatest seats of the Mother-goddess in works dating from the eighth century (*supra*, pp. 12ff.). Śiva was, however, usually worshipped along with the Mother-goddess in such seats (*Pīṭhas*) in a form styled Bhairava.[1] But the gradual increase in the importance of the Mother-goddess is also sometimes noticed as suggested by her independent installation for worship (cf. also *supra*, p. 10, note 1, l. 7). In the fifth century A.D., the Maukhari chief Anantavarman established the images of Bhūtapati and Devī in a cave in the Nagarjuni hills, while in another cave he installed an image of the Mother-goddess styled Devī, Bhavānī, Kātyāyanī and the one overpowering

---

[1] Cf. Mahiṣamardinī at the Śaiva establishments of Udaygiri (c. 400), Bhumara (c. 6th cent.), **Mamallapuram** (7th cent.), **Bhubaneswar** (Vaital Deul), etc.

the demon Mahiṣāsura. It should, however, be remembered that the chief was a worshipper of Śiva and Śakti and not of Śakti alone. The 'Divine Mothers', often associated with Mahāsena as in the records of the early Kadambas and Calukyas, are known to have usually been collectively adored (*Bṛhatsamhitā*, 60, 19). The construction of a temple for them, described as a 'terrible abode, full of *Ḍākinīs* (female ghouls), of the Mothers who utter loud and tremendous shouts of joy and who stir up the very oceans with the wind rising from the *Tantra* (magical rites)', by a Vaiṣṇava (the 'Mothers' being subordinate to Viṣṇu in this case) royal official for merit, is referred to in a Mandasor inscription of 423 A.D. (*Sel. Ins.*, pp. 284f.). For another early temple of the 'Divine Mothers', see the Deogarh rock inscription of about the sixth century A.D. (*E.I.*, XVIII, pp. 126f.). But whereas the kings of the Gupta age and their successors are usually described as devotees of Maheśvara, Śambhu, Aditya, Sugata, Buddha, Tathāgata, Bhagavat (Viṣṇu), Viṣṇu, Varāha, Cakrapāṇi, Narasimha, etc., we rarely find kings who were exclusively devoted to the worship of the Mother-goddess before the age of the Gurjara-Pratīharas (eighth to the eleventh century) of Kanauj, among whom Nāgabhaṭa II, Bhoja I and Mahendrapāla I claim to have been devotees of the goddess Bhagavatī (D. R. Bhandarkar, *op. cit.*, No. 25), while Mahīpāla had predilections for the worship of that goddess as well as of the sun-god (Tripathi, *Hist. Kanauj*, pp. 290-91).

Neither Śiva nor Śakti, however, has been free from aboriginal associations even to this day; but the latter bears the stigma in a far more marked degree than the former, although it has of course to be admitted that Śakti is now regarded as one of the *Pañcadevatā* (Sūrya, Gaṇeśa, Devī, Śiva and Viṣṇu) to be worshipped in all ceremonies (*Bṛhaddharma P.*, III, 9, 1). Certain late-medieval *Tantras* and other works dealing with the Śaiva and Śākta cults (e.g. *Annadāmaṅgala*, Vaṅgavāsī ed., p. 78) represent Śiva as an ardent lover of Koch girls. This trait, not found in earlier works, no doubt resulted from the identification of Śiva with a tribal deity of the Koch people after their Hinduization in the medieval period; but it shows that Śiva was particularly associated with non-Aryan barbarians even in comparatively modern times. We have already discussed (*supra*, p. 3, note 2) the contribu ion of the various non-Aryan elements in the Indian population to the conception of the Indian Mother-goddess as suggested by her names in Indian literature.[1] But the most glaring instance of her barbarian association in late-medieval and recent times is offered by the ceremony called Śabarotsava that was performed on the Daśamī *tithi* in connection with the autumnal worship of Durgā and is partially remembered in rural Bengal even to this day. The 'festivities on account of the excellent worship of the goddess Umā', celebrated by the people of Varendrī (North Bengal), is referred to by the twelfth century Bengali author Sandhyā-karanandin in his *Rāmacarita* (III, 25).[2] People taking part in the Śabarotsava used to cover their bodies with leaves, etc., and to besmear them with mud and other things in the style of the Śabaras who are a proto-Australoid aboriginal people of south-eastern India. Two verses occurring both in the *Kālaviveka* (Bib. Ind. ed., p. 514) by the Bengali jurist Jīmūta-vāhana (fifteenth century according to Jolly, but eleventh-twelfth century according to Kane, *Hist. Dharm.*, I, pp. 325-26) and in the *Kālikā Purāṇa*

---

[1] Names like *Kauśikī*, *Kātyāyanī* and *Dākṣāyaṇī* probably indicated deified ladies or deities worshipped by certain Aryan families or clans. See *supra*, p. 3, note 2.

[2] The oldest reference to the modern Bengali form of the worship of Durgā Mahiṣamardinī, accompanied by Kārttikeya, Gaṇeśa, Lakṣmī, and Sarasvatī, is found in the *Caṇḍīmaṅgala* (16th century).

(61, 21-22)[1] prove that the programme of this festivity included topics on and songs about the sex organs and possibly also about sexual intercourse with requisite movements of the body and that its violation incurred Bhagavatī's anger and curse. The Bṛhaddharma Purāṇa (III, 6, 81-83), a late-medieval Bengal work of about the seventeenth century,[2] introduces some modifications in the above programme when it says, 'People should not utter before others words which are expressive of such things as the male and female organs of generation; they should utter these during the days of the great worship of the goddess in the month of Āśvina. But even then they should never pronounce them before their mothers and daughters and before female disciples who have not yet been initiated to Śakti worship'. Still, however, the Purāṇa supports by arguments that a person worthy of worshipping the Mother-goddess should utter the indecent expressions with a view to pleasing her.[3]

[1] Cf. सुवासिनीभिः कुमारीभिर्वेश्याभिमन्तर्षिकया ।
मञ्जुनयनिनादैश्च सदर्पैः पटहेक्षणा ॥ १९
ध्वजेर्वेणैश्च विचित्रेर्लोजुप्यप्रकीर्षकैः ।
भूरिकर्दमविक्षेपैः श्रीडाकौतुकमङ्गलैः ॥ २०
भगलिङ्गाभिधानैश्च भगलिङ्गप्रगीतकैः ।
भगलिङ्गादिशब्दैश्च (v.l. °लिङ्गक्रियाभिश्च) श्रीदेवेयुरहं अमाः ॥ २१
परेनोन्दिष्यते यस्तु यः पराज्ञाविपेद्यादि ।
क्रुद्धा भगवती तस्य श्रापं दद्यात् सुदारुणम् ॥ २२

[2] The Brahmavaivarta Purāṇa (I, 10, 12 and 123), an East Indian adaptation of an old work and to be attributed to the fourteenth or fifteenth century (supra, p. 6, note 3), makes a distinction between the Ambaṣṭhas (probably the Ambaṣṭha-Kāyasthas of Bihar) and the Vaidyas (of Bengal), while the Bṛhaddharma (III, 14, 38-48) identifies the Vaidyas with the Ambaṣṭhas. Similarly, Kavikaṇṭhahāra's Sadvaidyaulapañjikā (1653 A.D.) is silent about the Ambaṣṭha origin of the Bengal Vaidyas (cf. Dacca ed., pp. 1-2), whereas Bharatamallika's Candraprabhā (1675 A.D.) definitely states that the Vaidyas were the same as the ancient Ambaṣṭhas (Calcutta ed., p. 4). The present-day Ambaṣṭhas of the Tamil land and Malabar (their early distribution in South India may have been wider) appear to be referred to as Vaidyas in inscriptions dating from the seventh century (E.I., IX, p. 101; VIII, pp. 317-21; XVII, pp. 291ff.; I.A., 1893, pp. 57f.). Their entry into Bengal during the rule of the Senas, hailing from Karṇāṭa or the Kanarese country in the Deccan, is very probable, as the Senas of Bengal must have patronized South Indians in the same way as the Muslim rulers of India entertained Musalmans of other countries at their courts. It is thus very probable that the crystallization of the professional community of the Vaidyas or physicians of Bengal into a caste was a result of their amalgamation with the tribal Ambaṣṭha-Vaidyas of Southern India. This seems to have been the background on which the theory identifying the Vaidyas with the Ambaṣṭhas of early Indian literature (Manu calling them physicians) was fabricated in the late-medieval period. The above facts would show that the date of the Bṛhaddharma Purāṇa is not much earlier than the seventeenth century. The reference to the stories of Kālaketu and Śrīmanta (III, 16, 45) seems to suggest for it more or less the same age as that of Mukundarāma's Caṇḍīmaṅgala (sixteenth century). It should also be noted that considerable influence of the late-medieval Tantric literature is discernible in this Purāṇa (cf. supra, p. 104, note 1). See Sircar, The Ambaṣṭa Jāti in J.U.P.H.S., XVIII, pp. 148-61.

[3] See History of Bengal (Dacca University), Vol. I, pp. 606-07. Cf.
प्रश्रयं वाग्श्रयं च नैव कुर्यादुद्धया कचित् ।
भगलिङ्गादिशब्दश्च नोचरेत् परमेश्वरम् ॥
उपरेदाश्विने मासि भद्रापूजादिषु द्वि ।
मातृणां सुतानां च सर्वोर्पे न तदापि च ॥
चशक्तिदीक्षितायाश्च शिष्यायाः सन्निधौ न च ।
देवी हि भगवत्येवं भगलिङ्गप्रप्रियाया ॥
तस्मातत्प्रियकाम्यायै तत्पूज्यार्थेव्यया वदेत् ॥

POSTSCRIPT

The *Devībhāgavata*, VII, 38, 5-30, containing an important medieval list of Śākta *tīrthas* (cf. *supra*, p. 66, note 1), is quoted below so that the names may be compared with those in the other lists quoted earlier.

कोलापुरं महास्थानं यत्र लक्ष्मीः सदा स्थिता ।
मातुः पुरं द्वितीयञ्च रेणुकाधिष्ठितं परम् ॥
तुळजापुरं तृतीयं स्यात् सप्तश्रृङ्गं तथैव च ।
हिङ्कुलाया महास्थानं ज्वालामुख्यास्तथैव च ॥
शाकम्भर्याः परं स्थानं भ्रामर्याः स्थानमुत्तमम् ।
श्रीरक्तदन्तिकास्थानं दुर्गास्थानं तथैव च ॥
विन्ध्याचलनिवासिन्याः स्थानं सर्वोत्तमोत्तमम् ।
अन्नपूर्णामहास्थानं काञ्चीपुरमनुत्तमम् ॥
भीमादेव्याः परं स्थानं विमलास्थानमेव च ।
श्रीचन्द्रलामहास्थानं कौशिकीस्थानमेव च ॥
नीलाम्बायाः परं स्थानं नीलपर्वतमस्तके ।
जाम्बूनदेश्वरीस्थानं तथा श्रीनगरं शुभम् ॥
गुह्यकाल्या महास्थानं नेपाले यत् प्रतिष्ठितम् ।
मीनाक्ष्याः परमं स्थानं यच्च प्रोक्तं चिदम्बरे ॥
वेदारण्यं महास्थानं सुन्दर्या समधिष्ठितम् ।
एकाम्बरं महास्थानं परशक्त्या प्रतिष्ठितम् ॥
मदालसापरं स्थानं योगेश्वर्यास्तथैव च ।
तथा नीलसरस्वत्याः स्थानं चीनेषु विश्रुतम् ॥
वैद्यनाथे तु बगलास्थानं सर्वोत्तमं मतम् ।
श्रीमच्छीभुवनेश्वर्या मणिद्वीपं मम स्मृतम् ॥
श्रीमन्त्रिपुरभैरव्याः कामाख्या योनिमण्डलम् ।
भूमण्डले क्षेत्ररत्नं महामायाधिवासितम् ॥
* * * *
गायत्र्याश्च परं स्थानं श्रीमत्पुष्करमीरितम् ।
अमरेशे चण्डिका स्यात् प्रभासे पुष्करेक्षिणी (°क्षणा) ॥
नैमिषे तु महास्थाने देवी सा लिङ्गधारिणी ।
पुरुह्रूता पुष्कराक्षे आषाढौ च रतिस्तथा ॥
चण्डमुण्डी महास्थाने दक्षिणी परमेश्वरी ।
भारभूतौ भवेद् भूतिर्नाकुले नकुलेश्वरी ॥
चन्द्रिका तु हरिश्चन्द्रे श्रीगिरौ शाङ्करी स्मृता ।
जप्येश्वरे त्रिशूला स्यात् सूक्ष्मा आम्रातकेश्वरे ॥

श्राङ्गेरौ तु महाकाले गर्वाणी मध्यमाभिधे ।
केदाराख्ये महाच्छेने देवी सा मार्गदायिनी ॥
भैरवाख्ये भैरवी सा गयायां मङ्गला स्मृता ।
स्थाणुप्रिया कुरुच्छेत्रे स्वायम्भुव्यपि नाकुले ॥
कनखले भवेदुग्रा विश्वेशा विमलेश्वरे ।
अट्टहासे महानन्दा महेन्द्रे तु महान्तका ॥
भीमे भौमेश्वरी प्रोक्ता स्थाने वस्त्रापथे पुनः ।
भवानी श्राङ्गेरौ प्रोक्ता रुद्राणी खर्डकोटिके ॥
अविमुक्ते विशालाक्षी महाभागा महालये ।
गोकर्णे भद्रकर्णौ स्याद्भद्रा स्याद्भद्रकर्णके ॥
उत्पलाक्षी सुवर्णाक्षे स्याखोग्रा स्यागूसंज्ञिके ।
कमलालये तु कमला प्रचण्डा छगलण्डके ॥
कुरण्डले त्रिसन्ध्या स्यान्माकोटे मुकुटेश्वरी ।
मण्डलेग्रे साण्डकी स्यात् काली कालञ्जरे पुनः ॥
श्रङ्कुकर्णो ध्वनिः प्रोक्ता स्थूला स्यात् स्थूलकेश्वरे ।
हानिनां हृदयाम्भोजे हृच्छेखा परमेश्वरी ॥

INDEX

Abdhisaṅgama 80
Abhayā 27, 69
Abul Fazl, on the Pīṭhas 14
Ācārya-Sātu 77, 70
Acchoda, Achchhabal in Kashmir 28, 70, 80
Adhirājendra, Cola king 25n
Ādinātha 81
Ādipīṭha 22n, 81
Aditipura 81
Āditya 81, 105
Adrikula 32n, 81
Advayasiddhi 17
Ādyādināthapīṭha 22n
Ādyantapura 27n, 81
Ādyā Śakti 3n
Āgamavāgīśa Kṛṣṇānanda 74-80
Āgameśvarī 74, 75n
Āgameśvarī-talā at Śrīdhāma Navadvīpa 74
Agasty-āśrama, Agastipurī near Nāsik 26n, 28n, 66n, 81
Aghoraghaṇṭa 10n
Ahicchatra 16
Ahom 16
Ai, Kāmarūpa goddess 16n
Allā 27n, 81
Aileyaka-vana 81
Aindrī 28n.
'Ain-i-Akbarī 14, 16n, 34n, 80, 82, 86-87, 92
Airāvatī. Irāvatī 29n, 81
Aitareya Brāhmaṇa 5, 71
Akampāditya-pīṭha 22n
Akbar 14
Akhilavardhinī 30n
Akhileśvarī 30n, 38n
Akṣayā 28n
Akṣayādya-vaṭa 25n
Akṣayagrīva 19, 20n, 81
Akṣayavaṭa 25n, 28n, 66n, 81
Ālāpura, 18, 19n, 81
Albīrūnī 6n, 10n, 15, 25n
'Alī 25
Allahabad pillar inscription 15
Āma, king of Kanauj 25n
Amala, same as Malaya 27, 67
Āma-Nāgabhaṭa 25n
Amara 35-36, 41, 45n, 47n
Amarakaṇṭaka, source of Sone and Narmadā 25n, 27, 28n, 66n, 69, 81
Amaranātha, *tīrtha* in Kashmir 44n

Amaraparvata, same as Meru 81
Amareśa, on south bank of Narmadā 28n, 31n, 81, 107
Amareśapura 22n
Amareśī 81
Amarī 36, 41, 47n
Ambā 28n
Ambara, modern Amber in Rajasthan 27, 36, 47n, 60, 67, 81
Ambaṣṭha, their relation with Bengal Vaidyas 106
Ambikā, goddess at Ambikā-Kālnā in Burdwan Dist. 3 and n, 11n, 30n, 35, 37, 40, 44, and n, 48 and n, 57, 59-60, 62-63, 81, 103
Ambikāpīṭha 22n
Ambujākṣapura 22n
Ambujapura 81
amma, mother 3n
Amoghākṣī 27, 68
Āmrātakeśvara, 20, 21n, 22n, 23n, 31n, 81, 107
Amṛtā 27-28, 37, 57n, 69-70
Amṛtakauśika 81
Amṛtākṣa 37, 57
Anala 36, 40, 53 and n, 60
Ānandapīṭha 22n, 81
Ānandarāma 79
Ānandārṇava Tantra 17n, 80
Anaṅga 28, 69n, 82
Anaṅgavajra, son of king Gopāla 12
Anantapura 22n, 81
Anantavarman Coḍagaṅga 25n
Aṅga, East Bihar 18, 81
Aṅganā 28, 69, 82
aṅga-nyāsa 7n
aṅga-pratyaṅga of Devī 35-66
Animāpura 22n, 81
Aniruddhapura, 22n, 81
Annadāmaṅgala 3, 23, 35, 39, 42, 43n, 51n 59
Annapurṇā 28n, 41, 81, 107
Antarvedi, Ganges-Yamuna Doab between Prayāga and Haridvāra 18, 81
Anu-Bel-Ea, trinity of Babylonians 17n
Aparājitā 30n
Aparārka 12n
Aparṇā 3 and n, 36, 40, 54 and n, 61, 65, 82
Apte, V. S. 28n
Araṇya 81

THE ŚĀKTA PĪṬHAS

Arbuda, Mt. Abu 20, 21n, 22, 23n,81
Ardhanālaka 81
Ardhanārīśvara 24
Arogā 27, 69
Arogyā 27, 69n
Artemes 20n
Arundhatī 28, 70
Aruṇekṣaṇā 29n
Āryāvarta 30n, 81
Asitāṅga, Aśitāṅga 28n, 36, 40, 52 and n, 60
Aśoka-stūpa, at Puṣkalāvatī 10n
Assam tribes 16
Aṣṭādaśapīṭha 18 80-100
Asurāntakapura 22n, 81
Āśusiddhipura, 22n, 81
Aśvamedhapura 81
Aśvaprada, hill near Gauhati 81
Aśvatīrtha, near Kanauj 26n, 81
Aśvattha 28, 70, 82
Atharvaśiras Upaniṣad 10n
Atharvaveda 102-03
Atiśaṅkarī 27, 69n
Ātmapīṭha 11
Aṭṭahāsa in Birbhum Dist. 21 and n, 22n, 23n, 30n, 32n, 37, 38n, 39, 41, 43n, 57 and n, 82, 108
Aujasa 82
Aurasa 82
Auṣadhi 28, 70n
Ausaja 66n
Avantī, Ujjayinī and the country round it 82
Avantī, goddess 37, 40, 55 and n, 61
Avanty-āśrama 26n, 82
Avimukta, same as Vārāṇasī 32n, 82, 108
Ayodhyā in Faizabad Dist., U.P. 17, 19 and n, 27n, 30n, 41, 64, 82

Badal pillar inscription 9n
Badarī, Badrīnāth in Gahrwal 19 and n, 26n, 28, 30, 70, 82
Bagalā, Bagalāmukhī 48n, 60, 63
Bagchi, P. C. 12n, 101n
Bāhudā, a tributary of the Rāptī 82
Bāhulā, Bāhulā, at Ketugrām in Burdwan Dist. 35, 40, 46 and n, 59, 82
Bahulākṣī 40
Baidyanātha 26n
Bālīḍāṅgā, near Dhaniākhāli in Hooghly Dist. 33 and n, 34, 82
Balipriyā 30n
Balipura, 22n, 82
Ballālasena, 12n
Banerjea, J. N. 11, 101
Banerji, B. N. 33n
Barbara 20n

Baṭakeśvara 62
Bāul of Bengal 24
Beṇā, tributary of the Kṛṣṇā 28, 70,82
Betāi Caṇḍī of Betor near Sibpur in Howrah Dist. 24n
Bhadra 27, 67, 82
Bhadrā 27, 28n, 41, 64-65, 67
Bhadrakāleśvara 26n, 82
Bhadrakālī, Bhadrakālikā, 27 29n, 30n, 31n, 63, 67n, 82
Bhadrakarṇa, Karnali on the Narmadā 82
Bhadrakarṇī, Bhadrakarṇikā 27, 29n, 31n, 32n, 67, 108
Bhadrasena 36, 40, 53 and n, 61, 64
Bhadrāsundarī 27, 68
Bhadrāśva 31n
Bhadreśvara 26n, 27, 29n, 41, 67n, 82
Bhaga 5, 6 and n, 8, 10n, 71-73
Bhagavadgītā 102
Bhagavat 105
Bhāgavata Purāṇa, 6, 73
Bhagavatī, deity possessing *bhaga* 8, 82, 105
Bhairava, associated with Devī 3, 7, 11, 24-25, 32, 35-66, 80, 82, 104
Bhairava-parvata in W. Malwa 37, 40, 55 and n, 61, 82
Bhairavī 40, 48n, 108
Bhandarkar, D. R. 104
Bhandarkar, R. G. 10n, 75
Bhañja kings 104
Bharatabhāṣya 12n
Bhāratacandra, author of *Annadāmaṅgala*, 3, 4n, 23, 37n, 39, 42, 50n, 58n
Bharatāśrama 28, 29n 69, 82
Bhāratī 29n
Bhāskaravarman 15
Bhattacharya, B. 12n, 76
Bhava 36, 50 and n, 60, 102
Bhavabhūti 10n, 16
Bhāvacūḍāmaṇi 4 and n
Bhavānī, goddess 15, 27, 30n, 32, 38n, 40, 47 and n, 60, 62-63, 67, 83, 87, 104, 108
Bhīmā, Bhīmādevī 9 and n, 28, 41, 69, 104, 107
Bhīmākālī 38n
Bhīmalocana 35, 39, 43, 59
Bhīmapīṭha, 32n
Bhīmarūpā 37, 41, 54 and n, 61
Bhīmaśaṅkara, at Ḍākinī near Poona, 46n
Bhīmā-tīrtha, Bhīmāstāna near Pañcanada (Punjab) 8, 9 and n, 11 and n
Bhīmeśvarī 32n, 108
Bhīruka 35, 40, 46, 60

INDEX

Bhīru-parvata 37, 55n, 82
Bhīṣaṇa 28n, 35, 40, 45 and n, 59, 62
Bhogeśvarī 39n
Bhogī, voluntary victim for sacrifice 16n
Bhoja I, Gurjara-Pratihāra king 25n, 105
Bhramarāmbā, Bhramarāmbikā 18, 19n, 20n, 54n
Bhramaravāsinī 20 and n
Bhrāmarī 20n, 36-37, 40-41, 47, 55 and n, 60-61, 63, 65, 107
Bhṛgu 21 and n, 23n, 73
Bhṛgupura, Bhṛgupurī, Balia in U. P. 38n, 82
Bhṛgutuṅga 26n, 66n
Bhūtapati 104
Bhūteśa 36, 41, 53 and n, 60
Bhuvaneśī 13n, 36, 41, 48 and n, 50, 60, 64-65
Bhuvaneśvara 65
Bhuvaneśvarī 31n, 38n, 48n, 107
Bībī Nānī 85
Bijāpur 82
Bilva, Bilvaka (Vilvaka) 26-27, 66, 83, 90
Binduka 66n
Bramhakalā 28, 70
Brahman 6, 11n, 24, 28, 70
Brāhmaṇa 5-6
Brahmānanda 18n, 25n, 75-76, 77n
Brahmāṇḍa Purāṇa 5
Brahmāṇī 28n, 29n, 38n, 83, 88
Brahmaputra river 13n
Brahmaśiras 29 n, 83
Brahm-āsya 83
Brahmavaivarta Purāṇa 6n, 106 and n
Brahmāvarta 26n, 30n, 83
Brahmayāmala 17n
Brāhmī 28n
Bṛhaddharma Purāṇa 48n, 106n
Bṛhan-Nīlatantra 17n, 20n, 22n, 25n, 28n, 37n, 39n, 80-100
Bṛhatsaṁhitā 3n, 10n, 105
Bsam-yas monastery 16, 17n
Buddha 7, 10n, 48n, 105

Caitraratha, 27, 67, 83
Cakradhāriṇī 41, 66, 83
Cakradvīpa, 41, 63, 66
Cakrapāṇi 40, 65, 105
Cakravartin of Yādava line 79
Cālukya 105
Cāmuṇḍā 10n, 16, 28n, 30n
Cāmuṇḍā Tantra 48n
Caṇḍa 28n, 36-37, 40, 53 and n, 57, 61
Caṇḍā 30n
Caṇḍadāyikā 41
Caṇḍamahāroṣaṇa Tantra 11n
Caṇḍamuṇḍī 107

Candana-parvata 38n, 83
Caṇḍanāyikā 65
Caṇḍapura 39n, 83
Caṇḍeśa 37, 41, 57n, 65, 73
Caṇḍeśvara 41
Caṇḍeśvarī 41
Caṇḍī, section of Mārkaṇḍeya Purāṇa 20
Caṇḍī, Caṇḍikā 12 and n, 13 and n, 17 and n, 27, 28n, 31n, 32n, 35, 40, 46, 59, 69, 81, 86, 107
Caṇḍīmaṅgala of Mukundarāma 6 and n, 24 n, 33, 34n, 49n, 80-100
Caṇḍīpura 22n, 83
Candrabhāgā, Chenab 28, 29n, 37, 40, 55 and n, 61, 66n, 70, 83
Candracūḍāmaṇi 4 and n
Candragarbhasūtra 7
Candraprabhā 106n
Candrapura, Chanda in Madhya Pradesh 21 and n, 22n, 23n, 38n, 83
Candrāsthira 20, 21n, 83
Candrikā 27, 68, 107
Carasthira, Carasthita 20, 21n, 23n, 83
Carcikā 28n
Carcitānanda 41
Caṭṭagrāma 40
Caṭṭala, Chittagong in East Bengal 36, 47 and n, 60, 83
Caturānanda, Sahajayāna concept of 'four' 11n
Catuṣpīṭha conception 11 and n
Catuṣpīṭha-parvata, near Jājpur in Orissa 11n
Catuṣpīṭha Tantra 11
Cauhāra 18, 83
Chagala, Chāgala, Chagalaṇḍa, Chāgalāṇḍa, Chāgalaṇḍa,
Chagalaṇḍaka 27, 32n, 69 and n, 83, 108
Chāgaliṅga, 26n, 27, 30n, 67n, 83
Chatreśvarī 39n
Chatterjee, R. N. 75
Chatterji, S. K. 10n
Chāyāchatrapura 21 and n, 23n, 83
Chāyāpura 22n, 83
Chinnamastā 48n
Christ 25
Chutiyā of Assam 15
Cidambaram 107
Citrakūṭa in Bundelkhand 27, 68, 83
Citta 83

Ḍākinī 105
Dakṣa 5-6, 11n, 72
Dakṣa (Dakṣiṇa)-Pañcanada 83
Dakṣa-Prajāpati 5-6
Dakṣa-yajña-bhaṅga, section of Mukundarāma's Caṇḍīmaṅgala 33

112　THE ŚĀKTA PĪṬHAS

Dakṣa-yajña-nāśa, legend of 5-6, 70-73
Dākṣāyaṇī 3n, 35, 40, 45, 59, 62
Dakṣiṇā 29n
Dakṣiṇa-Kālī image 74n
Dakṣiṇa- Pañcanada 66n
Ḍāmarī 65
Ḍāmunyā, in Burdwan Dist. 34
Daṇḍapāṇi 37, 41, 56, 65
Daṇḍinī 107
Dārukeśa 83
Daśāvatāra of Viṣṇu 39
Daśavidyā 3n
Dehalikā, Dehalikāśrama 28n, 83
Deogarh rock inscription 105
Deori, priest 15-16
Devadāruvana, Badrīnāth in Himalayas or Aundh in Deccan 28, 69, 83
Devagarbhā 36, 52 and n, 60
Devakī 27, 30n, 68
Devakoṭa, Devakoṭṭa, Devakūṭa 21 and n, 22n, 23n, 83
Devaloka 83
Devamātā 27, 69
Devanātha 75
Devī 3, 17, 24, 32-33, 35, 80, 100-106; presiding over Pīṭha 35-66
Devībhāgavata 6, 11n, 20n, 25, 66-70, 107
Devidaikoṭha 18, 83
Devikā river 27, 68
Devikā-taṭa 83
Devīkoṭa 38n, 83
Devīkoṭṭa, modern Bangarh in Dinajpur Dist. 17-18, 83
Devīkūṭa 13n, 17, 83
Devī-tīrtha 9n
Dharā 28, 70n
Dharmamāṇikya, king of Tripurā 47n
Dhṛti 28, 70
Dhūmāvatī 48n
Dhūminī 48n
Dhvani 28, 70
Dikkaravāsinī 13n, 17 and n, 64, 87
Dikṣu, Dikhu river 13n
Divine Mothers 28 and n, 70, 105
Drāviḍa 28n, 83
Durgā 3 and n, 25, 27n, 30n, 31n, 48n, 105-06; her worship 50n; tributary of Sābarmatī 83
Durmadā, v. l. Narmadā 28n
Dvāravatī, modern Dwarka 27 and n, 68, 84
Dyaus 5

Egypt 7
Eight Bhairavas 28n
Ekāgra 84

Ekāmra, Ekāmraka, Bhuvaneśvara in Orissa 20, 21n, 22n, 23n, 27, 38n, 67, 84
Ekavīrā 27, 68
Elāpura Ellora 21 and n, 22n, 23n 30n, 38n, 84
Elliot 14n

Fatimā 25
Female organ 3n, 7
Fīrūz, Sulṭān 15n

Gait, E. 16
Gajapura 22n
Gaṇakṣetra 31n, 84
Gaṇapati, 102
Gaṇḍaka 35, 46n, 59, 84
Gaṇḍakī, tributary of Ganges 35, 40, 46 and n, 59, 84
Gandhamādana, Himalayan peak 27, 67, 84
Gandhāra (Rawalpindi-Peshawar region) 9, 10n, 16
Gaṇeśvara 27n, 73, 84
Gaṅgā, Ganges 27, 28n, 66n, 68, 84
Gaṅgāvilva 84
Gaṅgādvāra, 26n, 27, 30n, 66n, 68, 72, 84
Gaṅgārāmācala 84
Gaṅgāsāgara-saṅgama 19 and n, 26n, 65, 66n, 84
Gaṅgāvāmācala 30n, 84
Gaṅgodbheda 84
garbhādhāna 8
Gargakṣetra 31n
Gargoccheda 84
Gauḍa 18, 84
Gauḍavaha 20
Gaurī 3, 27, 29n, 38n, 39n, 67; worshipped by Mongoloids of Himalayas 3n, 9
Gaurī-guru, father of Gaurī 9n
Gaurīśekhara 84
Gaurīśikhara 8, 9 and n, 11, 15, 41, 49, 63
Gautameśvara 26n, 84
Gaveśvarī, Gavīśvarī 28n, 30n
Gayā 9, 25n, 27, 28n, 68n, 84, 108
Gayāśīrṣa 66n
Gāyatrī 28 and n, 30n, 36, 38n, 40, 51 and n, 60, 64, 70, 107
Ghaṇṭākarṇa 19, 20n, 84
Ghaṇṭeśvara-Śiva 56n
Ghāṭaśilā, between Kharagpur and Tatanagar 33 and n, 84
Ghoṣa, modern Gusha 15

INDEX

Ghṛṣṇeśa, at Śivālaya (Ellora) 47n
Giri-pīṭha 23, 84
Giriśa 3n
Godāśrama 27, 68, 84
Godāvarī 19 and n, 27, 29n, 40, 65, 66n, 68n, 84
Godāvarī-tīra 37, 55 and n, 61
Gode 12n
Gokarṇa, modern Gendia near Goa 21 and n, 22n, 23n, 27, 32n, 38n, 67, 85, 108
Gomatī 27, 29n, 66n, 67, 85
Gomanta, in Goa region 27, 67, 85
Gopāla, founder of Pāla dynasty 12, 75
Gopalan, R. 10n
Gopāla-Pañcānana 79
Gopatha Brāhmaṇa 5, 72
Gorakṣacāriṇī 19 and n, 85
Gorakṣakāriṇī 19 and n, 85
Govardhana 19, 20n, 26n, 30n, 85
Gṛhyasūtra 102-03
Guhyakālī 31n, 107
Guhyapīṭha 11
Guhyātiguhya Tantra 48n
Guptapura 22n
Guptasādhana Tantra 76
Gupta dynasty 5, 8
Gurjara-Pratihāra 105
Guru Tantra 76
Haft Iqlim 16n

Haṁsatīrtha, modern Humza and Nagar 26n, 85
Haṁseśvarī 30n
Hara 35, 40, 45 and n, 59
Haratīrtha, Harakṣetra or Bhuvaneśvara 30n, 85
Hari 35, 45n, 79
Haridrāpīṭha 22n, 38n, 85
Harīdvāra 26n, 40, 65
Hari-Hara 24, 41
Harir̥ākṣī 30n
Harīnātha 79
Haripriyā 27, 68n
Hariścandra, Hariścandrapura 26n, 27, 30n, 68, 85, 107
Hārīta 26n, 30n, 85
Hārītī, Buddhist goddess 10n
Harivaṁśa 20n, 106
Harmacandra 27, 68n, 85
Haroccheda 85
Harodbheda 85
Hastināpura 21 and n, 23n, 27, 38n, 67, 85
Hayagrīva 19, 20n, 85
Hayakṣetra 85
Hazra, R. C. 10n, 12n

113

Hemakūṭa, part of N. Himalayas 28, 70, 85
Hevajra Tantra 12 and n, 80-100
Himācala 9
Himālaya 3n, 9 and n, 22n, 27-28, 67, 69, 85
Hima-parvata 39n
Himavat 85
Hiṅgalāja, Hiṅglāja, Hiṅgulā, Hiṅgulāta, modern Hinglaj in Baluchistan 18, 19 and n, 27n, 33n, 34n, 35, 39, 43 and n, 59, 62, 85, 107
Hiraṇyagarbha-mahādāna 8
Hiraṇyākṣa 27, 68n, 85
Hiraṇyapura, Herdoun(Hindaun) in Jaipur 21 and n, 22n, 23, 39n, 85
Hiuen Tsang 9, 10n, 11 and n, 15, 104
Hṛṣīkeśa 19 and n, 85
Human sacrifice 10n, 16; at Raṅkiṇī temple 33n
Huviṣka 3n, 104

Ilānta 85
Ilāntendupura 22n
Ilodayagiri 22n, 85
Incest of Prajāpati 5-6
Indirāpura 22n, 86
Indrabhūti 16-17
Indrākṣī 37, 41, 57
Indrānandapura 22n, 86
Indrāṇī 28, 70, 86
Indranīla 26, 30n, 86
Indrapāla, records of 15n
Indreśvarī 39n
Indreśvara 86
Indreśvarīpura 86
Indumatī 29n, 86
Indupura 86
Induvatīpura 86
Induvijayapura 22n, 86
Irāvatī 29n, 66n, 81, 86
Īśāna 35, 45n, 86, 102
Īśānendīśvarīpura 22n
Īśānyaiśapura 22n, 86
Isis, sister and wife of Osiris 7
Isis-Osiris-Horus, triad of Egyptians 17n
Iṣṭanābha 86
Iṣṭanāmabhapura 22n
Iṣṭapura 86
Īśvara 36, 41, 47 and n, 86
Īśvarī 29n
Īśvarayoga 86

Jaganmātā, in Yoni form 3n, 30n
Jagannātha 12 and n, 35, 41, 45

and n, 46n, 59, 65; temple at
 Puri 25n
Jahājapura, modern Jājpur 19 and n
Jāhnavī 86
Jāhnavī-saṅgama 29n, 86
Jaintia 16
Jāhnavī-taṭa 39n, 86
Jājpur 86
Jālandhara, in Punjab 45n, 12 and
 n, 13 and n, 14 and n, 16, 17 and
 n, 18, 19 and n, 21 and n, 22n,
 23n, 35, 38n, 40, 44, 59, 62, 69,
 84, 104
Jālandharabandha 12n
Jālandhara-giri 13
Jālandharī 14
Jalapriyā 27, 68
Jālaśaila, seat of Caṇḍī and Mahādeva 12 and n, 13, 86
Jalasthala 37, 55
Jaleśvara, in Balasore in Orissa
 12n, 21 and n, 23n, 86
Jaleśvarī 12n
Jāmadagnya 48n
Jambudvīpa 7
Janasthāna, Nasik region on Godāvarī 37, 40, 55, 61, 86
Japyeśvara 31n, 86, 107
Jarrett 14
jātakarman 8
Jaya 35, 40, 45n, 59
Jayā 27, 67
Jayadurgā 35, 37, 40, 45 and n, 56,
 59, 62
Jayamaṅgalā 30n, 38n
Jayanārāyaṇa 79
Jayanta 26n, 86
Jayantā 86
Jayantī 27, 30n, 36, 40, 50 and n,
 67, 86; Pīṭha at Sylhet in E.
 Bengal 50n, 60, 63
Jayantikā, Jayantī 21 and n, 23n, 86
Jayapura, Jaipur in Rajasthan 38n, 86
Jñānārṇava Tantra 18 and n, 20, 23,
 76, 80-100
Jñānasiddhi 16
Job Charnock 34n
Jolā caste 6n
Julāhā, weaver 6n
Jvālā 86
Jvālāmukhī 14 and n, 17, 19 and
 n, 27n, 31n, 33 and n, 34n, 35,
 38n, 40, 44 and n, 59, 62, 86, 107
Jvalantī 17, 86
Jyotiḥsara 86
Jyotirliṅga 46n

Kachāri 16
Kadamba 105

Kailāsa 21 and n, 22n, 23n, 38n, 87
Kakati, B. 15n
Kāla, time or death 3n, 36, 57
Kalā 28, 70n
Kālā 28, 70
Kālabhairava 47, 64
Kālamādhava 36, 40, 52 and n,
 60, 87
Kalambakubja, Kalambakuñjaka
 26n, 87
Kālāmukha 10n
Kālanidrā 3n
Kālañjara, in Banda Dist., U. P.
 27 and n, 67, 87, 108
Kālapīṭha 36, 50n
Kalāvatī 31n, 38n
Kālaviveka 105
Kāleśvara 21 and n, 23n, 87
Kalhaṇa 15, 20
Kālī 3 and n, 15-16, 20n, 27, 29n,
 36-37, 35n, 40, 48n, 52 and n,
 56, 60, 74-75
Kālidāsa 5
Kālīghāṭa 24 and n, 24n, 37, 39,
 41, 56, 87
Kālīghaṭṭa 27n, 31n, 39n, 87
Kālikā 24, 36, 41, 50 and n, 63, 87
Kālikā Purāṇa 6 and n, 12 and n,
 13n, 16, 17 and n, 28n, 80-100
Kālindī 28n
Kāliṅga 18, 73, 87
Kālīpīṭha 36-37, 41, 43n, 50 and n,
 56n, 60, 63, 87
Kālīpura 87
Kalkattā 34n
Kalki 48n
Kīlodaka 26n, 29n, 66n, 87
Kālya 27n
Kalyāṇī 27, 67n, 68
Kāmagiri 13n, 36, 47, 48n, 63, 87
Kāmākhyā 13 and n, 14, 15 and n,
 16n, 17, 33, 34n, 36, 46, 47 and
 n, 48n, 63, 87
Kāmakoṭa 38n, 87
Kāmakoṭi 87
Kāmakoṭṭa 21 and n, 22n, 23n, 87
Kāmākṣī 27, 67
Kāmakūṭa hill 13n
Kamalā 19, 20n, 27, 38n, 40, 48 and
 n, 60, 63, 67, 108
Kamalākṣī 28n, 32n
Kamalālaya 27, 32n, 67, 108
Kāmarūpa 9, 12 and n, 13, and n,
 14 and n, 15, 16n, 17 and n, 19,
 20n, 22n, 23n, 25n, 27, 30-31,
 33, 34n, 37n, 39-40, 43n, 48n,
 49 and n, 63, 67, 87, 104
Kāmeśa 37n
Kāmeśvara 13 and n, 21 and n, 23n,
 48n, 87, 104

INDEX
115

Kāmeśvarī 13 and n, 38n, 87
Kāmodaka 26n, 87
Kāmrāj 87
Kāmukā 27, 67n
Kāmukī 27, 67n
Kanakakāñcī 31n
Kanakāmaraparvata 38n, 31, 87
Kanakhala, near Hardwar 29n, 31n, 66n, 87, 108
Kāñcana, probably Kunchenjinga 13n
Kāñcī 17, 27n, 31n, 36, 40, 52 and n, 60, 64-87
Kāñcikāpurī 88
Kāñcīpura 107
Kangra 14
Kañja, same as Kunchenjinga 13n
Kaṇv-āśrama 26n, 66n, 88
Kanyā 38n
Kanyakāpura 38n
Kānyakubja 20, 21n, 22n, 23n, 27, 38n, 67, 88
Kanyāpura 88
Kanyāśrama 36, 37n, 51 and n, 60, 64, 88
kapāla 10n
Kapālakuṇḍalā 10n
Kapālamocana 28, 69, 88
Kapālin 28n, 35, 37, 40-41, 45 and n, 54n, 59, 61-62
Kāpālika 10n, 16, 104
Kāpālikavrata 10
Kapālinī 37, 54 and n
Kapilā 27, 67
Kapilāmbara 35, 40, 46 and n, 60
Kapileśvar 29n
Kapileśvara 35, 46n
Karālā 16
Karatoyā, river of North Bengal 13n, 49
Karatoyā-taṭa 36, 40, 54 and n, 61, 64-65, 88
Karavīra, Sukkur in Sind or Kolhapur in Maharashtra 27, 32n, 35, 44 and n, 69, 88
Karavīrapura 26n, 30n
Karkoṭa 27, 67n, 88
Karṇasūtra 19 and n, 88
Karṇāṭa 37n, 39, 43n
Karṇa-tīrtha 26n, 88
Kar, Sambhunath 19 and n
Kārttikeya 27, 69, 88
Kāśī 19 and n, 28n, 34n, 88
Kāśīnātha 79
Kāśmīra 16, 18, 19n, 20, 21n, 23n, 28, 35, 40, 44 and n, 59, 62, 69, 88
Kaṭaka 41, 88
Kaṭakeśvarī 41, 88
Kātyāyanī 3n, 12 and n, 13 and n,
17, 30n, 31n, 36, 38n, 53n, 64, 104
Kaulagiri 18, 88
Kaumārī 28n
Kauśikā 81
Kauśikī 3n, 26n, 29n, 66, 88, 107
Kauśītakipriya 29n
Kāverī 26n, 29n, 88
Kāvyamīmāṁsā 56n, 87
Kāyāvarohaṇa 28, 69, 88
Kedāra 21 and n, 22n, 23n, 26n, 27, 31n, 38n, 46n, 66n, 67, 88, 108
Kedāreśvara 88
Keśāi Khāti 15-16
Keśajāla 36, 41, 53n, 60, 88
Khotan 16
Kirātārjunīya 9n
Kirīṭa 27n, 31n, 36, 50 and n, 60, 64, 88
Kirīṭakoṇā 36, 41, 50n, 88
Kirīṭeśvarī 31n
Kirīṭin 41
Kīrtimatī 27, 67
Kishenganga river 15
Kiṣkindhya-parvata 28, 69, 88
Koch 16
Kokāmukha 40, 89
Kokeśvara 40
Kokeśvarī 40, 63
Kolāpura 107
Kolhāpura 18, 19n
Kol 20n
Kolva-giri (Kaula-giri) 18, 21 and n, 23n, 89
Koṭa 27, 67, 89
Koṭavī 27, 68
Koṭimudrā 18, 89
Koṭitīrtha 27, 68, 89
Koṭṭarī 35, 39, 43, 59
Koṭṭarīśā 35, 43n
Koṭṭavī 35, 43n
Kramadīśvara 36, 40, 50, 60
Krodha 28n
Krodheśa 37, 44n, 56n
Krodhīśa 35, 37, 39, 44, 56, 59, 62
Kṛṣṇa 25, 48n, 74, 75n
Kṛṣṇabenyā, Kṛṣṇbeṇvā 89
Kṛṣṇacandra 17
Kṛṣṇānanda Āgamavāgīśa 23, 74-80
Kṛṣṇanātha 36, 53n
Kṛṣṇaśaraṇa 79
Kṛṣṇaveṇā 26n, 29n
Kṛtaśauca 27, 69, 89
Kṣaṇā 31n
Kṣaṇamocana 30n
Kṣetrādhīśa, same as Bhairava 35
Kṣetravatī 65
Kṣīrikā, Kṣīragrāma 21 and n, 23n, 89
Kṣīragrāma, near Katwa in Burdwan Dist. 19, 20n, 21 and n, 23n, 33

116 THE ŚĀKTA PĪṬHAS

and n, 36, 41, 49n, 60, 89
Kṣīrakaṇṭha 36, 49n, 60
Kṣīrakhaṇḍa 36, 41, 49
Kṣīra-pīṭha 38n
Kṣīrapura 22n, 89
Kubjāmra, Kubjāmraka 27, 66n, 68n, 89
Kubjikā Tantra 19 and n, 20n, 39, 80-100
Kulānta, Kulāntaka 18, 21 and n, 23n, 89
Kulapañjikā 79
Kulārṇava Tantra 18, 77
Kulaśāstradīpikā 79
Kumāra 37, 40-41, 56n, 65, 89
Kumāradhāma 28n
Kumāradhārā 66n
Kumārākhya 26n
Kumārasambhava of Kālidāsa 5
Kumārī 27, 37, 38n, 41, 56, 61, 65, 68
Kumuda 28, 70n, 89
Kumudā 27, 67
Kuñcapaṭṭana 89
Kuñja-giri, same as Kañja 13n
Kūpānta, Kulānta 21 and n, 23n, 89
Kuraṇḍala 108
Kūrma 48n
Kūrma Purāṇa 5, 10n, 73
Kurukṣetra 19 and n, 29n, 31n, 36, 41, 51 and n, 60, 63, 89, 108
Kurukullā 16
Kuśadvīpa 28, 70, 89
Kuśapriyā 30n
Kuśavarta 26n, 27n, 30n, 66n, 89
Kuśodaka 28, 70
Kuṭuvī 62

Lagnikāśrama 26n, 89
Lakhyā, same as Lākṣā river 13n
Lākṣā 13n
Lakṣmaṇoccheda, °odbheda 89
Lakṣmī 107
Lakṣīṁkarā 16
Lalitā 26n, 27 ı, 29n, 36, 50, 60, 63, 67-68, 89
Lalitakāntā 17 and n, 87
Lalitapura 29n, 89
Lambakarṇa 37, 55, and n, 61
Laṅkā 18, 19n, 37, 39, 41, 43n, 57, 89
Lévi, S. 12n
Liṅga, male organ 7-8, 89, 101
Liṅgadhāriṇī 27, 66 and n, 107
Liṅgākhya 31n, 39n
Liṅgavāhinī 31n
Lokeśvara 16
Lolā 27, 69
Lomakhaṇḍa 65

Ma, Cappadocian goddess 20n

Madālasā 107
Madanta 30n, 89
Madantī, Madantikā 30n, 89
Mādhava 19, 20n, 64-65, 89
Mādhava-vana, Mādhavī-vana 27, 68, 89
Mādhavī 27, 30n, 31n, 67
Madhupurī, same as Mathurā 17, 19 and n, 89
Madhurā, same as Mathurā 30n, 89
Madhusūdana 79
Madotkaṭā 27, 67, 83
Madreśvara 27, 67n, 90
Magadha, Māgadha, 18, 37n, 39, 57n, 90
Mahābala 90
Mahābhadrā 30n, 82
Mahābhāgā 17, 27, 69
Mahābhārata 5, 8, 9 and n, 13n, 25, 73, 103-04
Mahabhāṣya 102
Mahābhīmā 41, 65
Mahābodhi 90
Mahābuddhi 29n, 30n
Mahācala 32n
Mahādeva 10n, 12 and n, 14, 102
Mahādevī 27, 31n, 37, 40, 56n, 61, 68
Mahāgaṅgā 26n, 66n, 90
Mahāgaurī 13n, 15n, 48, 87, 104
Mahākāla temple at Ujjayinī 27, 40, 46n, 69, 90
Mahākālī 62-63
Mahākāntā 30n
Mahākarṇa 19 and n, 90
Mahāmāyā 3n, 14, 31n, 35-36, 40, 44 and n, 45 and n, 52n, 59, 62
Mahālakṣmī, Pīṭha-goddess 18, 19n, 27, 28n, 36, 39n, 40, 48n, 52, 60, 64, 69, 90
Mahālakṣmīpura 18, 21 and n, 22n, 25n, 90
Mahālaya 27, 32n, 69, 90, 108
Mahāliṅga 27, 67, 90
Mahāl Kalkattā 34n
Mahānāda 26n, 30n, 90
Mahānala 90
Mahānandā 29n, 30n, 32n, 38n, 83, 90, 108
Mahānātha 12 and n
Mahā-Nīlatantra 25n, 58n
Mahāpadmā 27, 69n
Mahāpathapura 90
Mahāpīṭha 39
Mah°pīṭhanirūpaṇa, *Pīṭhanirṇaya* 3 and n, 4 and n, 23-24, 35, 38, 41-42, 59, 80-100
Mahārātri 79n
Maharudra 36, 40, 53, 60
Mahāryā 30n

INDEX

Mahāsena 105
Mahāsiddhi 30n
Mahāśmaśāna, at Padmāvatī in Gwalior (Gird) Dist., M.P. 10n
Mahātīrtha 90
Mahāvana 29n, 90
Mahāvegā 30n
Mahāvidyā 28n, 30n, 38n, 39, 48 and n, 49, 50n, 81
Mahāviṣṇupada 90
Mahāvratin 10n
Mahendra 21 and n, 22n, 23n, 32n, 90, 108
Mahendrapāla I 105
Mahendrapura 90
Mahendravarman I 10n
Māhendrī 28n
Maheśvara 9-10, 31n, 72, 104-05
Maheśvarapura, Māheśvarapura, on Narmadā 16, 27, 69, 90
Maheśvarī, Māheśvarī 27, 28n, 30n, 31n, 38n, 69, 81
Maheśvarīpura, Māheśvarīpura 27, 69n, 90
Mahīpāla 105
Mahiṣamardinī 35, 37, 39, 44, 57, 59, 62, 88
Mahiṣāsura 105
Māhiṣmatī 19, 20n, 90
Mahodara 37, 40, 56 and n, 61, 65
Mahodarī 29n
Māhvara 90
Maināka 30n, 90
Maithila Devanātha 76
Maitras of Maṇḍalajānī 74
Makarandaka 27, 69n, 81, 90
Mākoṭa 27, 32n, 67n
Makran 16
Malakūṭa 16
Mālatī 10n
Mālatīmādhava 10n, 16
Mālava 16, 21 and n, 23n, 30n, 35, 38n, 40, 45n, 90
Malaya 18, 21 and n, 23n, 27, 67, 90
Malay-ācala 27, 68n
Mālinī 30n
Mālinīvijaya 48n
Malladeva Naranārāyaṇa of Kāmtā 76
Mallikārjuna on Śrīśaila 46n, 54n
Mānasa 26n, 27, 29n, 35, 45, 59, 62, 67
Mānas-ācala 27, 68, 90
Manasāmaṅgala 24n, 34n
Mānasa-sarovara 40, 91
Mānava, Mālava 21 and n, 22n, 23n, 90
Mandā 27, 67n
Maṇḍaleśa 108
Maṇḍaleśvara 91
Mandara, Mandāra 27, 31n, 67, 91
Mandasor inscription 105

Māṇḍava 27, 69n
Māṇḍavī 27, 69
Māṇḍavya 27, 69, 91
Māṇḍavyapura, Mandor near Jodhpur 25n
Māṇḍukī 27, 69n
Maṅgalā 27, 31n, 35, 46 and n, 47, 60, 68, 108
Maṅgalacaṇḍī, Maṅgalacaṇḍikā 35, 40, 46n, 62
Maṅgalakoṭa 27n, 31n, 91
Maṅgaleśvarapīṭha 32n,
Maṅgaleśvarī 26, 67n
Maṇibandha, 37n, 39, 40, 43n, 51n, 64, 91
Maṇidvīpa 64
Maṇikarṇikā at Vārāṇasī 36, 51n, 64, 91
Māṇikī 91
Maṇipura 19 and n, 91
Maṇiveda 35-36, 40, 51, 60, 64, 91
Manmatha 28, 70
Mantracūḍāmaṇi 4 and n, 39
Marakaṇṭaka, Marakaṅkaṭa 27, 69, 81, 91
Mārgadāyinī 27, 67, 108
Mārīcī 16
Mārkaṇḍeya Purāṇa 9, 20n, 28n, 104
Markoṭa 27, 67n
Marshall, J. 101
Māruteśa 91
Māruteśvara 21 and n, 22n, 23n
Mātā 27, 28, 69
Mātā Lakṣmī 28, 69
Mātaṅga 91
Mātaṅgavāpī 26n, 66n, 91
Mātaṅgī 29n, 48 and n, 60, 63
Mathurā 27, 68, 91
Mathurānātha 79
Mātṛdarśa 30n, 91
Mātṛgaṇa 26n, 91
mātṛkā 28n
Mātṛ-maṇḍala 10n
Mātṛ-tīrtha 9n
Matsya Purāṇa 5, 25 and n, 66-70
Mattamedhā 28n, 81
Mattavilāsa-prahasana 10n
Māyā 27n, 38n, 91
Māyāpura 21 and n, 22n, 23n, 38n, 91
Māyāpurī 27, 68, 91
Māyāvatī, Pīṭha near Hardwar 17, 19 and n, 91
Medhā 28, 69
Meghabalā 30n
Meghasvanā 30n
Meghavana 26n, 30n, 91
Mehāra, Pargana of Tippera Dist. 3n, 91
Mekalā 18
Mekhalā 18, 63 and n, 91

Mekhalī 63
Meru 91
Merugiri 21 and n, 23 and n, 91
Merupīṭha 23
Merusvanā 3on
Mīnākṣī 107
Mitākṣarā 1on
Mithilā 18, 37, 40, 56 and n, 61, 65, 91
Mohenjodaro 3n, 7, 101-02
Mother-goddess 3 and n, 5, 7-8, 9 and n, 10 and n, 14-17, 20 and n, 25, 43, 101-06; of Mohenjodaro 101-02
Mother of Demons 1on
Mṛgī 27, 69n
Muḥammad Shāh bin Tughlak Shāh, Sulṭān 15n
Mukundarāma, Bengali poet 6, 24n, 33-34
Mukuṭa 28, 70, 91
Mukuṭeśvarī 27, 67, 108
Muṇḍakeśvarī 32n
Muṇḍamālā Tantra 48n
Muṇḍapṛṣṭha 29n, 92
Munīśvara 29n, 92

Nābhigayā, Jājpur 34n, 92
Naḍantikā 66n
Nādavaṭa 92
Nāgabhaṭa II 105
Nāgapura 31n
Nāgapurī 92
Nagarakoṭa 14, 33 and n, 92
Nagarasambhava, Nāgarasambhava 19 and n, 92
Nāga-tīrtha 29n, 92
Nāgeśa, at Dārukavana 47n
Nagna-Śabara 3n
Nagnik-āśrama 26n
Naimiṣ-āraṇya 27, 29n, 66 and n, 92, 107
Naipāla 92
Nakuleśa, , Nakulīśa 36, 41, 50 and n, 60, 63
Nakuleśvarī 107
Nala 36, 41, 47 and n, 60
Nalāhāṭī, Nalhāṭī in Birbhum Dist. 37, 39, 41, 43n, 56 and n, 92
Nalasthāna 41, 92
Nalīśa 36, 50n
Nāmāṣṭottaraśata 80-100
Namrakarṇa 37, 40, 55n
Nana, on Kuṣāṇa coins 43n
Nanaia 2on
Nandā 27, 67
Nandapura 29n, 92
Nandavaṭa 92
Nandataṭa 3on, 92

Nandikeśvara 37, 57 and n
Nandinī 27, 37, 41, 57, 68
Nandipura 37, 39, 41, 43n, 57, 92
Nandīśvara 41
Nandīśvarī 73
Nānyadeva 12n
Narasiṁha 105
Nārasiṁhī 28n
Nārāyaṇī 27, 3on, 36, 40, 53 and n, 60, 64, 68
Nārikela 19 and n, 92
Narmadā 16, 26n, 28n, 29n, 36, 40, 53 and n, 61, 92
Narmadā-tīra 66n
Narmadoccheda 92
Narmadodbheda 92
Navadurgā 40
Navadvīpa 74
Nāyikā 28n
Nepāla 13n, 19 and n, 20, 21n, 22n, 23n, 35, 37n, 40, 45 and n, 59, 62, 92, 107
Nidhi 28, 70
Nīlā 29n
Nīl-ācala 34n, 41, 65, 92
Nīla-parvata 12n, 31n, 38n, 40, 66n, 87, 107
Nīla-Sarasvatī 107
Nīlavāhinī 19, 20n, 92
Nimiṣa 36, 40, 51, 60
Niṣāda 102
Nitambā 27, 69n
Non-Vedic element in Hinduism 100n, 101n
Nṛsiṁha 48n

Oḍiyāna, Uḍḍiyāna in Swat valley 12-13, 92
Oḍḍiyāna 12n, 13n, 17 and n, 92
Oḍra, seat of Kātāyanī and Jagannātha 12 and n, 13 and n, 92
Oghavatī, Āpagā river 26n, 3on, 93
Ommo, on coins of Huviṣka 3n, 103
Oṅkāra-pīṭha 21 and n, 22n, 23n, 38n, 46n, 92
Oṣadhi 28, 70
Osiris myth 7

Padārthādarśa 76
Padma Purāṇa 5, 25, 66-70
Padmasambhava 16, 17n
Padmavajra, author of *Hevajra Tantra* 12
Padmāvatī, Padam Pawaya in Gwalior(Gird)Dist., M.P. 1on, 16
Pākhaṇḍa, Pākhaṇḍin 1on
Palusha 9
Pampāsaras 3on, 93

INDEX

Pañcakaṭī 93
Pañcanada (Punjab) 8, 9n, 29n, 93
Pañcāpsaras 93
Pañcasāgara 36, 40, 53, 60, 93
Pañcatantra 10n
Pañcatīrtha 93
Pañcavarga 30n
Pañcavaṭī 26n, 30n, 93
Pāṇḍarānanā, Pāṇḍavānanā 29n
Pāṇḍu, Pāṇḍya country 29n, 93
Pāṇini 10n, 102
Pāpaharā 40
Pāpamocana 38n
Pāpanāśinī 29n
Pārā 27, 69n
Paramānandā 38n
Parameśvarapura 93
Parameśvarī 27, 31n, 68
Parapīṭha 11
Paraśurāma 79
Pārasya, Persia 38n, 93
Pārā-taṭa 93
Pārāvāra-tīra 93
Parṇa-Śabarī, Buddhist deity borrowed from Parṇa-Śabaras 3n
Pārvatī 3 and n, 20n, 28, 32n, 39n, 41, 70
Pāśupata Yogin 10 and n, 16
Paśupati 72-73, 102
Paśupatinātha of Nepāl 45n
Pātāla 26n, 27, 29n, 68, 93
Pāṭalā 27, 68
Pāṭaleśvarī 19n
Patañjali 10n
Pauṇḍravardhana 20, 21n, 22n, 23n, 37n, 93
Pāvā 27, 69n
Pāvakya, Pārasya 22n
Payoṣṇī river 27, 69, 93
Phalgu-tīrtha 66n
Phallic worship 7, 101
Phullarā 37, 41, 57, 64
Piṇḍāraka, Piṇḍāraka-vana 26n, 28, 30n, 70, 93
Piṅga 93
Piṅgā 26
Piṅgaleśvarī 27, 69
Pīṭhas of Mother-goddess 3-8, 11-16, 17-18, 20 and n, 23-25, 32-66
Pīṭha-devatā, forms of Devī 35
Pīṭhamālā 4 and n
Pīṭhanirṇaya, Mahāpīṭhanirūpaṇa 3 and n, 4 and n, 9, 20n, 23-24, 34-35, 38-39, 41-42, 48n, 59, 80-100
Pīṭhanyāsa, Tantric ritual 4, 7 and n
Pīṭhasthala 3n
Pīṭhatattvanyāsa 14n
Pīṭhavinyāsa 7n
Piyālamārga 93
Plutarch 7

Prabalā 29n
Prabhā 28, 29n, 70
Prabhāsa, Prabhāsakhaṇḍa 26n, 27, 28n, 29n, 31n, 37, 40, 55 and n, 61, 65, 66n, 69, 93
Pracaṇḍā 27, 39n, 41, 69, 83, 108
Pracaṇḍacaṇḍikā 48 and n, 60, 63
Pradyumna 93
Prajāpati 5-6, 71-73
Prajñāpāramitā 11
Pramadā 30n
Prāṇatoṣaṇī Tantra 3, 14n, 23, 25n, 28n, 42, 66n, 76-100
Praṇava 93
Prāṇavallabha 79
Prapā 93
Prasaṅga 93
Pratāpgarh near Javlī 15
Prayāga 18, 19 and n, 21 and n, 22n, 23n, 27, 36, 40, 43n, 50 and n, 60, 63, 66n, 67, 93
Priyā 30n
Pṛthūdaka 26n, 36n, 94
Pulinda 20n
puṃsavana 8
Puṇḍra 41, 94
Puṇḍravardhana 27, 68, 94
Puṇyā 37n
Puṇyabhājana 41
Puṇyādri 94
Puṇyavardhana 27, 68n, 94
Puraścandra 30n, 94
Purasthira 94
Purasthita 20, 21n, 23n, 94
Pureśvarī 30n
Pūrṇa, Pūrṇaśaila, Pūrṇagiri 12 and n, 64, 94
Pūrṇā 37n
Pūrṇagiri 12 and n, 13 and n, 14n, 17 and n, 35, 94, 104
Pūrṇānanda 18n, 75, 76, 77 and n
Pūrṇanātha 12n
Pūrṇaśaila, seat of Pūrṇeśvarī and Mahānātha 12 and n, 20, 21n, 23n, 94
Pūrṇeśvarī 17 and n, 20, 21n, 23n
Pūrṇimā 29n
Pūruhūtā 27, 67
Puruṣottama 25n, 27, 31n, 68, 94
Pūṣan 5-6, 71-73
Puṣkalāvatī, Mirziyarat-Charsadda near Peshawar 10n
Puṣkara 25n, 27, 28n, 31n, 66n, 67, 94, 107
Puṣkarāvatī 27, 69
Puṣpatīrtha 27, 69n, 94
Puṣṭi 28, 69
Puṣyādri 22n

120

Rādhā, 18, 25n, 27, 31n, 68, 94
Rāghava Bhaṭṭa 76
Ragunātha Śiromani 74-75
Raghuvaṁśa 9n
Rahim 25
Rājabolahāṭa, near Serampur in Hooghly Dist. 33 and n. 34, 94
Rājagiri 36, 53n, 94
Rājagṛha 21 and n, 23n, 94
Rājalakṣmī 38n
Rājamālā, Bengali chronicle of Tripurā kings 4n, 20n
Rājaparvata 38n, 94
Rājataraṅgiṇī 10n, 15, 20
Rājeśvarī 33 and n
Rākiṇī 37, 56 and n, 65; same as Raṅkiṇī 33n
Rākṣaseśvara 37, 41, 57
Raktadantikā 107
Rāma 25, 48n
Ramā 29n, 38n
Rāmā 94
Rāmagiri, Ramtek in M. P. 19 and n, 36, 53, 61, 94
Rāmākiṇī 36, 53n
Ramaṇā 27, 69
Ramaṇa, Ramaṇaka 26n, 30n, 94
Rāmānanda 36, 47n
Rāmānuja 25n
Rāmaśobhana 79
Rāmatīrtha 26n, 27, 30n, 69, 94
Rāmatoṣaṇa Vidyālaṅkāra 23
Rambhā 27, 67
Rāmeśvara at Setubandha 26n, 29n, 30n, 47n, 94
Rāmeśvarī 31n
Rāmoccheda, Rāmodbheda 94
Raṇāditya 20
Raṇakhaṇḍa 40, 94
Raṇekṣaṇā 29n
Raṅkiṇī of Burdwan 33 and n
Rāsavṛndāvana 94
Ratipriyā 27, 68
Ratnāvalī 35,37,40, 56 and n, 65, 95
Ratnāvatī 37, 56 and n, 61, 95
Raudrī 38n
Rāvānanda 36, 40, 48n
Raychaudhuri 20n
retas of Prajāpati 5
Ṛgveda 5, 7, 71, 101-02
Ṛṇamocana 26n, 95
Rudra 3n, 5, 71, 102-03
Rudrakoṭi 27, 67, 95
Rudrāṇī 27, 38n, 81, 108
Rudrarāma 79
Rudra-Śiva 6, 102-03
Rudrasundarī 27, 68n
Rudrayāmala Tantra 12n, 17 and n, 18, 23, 80-100

THE ŚĀKTA PĪṬHAS

Rukmiṇī 27, 33 and n, 68
Rūpā 27, 69n
Rūpiṇī 38n
Ruru 28n, 36, 46, 52 and n, 60, 63

Śabara 20n
Śabdakalpadruma 3, 7n, 42, 48n
Sabhānandā 27, 68n
Sachau, E. A. 15, 25n
Sadānanda 40
Sadāśiva 64
Sādhanamālā 12n, 13, 16, 39, 80-100
Sadiyā, Copper temple at 16
Sāgara-saṅgama 31n, 80, 95
Sahajayāna school of Buddhists 11 and n
Sahasrākṣa 27, 68, 75n, 95
Sahyādri 27, 68, 95
Śaila 36, 53n
Śaiva 3n, 10n, 22
Śākambharī 66n, 107
Śākambharīpura 26n, 95
Sakhī-bhāva 74
Śakra 72-73
Śākta 3n, 8, 22, 74, 75 and n
Śākta-tīrtha 66n
Śakti 3 and n, 8, 10n, 16, 24, 28, 30, 39-40, 100-06
Śaktidhāriṇī 28, 70n, 80
Śaktisaṅgama Tantra 15, 76
Śālagrāma 27, 68, 95
Śāligrāma 27, 68n, 95
Samanakarman 40
Śamaneśvara-pīṭha 38n
Śamaneśvarapura 95
Samarānanda 36
Samayācāra Tantra 14n
Sambheda 95
Śambhu 10n, 102, 105
Śambhu-Śiva 10n
Saṁhāra 28n, 36, 41, 53, 60, 95
Saṁkrūra 36, 40, 53
Samudragupta 15
Saṁvarānanda 36, 52, 60
Saṁvarī 41
Saṁvarta 36, 41, 50
Saṁvṛtānanda 64
Sanātana 79
Śaṅkara 11n, 31n, 40
Śaṅkara Āgamācārya 18
Śaṅkarācārya 18
Śaṅkarī, Pīṭha-goddess 18, 19n, 27, 31n, 69n, 107-08
Śaṅkhoddhāra 28, 70, 95
Śaṅkhasaṁharaṇa 95
Śaṅkhasaṁhāriṇī 29n
Śani 6
Santāna 95
Śāntarakṣita, Śāntirakṣita 16

INDEX

Saptagodāvara 95
Saptagodāvarī 27n, 30n
Saptārci 95
Saptārṣa 66n
Saptaśṛṅga 107
Sāradā, goddess 15, 29n, 30n, 44n, 95
Sāradā-pīṭha, modern Sardi in Kashmir 14
Sāradā-maṭha in Kashmir 15
Sāradātilaka Tantra 76
Sāradā-tīrtha 26n
Sarasvatī, same as goddess Sāradā, 18, 19n, 26n, 27, 28 and n, 30n, 66n, 69-70, 95
Sarayu 26n, 29n, 95
Sarayutīra 66n
Sāre Mākhe Ḍherī 10n
Śarīrin 95
Śarkarāra 44n, 59, 95
Sarkar, J. N. 15
Sarkar Satgaon 34n
Sarva 41, 102
Sarvākṣiṇī 41
Sarvamaṅgalā of Citpur, Calcutta 24n, 38n
Sarvāṇa 40
Sarvānanda 3n, 36, 37, 40, 51 and n, 52n, 60, 64
Sarvānandamayī 57n
Sarvānandataraṅgiṇī 3n
Sarvāṇī 31n, 36, 51, 60, 108
Sarvaśaila 41, 95
Sarveśa 37n
Sarveśvarī 41
Ṣaṣṭhī 38n
Ṣaṣṭhīpura 22n, 38n, 95
Sastri, H. P. 11 and n
Śatadravā (Śatadrava) 29n
Śatadru 29n, 95
Śatadru-tīra 66n
Śatapatha-Brāhmaṇa 5, 71
Śataprabhā 29n
Śatarūpā 29n
Satgaon 34n
Satī, daughter of Dakṣa 4n, 5, 6 and n, 7, 11n, 13n, 25, 30n, 32-35, 39n, 50n, 51n, 95
Satīcala 41, 95
Ṣaṭtriṁśanmata 10n
Sātu 77, 79
Satyavādinī 28, 70
Saurabheśvarī 38n
Sāvitrī 9n, 10n, 25, 30n, 36, 40, 51 and n, 60, 64, 66n, 72, 105
Sen, D. C. 75
Sephālikā 41
Set, brother of Osiris 7
Setubandha 31n, 65, 95
Shams-i-Shrirāj 'Afīf 14n

Siddhapīṭha 3n, 6n, 19
Siddhapura 28, 69, 95
Siddhavana 28, 69n 95
Siddhavaṭa 28, 69n, 95
Siddeśvarī 40
Siddhi, perfection 3n
Siddhidā 29n, 35, 44 and n, 59, 62
Siddhidāyinī 28, 70n, 80
Siddhirūpā 36, 50 and n, 60
Siddhi-tīra 96
Sīmantonnayana 8
Siṁhala 18, 19 and n, 96
Siṁhanāda 19 and n, 96
Siṁhikā 27, 69
Sindhusaṅgama 28, 69n, 96
Sindhusthalī 38n
Sindhu-tīra 66n
Sircar, D. C. 24n
Sirihaṭṭa (Śrīhaṭṭa) 13, 14n, 96
Śiśnadeva, worshipper of Phallus 7
Sītā 27, 68
Sītākuṇḍa, on Chandranath hill 47n
Śiva 3 and n, 4n, 5-7, 10 and n, 11, 14, 16, 20n, 24 and n, 25,28, 31n, 37, 40, 56, 70, 100-06
Śivā 12n, 30n, 32n, 37, 39n, 40, 56n, 61
Śivabhadrā 37n
Śiva-bhāgavata 10n
Śivacaṇḍā 27, 68n, 96
Śivacarita 38, 39, 41n, 43n, 47n, 50n, 51n, 80-100
Śivadhāriṇī 28, 70n, 80
Śivadūtī 28n
Śivājī 15
Śiva-Kapāleśvara, in Cālukya inscription 10n
Śivakāriṇī 28, 70, 80
Śivakuṇḍa 27, 68, 96
Śivakuñja 27, 68n, 96
Śivaliṅga 27, 68, 96
Śiva-Mallikārjuna 16
Śivāmṛtā 28n
Śivānanda 36, 47n, 60
Śivānandā 27, 68
Śivānī 36, 40, 53 and n, 61
Śiva-Paśupati 3n
Śivapīṭha 31n, 96
Śiva Purāṇa 24n
Śivasannidhi 96
Śivātmikā 29n
Śivavallabhā 38n
Sixteen Mothers 28n
Skanda Purāṇa 24n, 25 and n, 66-70
Smith 2ₙn
Ṣoḍaśī 48 n
Śodhānyāsa 7n
Somākhyā 64
Somanātha near Veraval in Junagarh Dist., Gujarat 96

Someśvara 26n, 27, 69, 96
Soṇa 26n, 29, 36, 41, 53 and n, 96
Soṇajyotiṣā-saṅgama 28, 66n, 69
Soṇākṣī 40
Soṇa-saṅgama 96
Śraddhā 29n
Śrī 29n, 48n
Śrīcaitanya 74-75
Śrīgiri 29n, 96, 107
Śrīhaṭṭa, same as Sirihaṭṭa 13, 36, 40, 52, 69, 96, 104
Śrīkṛṣṇa-Śatanāma 24n
Śrīnagara 107
Śrī-Nīlaparvata 26n
Śrīparvata 10n, 16, 31n, 36-37, 40, 51n, 54 and n, 65, 66n, 96
Śrīpīṭha, Śrīhaṭṭa 21 and n, 23n, 96
Śrīpura 22n, 38n, 96
Śrīśaila, in Karnool Dist., A.P. 16, 18, 19n, 20n, 21 and n, 22n, 23n, 27, 36, 38n, 41, 52, 64, 67
Śrītattvacintāmaṇi 75-76, 77 and n
Śrīvidyā 30n
Stambheśvarī 104
stana, hills regarded as breasts of Devī 8
Stanakuṇḍa 7-8, 9n, 15
Sthala 96
Sthāṇu 36 40, 51 and n, 60
Sthāneśvara 27, 67n
Sthāṇvīśvara, modern Thanesar 27, 32n, 51n, 67, 96
Strīrājya 18, 96
Stūpa 7
Subalā 29n
Śubhacaṇḍī 40
Subhadrā 28, 69, 96
Śubhānandā 27, 68n
Śubhavāsinī 29n
Śubheśvarī 30n
Śuci 36, 53, 60, 64, 96
Śuddhā 28, 69n
Śuddhabuddhi 29n
Śuddhi 28, 69, 88
Sugandhā, Shikarpur in Buckergunge Dist. 26n, 27, 35, 40, 44 and n, 59, 62, 66n, 68, 96
Sugatā 105
Sukathā 29n
Śukla-tīrtha 26n, 29n, 96
Śukra-tīrtha 29n
Śūlagava sacrifice 103
Śūlapāṇi 41, 66
Śūlinī 20n
Sunandā 27, 35, 40-41, 44 and n, 59
Sunandānanda 37, 54n
Sundarānanda 37, 40, 54 and n, 61
Sundarī 37, 40, 48n, 54 and n, 61, 65, 107
Suparṇa 96

Suparṇākhya 32n
Supārśva 27, 68, 96
Surapūjitā 28n
Surasā 29n, 30n
Sureśa 41
Sureśī 41
Sūrya 6 and n
Suvarṇākhya 32n
Suvarṇākṣa 108
Svadhā 29n
Svāhā 27, 31n, 69
Svargadā 29n
Svargalakṣmī 38n
Svargamārga 2 n, 66n, 96
Svargoccheda, °dbheda 29n, 97
Svayambhū-liṅga of Śiva 8
Śvetabandha 41, 97
Śyāmā (Kālī) 48n, 75
Śyāmārahasya of Pūrṇānanda 75-76, 77n
Śyāmasundara 79
Syria 7

Tailaṅga 41, 65, 97
Taittirīya Saṁhitā 29n
Tamoghnī 31n
Tamoliptā 31n, 97
Tāmra 40
Tāṇḍyamahābrāhmaṇa 5
Tantracūḍāmaṇi 3, 4 and n, 20n, 39, 42, 48n, 58n
Tantrakaumudī 76
Tantrasāra 4, 7n, 14n, 16, 18n, 20,23 and n, 28n, 48n, 51n, 74-80
Tapasvinī 30n
Tapolakṣmī 38n
Tārā 16, 28, 39, 48n, 69, 97
Tārādyā 62
Taraṅgā 28, 69n, 82
Tārārahasya 25n, 77n
Tārārahasya-vṛttikā 18
Tāriṇī 39
Tarkaratna, Pañcānana 80
Tarkavācaspati, Tārānātha 42
Tathāgata 105
Tattvacintāmaṇididhīti 75
Teshub 20n
Thomas, F. W. 17n
Thuggee 15
Tibet 16
Tilottamā 28, 70
Tippera Dist. 3n, 16
Tīrabhukti, Tirhut in North Bihar 47n
Tīrotā 36, 47n, 97
Tīrthika 10, 16
Tīrthasaṅgama 97
Tivraka 35, 46n
Traipura 27n, 97

INDEX

Tribal deities 3n
Trihalikāgrāma 66n
Trihuta (Tīrabhukti) 41, 97
Trikūṭa 27, 68, 97
Trimūrti 24
Trinetreśvara 35, 44n
Tripada 97
Tripathi, R. S. 105
Tripura 97
Tripurā 4n, 19, 20n, 36, 41, 47 and n, 48 and n, 60, 63, 97
Tripurākṣa 36, 47n, 60
Tripuramālinī 35, 40, 45, 59, 62, 86
Tripuranāśinī 35, 45n, 59, 86
Tripurā Rājamālā 58n
Tripurasundarī 36, 38n, 43, 47, 63
Tripureśa, Śiva of Tripurā 4n, 36
Tripuṭā 40
Trisandhyā 27, 40, 68, 108
Trisandhyeśvara 35, 44, 59, 62
Trisrotā, Tista river in North-Eastern India 20, 21n, 23n, 36, 38n, 40-41, 47, 63
Triśūlā 107
Triśūlinī 31n
Triveṇī 19 and n, 97
Tṛpti 29n
Tryambaka 35, 40, 44 and n, 47n, 59
Tryambakeśvara temple at Ponabalia 44n
Tuljā Bhavānī 14, 82
Tuljāpura 107
Turjā (Tuljā) Bhavānī, 14, 82
Turkish Musalman 17
Tuṣṭi 28, 69n

Ucchiṣṭacaṇḍālinī 66
Uḍḍīna 22n
Uḍḍīnapura 97
Uḍḍīśa, from *Oḍḍaviṣa*, same as Orissa 21 and n, 23n, 97
Uḍḍiyāna in Swat Valley 12 and n, 13 and n, 14n, 16, 17 and n, 18, 19 and n, 21 and n, 23n, 30-31, 35, 97, 104
Uḍḍiyānabandha 12n
Udyatparvata 8, 9 and n, 11
Ugra 102
Ugrā 108
Ugratārā 34n, 97
Ujānī, same as Kogrām in Burdwan Dist 35, 40, 46n, 97-98
Ujjani 35, 46n, 98
Ujjayinī 21 and n, 22n, 23n, 35, 38n, 45n, 46 and n, 47, 59, 98
Umā 3 and n, 27, 36, 37, 39n, 41, 53 and n, 64, 69, 72, 105
Umālakṣmī 28, 69n

Umānanda 36, 40, 48
Umāvana 36, 53n, 60
Unmatta 35, 39, 40, 44 and n, 59, 62
Unmatta-bhairava 28n
Upaniṣad 102
Upa-pīṭha 39, 41
Ūrdhvapāda-Vajravārāhī 16
Urjanī 35, 46n, 98
Urjayinī 35, 46n
Urvaśī 28, 70
Uṣas 5
Uṣṇatīrtha 27, 69, 98
Utkala 35, 40, 45, 59, 62, 98
Utpalā 27, 32n, 68
Utpalākṣī 27, 68n, 108
Utpalāvartaka 27, 69, 98
Uṭsādana 41
Uttarā 41, 98
Uttarakuru 28, 70, 98
Uttaramānasa 29n, 66n, 98
Uttariṇī 41

Vācaspatya 7n, 25n, 43
Vaḍavā 66n
Vagalāsthāna 107
Vāgmatī 19, 20n, 98
Vaidyanātha, Deoghar-Vaidyanāthdhām 19n, 26n, 25n, 27, 35, 40, 45 and n, 59, 62, 69, 98, 107
Vaiṣṇava 22, 75 and n
Vaiṣṇavī 28 and n, 30n, 65, 70
Vaiśravaṇa 28, 70
Vaiśravaṇ-ālaya 98
Vaitaraṇī river 19 and n
Vaivasvata 40, 51n, 98
Vājasaneyi Saṁhitā 24n
Vajradhātvīśvarī 11n
Vajrasattva 11 and n
Vākpatirāja 20, 104
Vakra 40
Vakranātha, 37, 40, 57, 98
Vakratuṇḍa 37, 40, 55 and n, 61
Vakreśvara in Birbhum Dist. 37, 39-40, 43n, 57, 98
Vakreśvarī 40
Vāmācāra 10n
Vāmadeva 41, 64
Vāmana 21 and n, 23n, 36, 48n, 54, 61, 65, 98
Vāmeśa 37, 40, 54n
Vaṁśīdāsa of Mymensing 24n, 34n
Vanamālā, records of 15n
Vandinikā 28, 70n
Vandanīyā 28, 70
Vaṅga 18, 98
Varadā 38n
Varāha 105
Varāha-parvata 25n, 28n, 66n, 98

124   THE ŚĀKTA PĪTHAS

Varāha-śaila 27, 67
Vārāhī 19, 20n, 28n, 36, 40, 53, 60, 65, 98
Vārāṇasī 17, 18 and n, 19n, 20, 21n, 27n, 27, 33, 34n, 36, 37n, 41, 43n, 51 and n, 64, 66 and n, 98
Varārohā 27, 69
Vardhamāna 98
Vardhamānaka 81
Vareṇya 81, 98
Vasiṣṭha 30n
Vasiṣṭha-tīrtha 26n, 98
Vāstoṣpati 71
Vastrapāda 32n, 98
Vastreśvara 28, 69, 99
Vasu, N.N. 39, 74 and n, 75 and n, 77
Vaṭakeśvara 40
Vaṭaparvatikā 30n, 99
Vaṭīparvatikā 30n, 99
Vatsanābha 37, 56n
Vedagarbhā 40, 64, 87
Vedamastaka 99
Vedamātā 30n
Vedāraṇya 107
Vedaśiras 99
Vedavadana 99
Vedeśa 99
Vedic Rudra 3n
Vegala 27, 69n, 99
Veṇā 99
Veṇīmādhava 40, 50n
Veṇumatī 99
Veṇuvatī 29n
Vetravatī 66n
Vibhāsa 37, 41, 54, and n, 61, 99
Vidiśā, modern Besnagar 45n
Vidyā 31n
Vidyālaṅkāra, Rāmatoṣaṇa 77-80
Vidyāpura 27n, 31n, 99
Vidyābhūṣaṇa, Rāmalobhana 79
Vidyābhūṣaṇa, Rāmalocana 78-79
Vidyābhūṣaṇa, S.C. 75
Vidyāvāgīśa, Kṛṣṇamaṅgala 79
Vijayā 30n, 35, 39n, 40, 45n, 99
Vijayanta 26n, 30n, 99
Vikramāditya 5
Vikṛta, Vikṛtā 37, 55 and n, 61
Vikṛtākṣa 37, 40, 55n
Vilvā 27, 67n
Vilvaka 26n, 27, 66, 99
Vilvala 27, 67n 99
Vilvapatrikā 27, 67
Vilvapīṭha 27n, 38n
Vimalā 19, 20n, 27, 31n, 35-36, 38n, 41, 45 and n, 50 and n, 59, 64-65, 68, 99, 107
Vimaleśvara 31n, 99
Vimukti 30n
Vināyaka 27, 69, 99
Vindhya 21 and n, 23n, 27, 30n,65,
68, 99
Vindhyācala 107
Vindhyagaṅgā 30n
Vindyagaṅgāsaṅgama 99
Vindhyagiri 19, 20n
Vindhyakandara 99
Vindhyavāsinī, non-Aryan goddess 20 and n; her temple near Mirzapur, U. P. 20, 27, 30n, 35, 41, 68, 104
Vindhyaśekhara 41
Vipāśā 27, 29n, 66n, 68, 99
Vipradāsa 24n
Vipula 27, 68
Vipulā 27, 68, 99
Vīrabhadra 6, 73
Virācāra 10n
Virajā 19 and n, 21 and n, 23n, 31n, 33 and n, 38n, 65, 86
Virajākṣetra in Utkala 35, 45 and n, 59
Virajāpura 99
Virāṭa, Virāṭadeśa 39, 43n, 57 and n, 99
Virūpākṣa 41
Viśāla 100
Viśālā 29n
Viśālākṣī, Pīṭha-goddess 18, 19n, 27, 29n, 32n, 33, 34n, 36, 41, 51, 64, 66, 108
Viśālalocanī 33 and n
Viṣṇu 6-7, 10n, 11n, 24 and n, 73-74, 75 n, 104-05
Viṣṇupada 29n, 66n, 100
Viṣṇupriyā 29n
Viṣṇusaṁhitā 66n
Viṣṇuvardhana, Hoysala king 25n
Viśvā 27, 67
Viśvakāmā 37, 67n, 81
Viśvakāyā 27, 67, 81
Viśvamātā 41
Viśvamātṛkā 40
Viśvamukhī 28, 69
Viśvanātha 41, 79
Viśvāsa, Prāṇakṛṣṇa 77
Viśveśa 37, 40, 57
Viśveśī 37, 55 and n, 61
Viśveśvara 27-28, 41, 47n, 67, 69n, 100
Vitastā 66n
Vrajeśvarī 30n, 38n, 83
Vṛndāvana 25n, 27 and n, 36, 41, 53 and n, 68, 100
Vyāghrapura 32n, 100
Vyomakeśa 57n

Watters 10, 16

Yādaveśvarī 30n
Yāgapura 31n

INDEX

Yāgapurī 100
Yāgeśvarī 38n
Yājapura in Orissa 33 and n, 100
yajña, sacrifice 5
Yajurveda 24n, 102-03
Yamunā 26n, 27, 28n, 69, 100
Yamunā, river of North Bengal 13n
Yamunā-tīra 66n
Yaśaskarī 27, 69
Yaśora, Īśvarīpura in the Khulna Dist. 37, 39, 41, 43n, 57 and n, 100
Yaśoreśvarī 37, 41, 57
Yaśovarman 20, 57n
Yogācāra doctrine 16
Yogādyā 33 and n, 36, 41, 49n
Yogamāyā 3n

Yogapīṭha 11
Yogeśa 37, 56n
Yogeśvarī 107
Yoginī 10n, 11, 28n
Yoginī Tantra 13n
Yogin, ascetic 3n
Yogīśa 35, 37, 41, 56
Yoni 3n, 7-8, 9n, 13n
Yonikuṇḍa 7-8, 9n
Yoni rings 101
Yonistotra 3n
Yoni Tantra 7
Yoni-tīrtha 15
Yugādyā 36, 38n, 39, 41, 49 and n 60, 100
Yugalā, Pīṭha-goddess 18, 19n

Addenda et Corrigenda

Page 1, line 20.	*Read*—from *for*—form
,, 2, line 19.	*Read*—Mahāpīṭhanirūpaṇa
,, ,, line 21.	*Read*—Śivacarita
,, 3, note 2.	*Add*—As regards the maiden (Kumārī) aspect, we may note that, in every Bihāl (*vihāra*) of the Newars of Nepal, a young girl having no scar on her body is worshipped as the living form of Kālī or Durgā. There is also a similar Kumārī for the whole kingdom. The State Kumārī is periodically selected from amongst the girls of the Vanra or priestly community on the last day of the Navarātra, after a trying test. The Newars believe that the valley of Nepal belongs to the Kumārī and therefore every year the king has to receive from her a fresh mandate for ruling the country. The Kumārī is replaced by another before she approaches her first menstruation. See Gopal Singh Nepali, *The Newars*, reviewed in *Swarajya*, March 26, 1966, p. 27
,, 5, line 15.	*Read*—Uṣas
,, ,, lines 35 ff.	*Add references*—*Bhāgavata Purāṇa*, IV. 2-7; cf. allusion to the story of the destruction of Dakṣa's sacrifice in the *Rāmāyaṇa*, I. 66.9.
,, ,, note 1.	*Add*—In the *Tāṇḍyamahābrāhmaṇa* (VII. 9.16), we are told that the gods were once sharing among themselves the animals sacrificed to them in ceremonies, but that they avoided Rudra in this sharing. *Read*—Appendix III.
,, 7, line 5.	*Read*—Viṣṇu
,, ,, line 19.	*Read*—afterwards

Page 8, lines 9 ff. *Read*—As will be seen below, there is reason to believe....the *Yoni* of the Mother-goddess.

Add note—George MacMunn says, "at Malabar in Bombay, a great cleft in the rock is known as the *Yoni*, and through it pass barren women desirous of child, who travel from far and wide to do so" (*The Underworld of India*, 1933, p. 99).

,, 11, note 1. *Add*—We have also legends connecting holy places with the limbs of other divinities. The *Vāyu Purāṇa* (Chap. 104) relates a story about Vyāsa who is said to have noticed the following holy places and rivers in the limbs of the Vedas incarnate—(1) Mathurā in their heart, (2) Kāśī between the eye-brows, (3) Kāñcī in the organ of generation, (4) Avanti in the navel, (5) Dvārakā in the throat, (6) Prayāga in the life breath, (7) the Gaṅgā and Yamunā on their left and right, (8) the Sarasvatī in the middle, (9) Gayā in the face, (10) Prabhāsa between the jaw and neck, (11) Badarī in the crown of the head, (12) Puṇḍravardhana-pīṭha and Nepāla-pīṭha in the two eyes, (13) Pūrṇagiri-pīṭha on the forehead, (14) Mathurā-pīṭha on the neck, (15) Kāñcī-pīṭha on the loin, (16) Jālandhara-pīṭha on the breast, (17) Bhṛgu-pīṭha in the ear, and (18) Ayodhyā in the nostril. While there are a few cases of repetition (cf. Nos. 1 and 14, 3 and 15), it is difficult to say whether Bhṛgu (No. 17) is the same as Bhṛgukaccha. It may be noted that only Puṇḍravardhana, Nepāla, Pūrṇagiri, Mathurā, Kāñcī, Jālandhara and Bhṛgu are called *pīṭha*, but that Kāmākhyā is a significant omission.

ADDENDA ET CORRIGENDA

Page 12, note 5,   Read—c. 1159-79 A. D.
line 16.

„ „ note 6.   Add—p. 13 and notes, and p. 23 and note 3 (refering to the separate mention of Uḍḍīyāna and Uḍḍīśa or Orissa side by side in the same list).

„ 13, note 1, line 4.   Add—See below p. 17, note 3. The *Kālikā Purāṇa* (62. 76 ff.) applies the name Kāmeśvarī to the goddess Kāmākhyā.

„ „ line 13.   Read—mountain

„ „ last line.   Add—The goddess worshipped in the Tāmreśvarī temple near Paya in the Lohit District of NEFA is called Dikkaravāsinī in an inscription of Śaka 1364 (1442 A.D.). See *Journ. Anc. Ind. Hist.*, Vol. I, pp. 17ff.

„ „ note 2,   Omit—For the same confusion...*Mahā-*
lines 14-16.   *bhārata*, II. 14.19. Read instead—See p. 13 and notes, and p. 23 and note 3 for the separate mention of Uḍḍīśa (Orissa) and Uḍḍīyāna. See Sircar, *Stud. Geog.*, 1971, pp. 181 ff.

„ 16, line 17.   Read—*op. cit.*

„ „ lines 20-21   Read—Andhra Pradesh *for*—Madras Presi-
and some other   dency
places in the book.

„ 18, line 1 and   Read—Tamil Nadu *for*—Madras Presidency
some other
places in the book.

„ „ line 23 and   Read—Asiatic Society, Calcutta *for*—Royal
elsewhere in the   Asiatic Society of Bengal.
book.

„ 19, note 1, line 3.   Read—*Pradyumno*

„ „ „ line 7.   Read—*Kāmarūpī (pā)*.

„ „ „ line 8.   Read—*Gayā (yāṁ*)*.

„ „ note 2, line 13.   Read—*Uḍḍiyānaṁ*

„ 20, line 6, and   Read—Uttar Pradesh *for* United Provinces
elsewhere in the
book.

„ „ line 8.   Read—c. 725-53 A. D.

Page 21, note.	*Add*—Note the separate mention of Uḍḍiśa (Orissa) and Uḍḍīyāna.
„ 23, note 3, line 19.	Read—*hṛdādyudara*
„ „ note 3.	*Add*—The separate mention of Uḍḍiśa (Orissa) and Uḍḍīyāna is worthy of note.
„ 24, note 3.	*Add*—For the Avatāras, see also Sircar, *Stud. Rel. L. Anc. Med. Ind.*, pp. 41ff.
„ 25, note 1.	*Add*—For the god Puruṣottama-Jagannātha, see now Sircar, *Stud. Rel. L. Anc. Med. Ind.*, pp. 59ff., to note modification in the views.
„ „ note 2, line 5.	*Read*—c. 725-53 A. D.
„ 30, note, last line.	Read—*Madhurāyāñ = ca*.
„ 31, note, line 33.	Read—*Kurukṣetre*.
„ 33, line 5.	*Read*—S.E.R. *for*—B.N.R.
„ 37, note, line 7.	*Read*—in Kāmarūpa
„ 39, line 13.	*Read*—suggest
„ 43, note 5, line 1.	Read—*mam = āsya vapuṣo*
„ 46, note 4, line 1.	Read—*kurparañ = c = aiva*.
„ 47, note 2, lines 6 and 8 and elsewhere in the book.	*Read*—Tripura State in East India and Jabalpur in Madhya Pradesh.
„ „ note 2.	*Add*—For the correct date of Dharmamāṇikya, see *JAIH*, Vol. V, pp. 32-33.
„ „ note 7, line 2.	Read—*Umānando = tha*.
„ 49, note 9.	*Add*—See also *JAIH*, Vol. I, pp. 19ff.
„ 53, note 3, line 2.	*Read*—Nagpur in Maharashtra.
„ 55, note 1, line 5 and elsewhere in the book.	*Read*—Kathiawar (Gujarat).
„ „ note 6, lines 4-5.	*Read*—Nasik region of Maharashtra.
„ 63, note, line 3.	*Read*—Cooch Bihar District of the West Bengal State.
„ 74, note.	*Add*—*Lola-jihvā ālola-jihvā, lelihāna-jihvā* or *lalaj-jihvā* was really a characteristic of several Tantric gods and goddesses. See *Tantrasāra*, Vaṅgavāsi ed., pp. 301, 462-63, 470, 502, 514, 596.
„ 80, line 38.	*Add*—Vāyu = Vāyu Purāṇa
„ 80, line 44.	*Read*—Achchhabal
„ 81, line 17.	*Omit*—possibly a mistake for Elāpura.

ADDENDA ET CORRIGENDA 131

	Read—modern Alampur in the Mahbubnagar District of Andhra Pradesh.
,, ,, line 21 and some other places in the book.	*Read*—Madhya Pradesh *for*—C. P.
,, ,, lines 27 and 46-47.	*Read*—District, Rajasthan *for*—State, Rajputana.
,, ,, line 50.	*Add*—See also Sircar, *Stud. Geog. Anc. Med. Ind.*, 2nd ed., p. 106.
,, 82, lines 9, 25 and 27.	*Read*—West *before*—Bengal.
,, ,, last line.	*Read*—in Maharashtra
,, 83, line 4.	*Read*—in Haryana
,, ,, line 12.	*Read*—Punjab (Pakistan)
,, ,, line 13.	*Read*—in Maharashtra
,, ,, line 49.	*Read*—North Bengal
,, 84, line 8.	*For*—Hyderabad State *read*—Aurangabad District of Maharashtra; may also be a mistake for *Ālāpura*.
,, ,, line 31	*Add*—According to the *Rājataraṅgiṇī* (I.35), it was the Bheḍa hill in Kashmir and the goddess Sarasvatī appeared there in the form of a swan in a lake. The Bheḍa is identified by Stein with Buḍbrār in the valley of the Birnai (trans., Vol. II, p. 472).
,, ,, lines 44-45.	*Read*—South-Eastern Railway.
,, 85, lines 24 and other places in the book.	*Read*—Rajasthan *for*—Rajputana
,, ,, line 48.	*Read*—Jaipur District
,, 86, lines 38-39.	*Read*—region in Maharashtra
,, ,, line 41.	*Read*—West Bengal
,, ,, line 45.	*Read*—District, Bangladesh
,, ,, line 52.	*Read*—Himachal Pradesh *for*—Punjab
,, 87, penultimate and last lines.	*Read*—Tamil Nadu *for*—Madras *and* West Bengal *for*—Bengal
,, 88, line 11.	*Add*—For modern Degām = ancient Kapālamocana in Kashmir, see Stein, *Rājatar.*, trans., Vol. II, p. 472.
,, ,, line 18.	*Read*—in Haryana.

Page ,, line 41.	*Read*—Baroda District, Gujarat
,, ,, penultimate and last lines.	*Read*—modern Bellary District of Karnataka *and* Jodhpur Division, Rajasthan
,, 91, line 31.	*Add reference*—Vāyu.
,, 92, line 41.	*Add reference*—Vāyu.
,, 94, line 5.	*Add reference*—Vāyu.
,, ,, line 17.	*Add reference*—Vāyu.
,, ,, line 35.	*For*—Gaya *read*—Patna
,, 99, last line.	*Add*—See also Sircar, *Stud. Geog. Anc. Med. Ind.*, 2nd ed., pp. 100-01.
,, 101, line 7.	*Add*—See *The Bhakti Cult and Ancient Indian Geography*, ed. Sircar, pp. 36 ff.
,, ,, note.	*Add*—On the same subject, see also *The Vedic Age* (*The History and Culture of the Indian People*, Vol. I), pp. 147 ff.
,, 104, lines 31 ff.	*Add note*—The deity Stambheśvarī is still worshipped by the people of the different castes of Orissa in some parts of the country under the local name Khambeśvarī and in the shape of a post or pillar without any special association with the Śivaliṅga (*Ep. Ind.*, Vol. XXVIII, p.112).
,, 105, note 2.	*Add*—The autumnal worship of Durgā was prevalent in the Ayodhyā region of U. P. in the seventh century A. D. See *Life of Hiuen-Tsiang*, trans. S. Beal, p. 86; Sircar, *Stud. Rel. L. Anc. Med. Ind.*, p. 230.